POETIC VISUAL MUSIC

POETIC VISUAL MUSIC

Praveen Patnaik

Commonwealth

Poetic Visual Music

ISBN : 81-311-0005-7

Edition : 2026

Published by :
COMMONWEALTH PUBLISHERS (P) LTD.
4831/24, Govind Lane,
Ansari Road, Darya Ganj,
New Delhi - 110002
Ph. : 23272541, 23242541
e-mail : commonwealthpublishers2016@gmail.com

Distributed by :
ARJUN PUBLISHING HOUSE
4831/24, Govind Lane,
Ansari Road, Darya Ganj,
New Delhi - 110002
Ph. : 23272541, 23242541
e-mail : arjunbooks2001@gmail.com

Laser Typesetting by :
Dimple Computers
Delhi

Printed at :
Milan Enterprises
Delhi

Preface

Music has been associated with moods and emotions for centuries. It was natural for music to play an important part in the formation of an image culture in spite of it not being apprehended by eye—because of this close tie to the emotional part of being. Visual music is a means of expressing music in visual form requiring the active involvement of an artist, designer or director to interpret the music and find the means to express it visually.

Visual music compositions can be created that will elicit responses in the viewers that are similar to the responses of those who listen to music. These responses will mirror what the essence of music carries—the deeper emotional connections, the energy, the meditative possibilities, or the engrossing enveloping characters of music. These explorations will include the troublesome issues of rhythm, musical sound decay, repeatability, melody and harmony—attempting to bridge the divide between the aural and the visual.

It is possible to compose music using a visual aesthetic—rather than the customary aural one—and listeners will recognise the resulting sounds as music. For this be fully realised the visual composers must have no awareness, during the compositional activity, of what the resulting "music" will sound like. The visual composer must be focused fully on the visual content of their compositions—ignoring the possible auditory connections that might be made.

The present volume is a philosophic and artistic exploration of the creation of visual music. The problem it explores is whether music can be composed in this image/electrate era using the image and its associated aesthetic instead of resorting to the auditory process—where music is primarily composed with an oral and literate manner. The work will serve as a highly valuable reference tool for all those concerned.

Praveen Patnaik

Contents

1

Poetic Visual Music

Music is magic. It influences our emotions. It has the power to make us happy or sad, just as it can make us relaxed or aggressive. Often it is associated with some very special moments in our lives. Moreover, music is an important part of our cultures and identities. However, the most fascinating aspect of music might be the fact that the annual turnover for record sales only within the US has a magnitude of several billion USD. This huge industry would not exist without its customers, who are always looking for something new to listen to. There are many ways in which customers find their desired products.

For example, one way is to listen around. Customers might listen to what is being played on the radio or to what friends are listening to. However, this type of search is restricted to the subjective taste of others. Furthermore, it might take a while until a new release reaches ones ears. Another approach is to follow the development of artists, who have been appreciated in the past, assuming that their work will also be appreciated in the future. However, this kind of search does not include unknown artists or newcomers.

Customers might also follow the development of a genre like Jazz, Hip Hop, Classic or Funk. Relying on the classification skills of other people it is possible to search music stores for new releases in certain genres. However, classifying music into a limited number of genres is not an easy task. Lots of music is located somewhere in between many genres.

Genres of music are represented by islands and continents. Similar genres are located close together and might even be connected through some land passage. On these islands there might be some further sub-genres that are represented as mountains and hills. Again these sub-genres might be more or less similar to each other and are arranged accordingly. The mountains and hills on the map are labeled with words that describe certain attributes of the associated genre, for example the type of rhythm is described rather than using words like Pop, Jazz or Classical.

The pieces of music in the collection are placed on the map according to their genre or sub-genre. Most of the music will be located around the mountains. However the few located in the valleys between typical genres might be the most interesting ones. The user can listen to the music by clicking on its representation on the map and can explore island after island according to his or her musical taste. Furthermore, music known to the user can be used as landmarks, to identify interesting regions on the map.

The maps with the islands of music could easily be placed on a web page of an internet store. Or they could be used in any conventional music store. Simple earphones and a touch screen monitor connected to a server would be sufficient. These maps could also be applied to digital libraries containing music, or simply at home to organize the private music collection. They could reveal some interesting properties of the inherent structure of the music collection that might not have been obvious before.

The technical requirements to develop music maps have only recently been met by the tremendous increase in computational power as well as the availability of affordable large storage. Now it is possible to handle the huge amount of data within music collections and to do the complex calculations leading to the music maps described above within reasonable time.

Music has been analyzed since the ancient Greeks. Pythagoras is credited with recognizing that strings whose lengths are related as the ratio of small integers sounds good when plucked at the same time. Since then a lot of research has been conducted and very sophisticated models and systems have been developed.

Content-Based Music Retrieval

There are several possibilities to search for music based on its content. One is to use metadata information consisting of descriptions which have manually been assigned to each piece of music. These descriptions can be as simple as the name of the piece of music, but also more complex like an assignment to a specific genre or a verbal description of the music. The necessary standards are provided, for example, by the MPEG 7 standard. A system based on MPEG 7 to compare sounds has, for example, been presented by [PMH00]. Often pieces of music have lyrics, thus another possibility would be to apply methods from text document retrieval to search for music.

Such systems are currently in use, for example, BigLyrics.com and LyricCrawler.com are two of the currently biggest music lyric search engines on the web. Using the lyrics as descriptions of the music it is possible to create an interface to allow an exploration of music archives where pieces of music with similar lyrics are located close to each other on a 2-dimensional map display using methods which have been developed mainly for text document collections, such as the SOMLib [RM99] or the WebSOM [KHLK98].

Sometimes music is available in the MIDI format [MID96] and for a limited subset of music automatic transcription to the MIDI format is possible (e.g. [Moo77, MSW96b]). Music archives in MIDI format contain information on the exact melody for each song. Hawley presented a system [Haw90], where the user enters a melody on a keyboard and tunes whose beginnings exactly match the input are retrieved. Ghias et al. [GLCS95] presented a system where the user hummes a query, which is reduced to relative information such as if a note is higher, lower or about the same as the previous, and retrieves songs which have similar melodies. One of the best known representatives of such systems is the New Zealand Musical Digital Library [MSW+96a, BNMW+99].

Additionally to the melody of a piece of music information on its style can be abstracted from the MIDI data. Dannenberg et al. [DTW97] described a system, which classified solo improvised trumpet performances into one of the four styles: lyrical, frantic, syncopated, or pointillistic.

However, not always metadata is available and the metadata available might be erroneous, incomplete or inaccurate due to the deficiencies of manual labor. Likewise song lyrics are not always available, speech recognition systems only have a limited capability of extracting the lyrics automatically. And finally most music is available in

MP3 or other similar formats rather than in MIDI. Thus content-based systems which directly analyze the raw music data (acoustical signals) have been developed. The models of these systems for music processing are usually sub-symbolic [Lem89] since they operate directly on acoustical signals and do not involve an explicit symbolizationc step as, for example, in [Wid01], where the musical structure is analyzed on a very abstract level.

Wold et al. [WBKW96] presented a system which analyzes sounds based on their pitch, loudness, brightness, and bandwidth over time and tracked the mean, variance, and autocorrelation functions of these properties. They analyze sounds such as speech and individual musical notes, but do not focus on whole music collections. Other approaches (e.g. [Foo97, BKWW99, Log00]) are based on methods developed in the digital speech processing community using Mel Frequency Cepstral Coefficients (MFCCs).

MFCCs are motivated by perceptual and computational considerations, for example, instead of calculating the exact loudness sensation only decibel values are used. Furthermore the techniques appropriate to process speech data are not necessarily the best for processing music. For example, the MFCCs ignore some of the dynamic aspects of music. Recently Scheirer presented a model of human perceptual behavior and briefly discussed how his model can be applied to classifying music into genre categories and performing music similarity-matching. However, he has not applied his model to large scale music collections.

Approaches using Self-Organizing Maps

Fruhwirth and Rauber, who have shown that it is possible

to cluster and organize music using neural networks. In their work they extract features from MP3 files which enable a self-organizing map (SOM) [Koh01] to learn the inherent structure within a music collection. The feature 6 extraction process consists of several steps. They first transform the audio signals into the frequency domain using a fast Fourier transformation (FFT) with about 20 millisecond windows. In the frequency domain they select 17 frequencies for further processing. They split each piece of music into 5-second sequences. They remove the first and the last sequences to avoid fade-in and fade-out effects. From the remaining they select a subset using only every second to third sequence. Each frequency band from the selected sequences is then transformed into the frequency domain yielding 256 coefficients. They combine these 256 values for the 17 bands in a 4352-dimensional vector representing a 5-second sequence. These vectors reflect the dynamic properties of the selected frequencies.

A SOM is used to organize the large number of 5 second sequences on a 2-dimensional map in such a way that similar sequences are located close to each other. The different sequences of one piece of music might be scattered across the map if it contains a lot of variations. To get the pieces together again another feature vector is created using the information on where the different sequences of one piece of music are located. With this information another SOM is trained which organizes the pieces of music on a 2-dimensional map.

Psychoacoustics deals with the relationship of physical sounds and the human brain's interpretation of them. For example, Feiten applies psychoacoustics to cluster about 100 different music instruments according to their sounds. He uses the concepts of critical-bands and specific loudness. Feiten divides the sounds into sequences of very short (6 milliseconds) steady-state components, assuming that similar sounds are similar sequences of steady-state sounds. He then applies the SOM algorithm to order them according to their similarity on a 2-dimensional map. Each dynamic sound is represented by a trajectory on this map, and similar dynamic sounds have similar trajectories, which Feiten uses to create a (SOM) map of the music instruments.

Feiten's approach is very accurate and works very well with music instruments. However it is computationally expensive. Using only 300 millisecond sounds to describe each of the 100 music instruments, yields 5000 different steady-state sounds. A small music collection with about 10 hours of music would result in about 6 million steadystate sounds. A similar approach as Feiten's where a SOM was used to cluster music instruments was presented by Cosi et al. [CPL94]. While Feiten applies general psychoacoustic models, Cosi et al. rely on specific methods developed by the speech processing community to process the audio signals.

Another approach using the SOM was published by Leman. Leman used the SOM to represent tonality in music and using this 2-dimensional representation 7 to analyze cadence sequences of pieces of music. Leman's goal is to analyze music and he is especially interested in musicology and hopes to provide tools of interest for music theorists in understanding the nature of music.

Feature Extraction

Music with a duration of 5 minutes is usually represented by 13 million values. These values describe the physical properties of the acoustical waves, which we hear. When analyzing this data it is necessary to remove the irrelevant parts and emphasize the important features. The extraction of these features from the raw data is the most critical part in the process of creating a content-based organization in a music collection. If it were possible to extract one single feature that directly indicates which genre a piece of music belongs to, everything else would be trivial.

Good features should be intuitively meaningful, based on psychoacoustic findings, and robust towards variations which are insignificant to our hearing sensation. Furthermore, they should lead to an organization of the music collection that makes sense and not be too expensive to compute. It is necessary to consider computational aspects because the raw data of even small music collections easily consumes several gigabytes of storage. A detailed analysis of all this information and all its possible meanings would be computationally prohibitive. It thus is necessary to reduce the amount of information to what is relevant in respect to the overall goal, which is to organize music according to its genre. These genres are not clearly defined and different people might assign the same piece of music to different genres. However, there are some attributes of the raw data, which definitely do not determine the genre. For example, removing the first second of a piece of music does not change its genre, but the raw data compared bit wise will be completely different.

Generally the duration of a piece of music is not relevant. Neither does a particular melody define a genre. The same melody can be interpreted in different genre styles just as different melodies might be members of the same genre. Likewise, the number of instruments involved plays a minor role in defining the genre.

In the frequency-domain several transformations are applied to obtain the specific loudness per critical-band. Based on the specific loudness per critical-band the loudness fluctuation in a time interval of about 6 seconds is analyzed and an image in the dimensions of critical-band, modulation frequency, and fluctuation strength is created. To this image gradient and Gaussian filters are applied to emphasize important characteristics and remove insignificant ones. The modified fluctuation strength is used as final feature for the clustering algorithms.

Raw Audio Data

There are different possibilities to code digitized music. Pulse Coded Modulation (PCM) audio data to which any digital music representation can be transformed. For example, MP3 files can easily be decoded to PCM using almost any of the currently available audio players. The PCM data is the discrete representation of a continuous acoustical wave. The amplitude is usually represented by 16 bits, which allows the description of more than 65,000 different amplitude levels. The time axis is usually sampled 44,100 times per second, which is one amplitude value approximately every 23 microseconds. The unit of the sampling frequency is Hertz (Hz), measured in cycles per second. The amplitude values are dimensionless although they correspond to sound pressure levels. The actual level depends on the sound system used to create physical acoustic waves.

The song Freak on a Leash by Korn is rather aggressive, loud, and perhaps even a little noisy. At least one electric guitar, a strange sounding male voice, and drums create a freaky sound experience. In contrast Fur Elise by Beethoven is a rather peaceful, classical piano solo. These two pieces of music will be used throughout illustrate the different steps of the feature extraction process. The envelope of the acoustical wave in Fur Elise over the interval of one-minute has several modulations and seldom reaches the highest levels, while Freak on a Leash is constantly around the maximum amplitude level. There is also a significant difference in the interval of only 20 milliseconds (ms), where Freak on a Leash has a more jagged structure than Fur Elise.

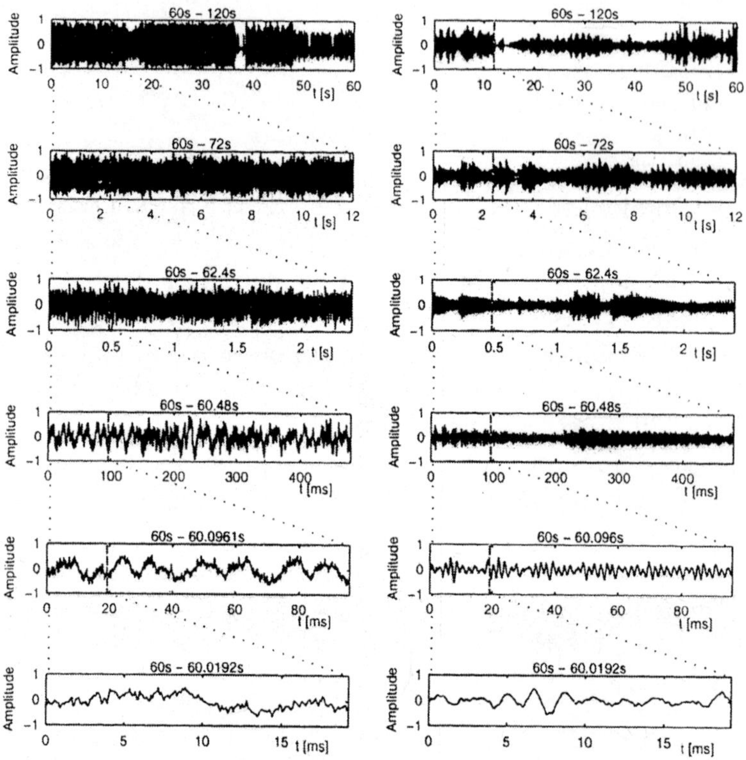

(a) Korn, Freak on the Leash (b) Beethoven, Für Elise

Figure 1. 44kHz PCM data at different magnitude levels

Obviously some basic descriptions of the audio signals would be sufficient to distinguish the peaceful-classical from the aggressive-noisy. One commonly used feature of signals is their zero-crossings, counting the times the signal crosses over the zero line. Another possibility is to analyze the envelope of the signal and extract beat information, based on the correlation between the magnitude of the envelope and the loudness [Dix00]. The main advantage of any features extracted directly from the PCM data is that they avoid computationally expensive preprocessing, which is necessary to transform the PCM data into data more representative of what we perceive.

For example, it is not possible to recognize if there are vocals or not, or if the energy in the audio signal derives from instruments with high or low pitch. Besides finding a representation that corresponds with our perception, it is also necessary to reduce the amount of data. A 5-second stereo sound sampled at 44kHz with 16 bit values equals almost 7 megabytes of data. For this reason the music is down-sampled to 11kHz, the two stereo channels are added up to one (mono), and only a fraction of every song is used for further processing. Specifically only every third 6-second sequence is further processed, starting after the first 12 seconds (fade-in) and ending before the last 12 seconds (fade-out). Additionally, zeros at the beginning or end of the music are truncated. This leads to a data reduction by a factor of over 16.

In figure 1, the 44kHz PCM data of two very different pieces of music at different time scales. The titles of the subplots indicate their time intervals. The second minute was chosen since the first minute includes fade-in effects. Starting with an interval of 60 seconds each subsequent subplot magnifies the first fifth of the previous interval. This is indicated by the dotted lines. For each of the two pieces of music, the amplitude values are relative to the highest amplitude within the one-minute intervals.

Changing stereo to mono has no significant impact on the perception of the music genre. Using only a small fraction of an entire piece of music should be sufficient since humans are able to recognize the genre within seconds. Often it is possible to recognize the genre by listening to only one 6-second sequence of a piece of music. A more accurate classification is possible if a few sequences throughout the piece of music are listened to.

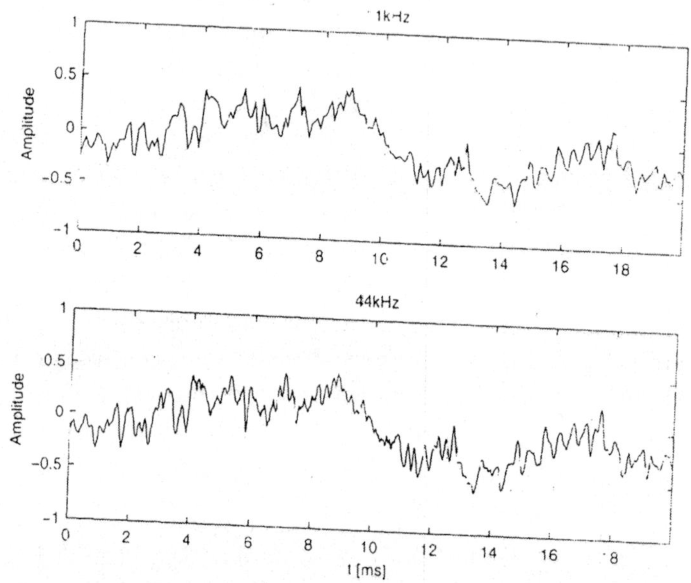

Figure 2. The effects of down-sampling on a 20ms sequence of Freak on a Leash. This sequence is the same as the one in the last subplot of Figure 1(c).

However, the first and the last seconds of a piece of music usually contain fade-in and fade-out effects, which do not help in determining the genre. Neither should the down-sampling affect the ability to recognize the genre. In simple experiments using average computer speakers it was hardly possible to recognize the difference between 44kHz and 11kHz for most songs, while the genres remain clearly recognizable.

Figure 2 depicts the effect of down-sampling. Notice that some of the fine details are lost, however, the signals still look alike. It is important to mention that down-sampling to 11kHz means that only frequencies up to 5.5kHz are noticeable. This is definitely far below the 16kHz an average human can hear, however, 5.5kHz are sufficient to cover the spectrum we use in speech, and almost all frequencies used in music [ZF99]. Furthermore, very high frequencies are usually not perceived as pleasant and thus do not play a very significant role in music.

Loudness Sensation

Loudness belongs to the category of intensity sensations. The loudness of a sound is measured by comparing it to a reference sound. The 1kHz tone is a very popular reference tone in psychoacoustics, and the loudness of the 1kHz tone at 40dB is defined to be 1 sone. A sound perceived to be twice as loud is defined to be 2 sone and so on. To calculate the loudness sensation from raw audio data several transformations are necessary. The raw audio data is first decomposed into its frequencies using a discrete Fourier transformation. These frequencies are bundled according to the nonlinear critical-band rate scale (bark). Then spectral masking effects are applied before the decibel values are calculated. The decibel values are transformed to equal loudness levels (phon) and finally from these the specific loudness sensation is calculated (sone).

Discrete Fourier Transformation

Complex acoustical signals consist of several waves with different frequencies and amplitudes. The inner ear (cochlea) of humans decomposes the incoming acoustical waves into separate frequencies. The energy of different frequencies is transferred to and con- centrated at different locations along the basilar membrane. Thus, it is appropriate to transform the PCM data into the frequency domain before analyzing it further. This can be achieved using, for example, Fourier Transformations. Alternatives include Wavelets, but are not considered in this thesis.

Theory

Using the linear Fourier transform, a continuous signal can be transformed between its time domain representation, denoted by $h(t)$, and the frequency domain representation $H(f)$. The respective equations are

$$\begin{aligned} H(f) &= \int_{-\infty}^{+\infty} h(t) e^{2\pi i f t} \mathrm{d}t, \quad \text{and} \\ h(t) &= \int_{-\infty}^{+\infty} H(f) e^{-2\pi i f t} \mathrm{d}f. \end{aligned} \tag{1}$$

Note that $i^2 = -1$ and $e^{ix} = \cos(x) + i \sin(x)$.

Pharseval's theorem, states that the total power in the signal is the same whether calculated in the time domain or the frequency domain. This is important for the loudness calculation of a sound and is formulated as

$$\int_{-\infty}^{+\infty} |h(t)|^2 \mathrm{d}t = \int_{-\infty}^{+\infty} |H(f)|^2 \mathrm{d}f. \tag{2}$$

The one-sided power spectral density $P_h(f)$, defines how much power is contained within the frequency interval between f and $f + df$. For real valued signals it is calculated as $P_h(f) = 2H|(f)|^2$.

As mentioned before, the audio signal is sampled at a fixed sampling rate, so the function is not continuous $h(t)$ but discrete $h(k\Delta t)$ with k denoting the whole-numbered index of the sample. The constant Δt denotes the time interval between two samples, which is determined by the sampling frequency (for 11kHz data Δt is less then 0.1ms).

For any sampling interval Δt there is a special frequency f_c, called the Nyquist critical frequency, given by $f_c \equiv 1/(2\Delta t)$. To describe a sine wave two samples per period are necessary. One sample point to define the positive peak and one for the negative peak.

Shannons sampling theorem states that a sampled continuous bandwidth limited function $h(t)$ is completely determined by its samples (measured at $k\Delta t$) if all its frequencies are smaller in magnitude than f_c. More accurately, if $H(f) = 0$ for all $|f| > f_c$, then $h(t)$ is given explicitly by the formula

$$h(t) = \Delta t \sum_{k=-\infty}^{+\infty} h(k\Delta t) \frac{\sin(2\pi f_c (t - k\Delta t))}{\pi(t - k\Delta t)}. \qquad (3)$$

This is remarkable since the information of a signal with a potentially infinite amount of information is reduced to a finite amount. On the other hand physical signals, such as audio signals are usually not bandwidth limited. Sampling and applying a discrete Fourier transformation to audio signals will fold the energy contained in the frequencies beyond f_c into the range within f_c. More accurately the energy of the frequency $f_c+\Delta f$ is moved to $f_c-\Delta f$. This is know as aliasing. The only way to avoid this is by low-pass filtering the original signal before sampling.

Putting it all together, when down-sampling the 44kHz PCM signal to 11kHz it is necessary to apply a low-pass filter that cuts off frequencies beyond 5.5kHz. From the PCM signal sampled at 11kHz it is possible to obtain the true Fourier transform for frequencies up to 5.5kHz.

The discrete Fourier transform is applied to $h(k\Delta t)$ with $k = 1, \ldots, N$ assuming that the period length of $h(t) = N\Delta t$. For simplicity N is assumed to be even. Since the Fourier transformation is linear, N inputs can only produce N independent outputs, which correspond to the frequencies given by

$$f(n) \equiv \frac{n}{N\Delta t}; \quad n = -\frac{N}{2}, \ldots, \frac{N}{2}. \tag{4}$$

Notice that there are N+1 values, however, the two extremes of n are equal. For real valued signals $H(f(n))$ is symmetric resulting in a frequency resolution of

$$f_{res}(n, N, \Delta t) \equiv \frac{n}{N\Delta t}, \quad n = 0, \ldots, \frac{N}{2}. \tag{5}$$

The estimation of the discrete Fourier transform which maps N complex numbers to N complex numbers is given by

$$H\left(f\left(n\right)\right) \approx \Delta t \sum_{k=1}^{N} h(k\Delta t)\, e^{2\pi i(k-1)n/N} \tag{6}$$

The Fast Fourier Transformation (FFT) calculates the discrete Fourier transform in $O(Nlog_2N)$ instead of $O(N_2)$ operations. Especially if N is a power of 2, the Fourier transform can be calculated very efficiently. The Matlab FFT functions used on the bases of the FFTW1 library which has been developed at the MIT.

The assumption is that the function $h(k\Delta t)$ has a period of N. This is rather unlikely when an arbitrary sequence is taken out of a music signal.

For example, the signal might start with a high amplitude at k = 1 and have a low amplitude at $k = N$. This leads to a discontinuity which gives rise to ringing (leakage) or sidelobes, which can be seen as errors in the frequency-domain. To reduce these effects, window functions $w(k)$ are used and multiplied with the signal function $h(k\Delta t)$ in the time-domain. A common choice for a windowing function is the Hanning window. Figure 3 depicts the Hanning window and its effect on a signal and its power spectrum. The Hanning window is calculated as

$$w(k) = \frac{1}{2}\left(1 - \cos\left(2\pi\frac{k-1}{N-1}\right)\right), \quad k = 1, \ldots, N. \tag{7}$$

Figure 3 illustrates, the upper subplot shows the Hanning function over an interval of 256 samples plotted with the solid line. The dotted lines indicate the values for the Hanning functions with 50% overlap. The center subplot depicts the effects of the Hanning function applied to a signal. The signal is the same as the one in Figure 2. It is taken from Freak on a Leash, sampled at 11kHz, in the interval 60s to 60s+23ms. The solid line is the result of multiplying the Hanning window with the sample values, the dotted line is the original waveform. Notice that while the original signal starts with an amplitude of about -0.25 and ends with an amplitude of 0.17, the signal multiplied with the Hanning function starts and ends at zero. The lower subplot shows the effects of the Hanning function in the frequency domain. Again the solid line represents the signal to which the Hanning function has been applied, and the dotted line represents the original signal. The decibel (dB) values will be explained in subsection 2.

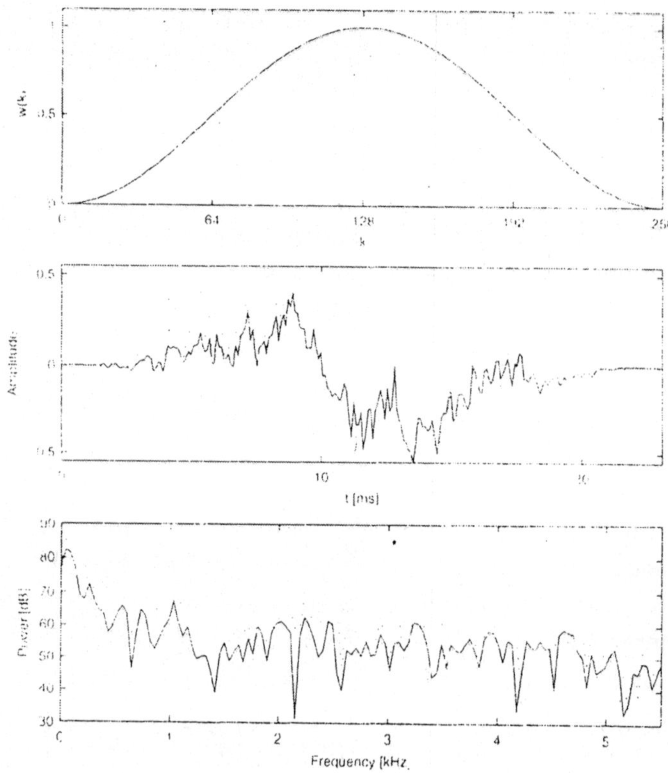

Figure 3. Hanning function

Application

One of the aspects of music is that the frequencies change continuously, however, within very short time frames the frequencies are approximately constant. These very short sequences can be seen as fundamental building blocks of music. Thus, a piece of music can be described with subsequent frequency patterns, each representing a time quantum. A common choice for this interval is 20ms. To optimize the FFT the number of samples N should be a power of 2.

However, this does not mean that it is necessary to have N samples. Shorter signals can be padded with zeros. Using 23ms time frames corresponds to 256 samples and results in a frequency resolution of about 43Hz in a range from 0 to 5.5kHz. As indicated in Figure 3 a 50% overlap between the windows is used. Notice that the sum of the two overlapping Hanning windows at any point always equals 1. A 50% overlap increases the time resolution by a factor 2 to about 12ms. The calculations are implemented as follows. The raw audio data is given in vectors y_t of length N corresponding to 23ms at the time frame t. The power spectrum matrix $P(n, t)$, where n is the index for the frequency and t for the time frame can be calculated using,

$$\begin{aligned} \mathbf{y}'_t &= \mathbf{W}_N \mathbf{y}_t, \\ \mathbf{Y}_t &= \text{fft}(\mathbf{y}'_t), \quad \text{and} \\ \mathrm{P}(n, t) &= |\mathbf{Y}_t(n)|^2 \frac{1}{N}. \end{aligned} \tag{8}$$

The index n ranges from 1 to $N/2+1$. The matrix W_N contains the Hanning function weights for N points on the diagonal with zeros elsewhere where $N = 256$ at 11kHz. The *fft* function is taken from the previously mentioned FFTW library. The data after this feature extraction step basically still has the same size. While the discrete Fourier transformation yields 129 values for 256 sample values, the 50% overlap increases the amount of data by 2.

Critical-Bands

So far a piece of music is represented by a frequency snapshot every 12ms. These have one value every 43Hz starting at 0Hz up to 5.5kHz, where each value represents the power of the respective frequency. The inner ear separates the frequencies, transfers, and concentrates them at certain locations along the basilar membrane. The inner ear can be regarded as a complex system of a series of band-pass filters with an asymmetrical shape of frequency response. The center frequencies of these band-pass filters are closely related to the critical-band rates. Where these bands should be centered or how wide they should be, has been analyzed throughout several psychoacoustic experiments.

While we can distinguish low frequencies of up to about 500Hz well, our ability decreases above 500Hz with approximately a factor of $0.2f$, where f is the frequency. This is shown in experiments using a loud tone to mask a more quiet one. At high frequencies these two tones need to be rather far apart regarding their frequencies, while at lower frequencies the quiet tone will still be noticeable at smaller distances. In addition to these masking effects the critical-bandwidth is also very closely related to just noticeable frequency variations. Within a critical-band it is difficult to notice any variations. This can be tested by presenting two tones to a listener and asking which of the two has a higher or lower frequency.

Since the critical-band scale has been used very frequently, it has been assigned a unit, the *bark*.

The name has been chosen in memory of Barkhausen, a scientist who introduced the phon to describe loudness levels for which critical-bands play an important role. Figure 4 shows the main characteristics of this scale. At low frequencies below 500Hz the critical-bands are about 100Hz wide. The width of the critical bands increases rapidly with the frequency. The 24th critical-band has a width of 3500Hz.

The 9th critical-band has the center frequency of 1kHz. The critical-band rate is important for understanding many characteristics of the human ear.

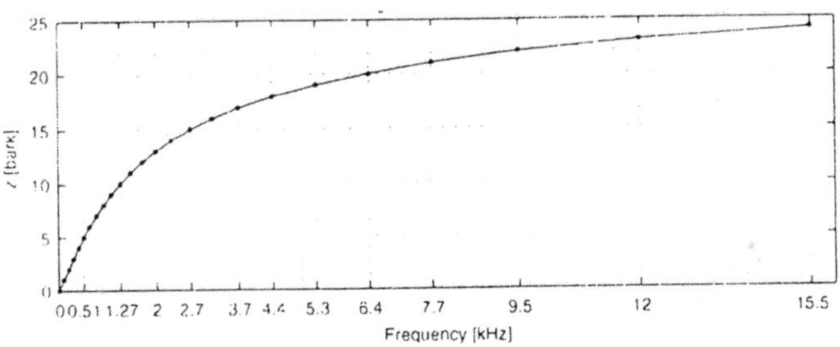

Figure 4. The basic characteristics of the critical-band rate scale. Two adjoining markers on the plotted line indicate the upper and lower frequency borders for a criticalband. For example, the 24th band starts at 12kHz and ends at 15.5kHz.

A critical-band value is calculated by summing up the values of the pow within the respective lower $f_a(i)$ and upper $f_b(i)$ frequency limits of the *i*-th criticalband. This can be formulated as

$$\mathbf{B}(i,t) = \sum_{n \in I(i)} \mathbf{P}(n,t), \quad I(i) = \{n \mid f_a(i) < f_{res}(n-1, 256, 1/11025) \leq f_b(i)\} \tag{9}$$

where *i*, *t*, *n* are indexes and B is a matrix containing the power within the *i*-th criticalband at a specific time interval *t*. P is the matrix representing the power per frequency and time interval *t* obtained from Equation 8. The relation between actual frequency and the row index *n* of *P* can be obtained using f_{res}(n–1, 256, 1/11025) (cf. Equation 5). The necessary upper and lower limits for each critical-band are listed in Table 1. Notice that P(*1*, *t*), which represents the power at 0Hz, is not used.

While the critical-band rate is defined having 24 bands, only the first 20 are used, since the highest frequencies in the data are limited to 5.5kHz. The 129 power spectrum values are now represented by 20 critical-bands values. This corresponds to a data reduction by a factor of about 6.5.

Masking

As mentioned before, the critical-bands are closely related to masking effects. Masking is the occlusion of one sound by another sound. A loud sound might mask a simultaneous sound (simultaneous masking), or a sound closely following (post-masking) or preceding (pre-masking) it. Pre-masking is usually neglected since it can only be measured during about 20ms. Post-masking, on the other hand can last longer than 100ms and ends after about a 200ms delay. Simultaneous masking occurs when the test sound and the masker are present simultaneously.

Table 1: Critical-band rate z, lower (f_a) and upper (f_b) frequency limits of the critical bandwidths, $f\Delta$, centered at f_c.

z	$f_{a,}$	f_b, f_c	z	$f\Delta$
Bark	Hz	Hz	Bark	Hz
0	0			
			50	0.5
1	100			
	150	1.5	100	
2		250	2.5	100
3	300			
		350	3.5	100
4	400			
		570	4.5	110
5	510			
		570	5.5	120
6	630			
		700	6.5	140
7	770			
		840	7.5	150
8	920			
		1000	8.5	160
9	1080			
		1170	9.5	190
10	1270			
		1370	10.5	210
11		1480		
		1600	11.5	240
12	1720			
		1850	12.5	280
13	2000			
		2150	13.5	320
14	2320			
		2500	14.5	380
15	2700			
		2900	15.5	450
16	3150			
		3400	16.5	550
17	3700			
		4000	17.5	700
18	4400			
		4800	18.5	900

19	5300			
		5800	19.5	1100
20	6400			
		7000	20.5	1300
21	7700			
		8500	21.5	1800
22	9500			
		10500	22.5	2500
23	12000			
		13500	23.5	3500
24	15500			

The spreading function defines the influence of the *j*-th critical-band on the *i*-th and is calculated as

$$\begin{aligned} S(i,j) &= 15.81 + 7.5(i - j + 0.474) \\ &\quad - 17.5\sqrt{1 + (i - j + 0.474)^2}. \end{aligned} \tag{10}$$

The spread critical-band rate spectrum matrix BS is obtained by multiplying B with S as follows

$$\begin{aligned} B_S(i,t) &= \sum_{j=1}^{20} S(i,j)\, B(j,t), \quad \text{which is equivalent to} \\ B_S &= SB. \end{aligned} \tag{11}$$

The simultaneous masking asymmetrically spreads the power spectrum over the criticalbands. The masking influence of a critical-band is higher on bands above it than on those below it.

Decibel

Before calculating sone values it is necessary to transform the data into decibel. The intensity unit of physical audio signals is sound pressure and is measured in Pascal (Pa). The values of the PCM data correspond to the sound pressure. It is very common to transform the sound pressure into decibel (dB). Decibel is the logarithm, to the base of 10, of the ratio between two amounts of power.

The decibel value of a sound is calculated as the ratio between its pressure and the pressure of the hearing threshold given by 20μPa. The sound pressure level in dB is calculated as

$$s_{dB} = 10 \log_{10} \frac{p}{p_0}. \tag{12}$$

where p is the power of the sound pressure, and p0 is the power of the sound pressure of the hearing threshold. The power is calculated as the squared sound pressure. Parseval's theorem states that the power of the signal is the same whether calculated in the time domain or the frequency domain, so the dB values can be calculated for the spread critical-band matrix BS. A parameter to adjust is the reference value p0. Note that the influence of the hearing threshold p0 on the decibel calculations is non-linear. If the hearing threshold is too low insignificant sounds will become significant, on the other hand if it is too high significant sounds will become insignificant.

Knowing that the sound pressure of the signals is digitized using 16 bit, it could be assumed that the most quiet, just noticeable power of the sound pressure level corresponds to 1 (or -1). When using p0 = 1 the notation db(SPL) is used, where SPL stands for sound pressure level.

The maximal decibel value for the energy at a certain frequency using db(SPL) is 96dB. However, the use of this assumption has led to sone values beyond the limit of damage risk in the experiments. This occurs because the energy of the frequencies are added together in the critical-bands and the masking function used is additive. The problem with decibel values beyond the limit of damage risk is that only equal loudness contours for levels below the limit are available, thus it is not possible to calculate accurate phon values, which have a non-linear correlation to the decibel values.

To be able to calculate the phon values the PCM amplitudes of the music collection were scaled so that all sounds are below the limit of damage risk. This corresponds to turning down the volume to a level at which the loudness of all music listened to, is within healthy ranges. The hearing threshold parameter p0 was set to 1/0.35. The loudness matrix in decibel, L_{dB}, is calculated as follows,

$$\begin{aligned} B'_S(i,t) &= \min(B_S(i,t), p_0), \quad \text{and} \\ L_{dB}(i,t) &= 10 \log_{10} \frac{1}{p_0} B'_S(i,t). \end{aligned} \tag{13}$$

The respective sone values are 0, 0.15, 1, 4, 16 and 64 sone. The dotted vertical lines indicate the positions of the center frequencies of the critical-bands (see Table 1). Notice how the critical-bands are almost evenly spaced on the log-frequency axis around 500Hz to 6kHz. The dots correspond to the values of the Celc matrix used to estimate the phon values from the dB values. The dip around 2kHz to 5kHz corresponds to the frequency spectrum we are most sensitive to.

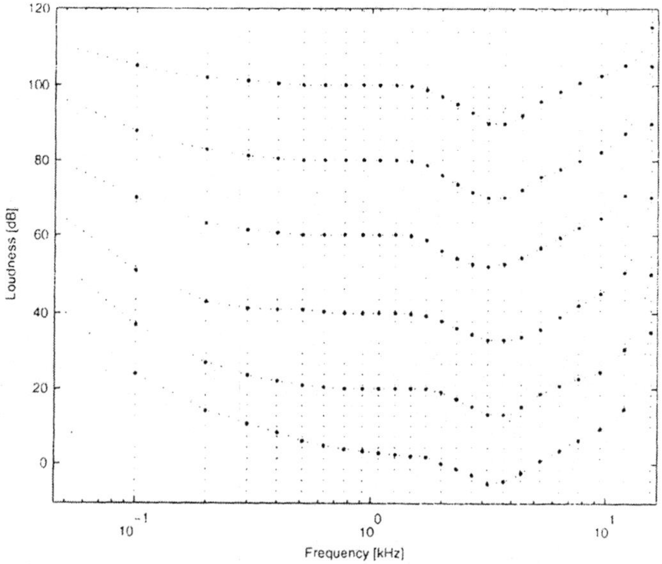

Figure 5. Equal loudness contours for 3, 20, 40, 60, 80 and 100 phon.

Phon

The relationship between the sound pressure level in decibel and our hearing sensation measured in sone is not linear. The perceived loudness depends on the frequency of the tone. Figure 5 shows so-called loudness levels for pure tones, which are measured in phon. The phon is defined using the 1kHz tone and the decibel scale. For example, a pure tone at any frequency with 40 phon is as loud as a pure tone with 40dB at 1kHz.

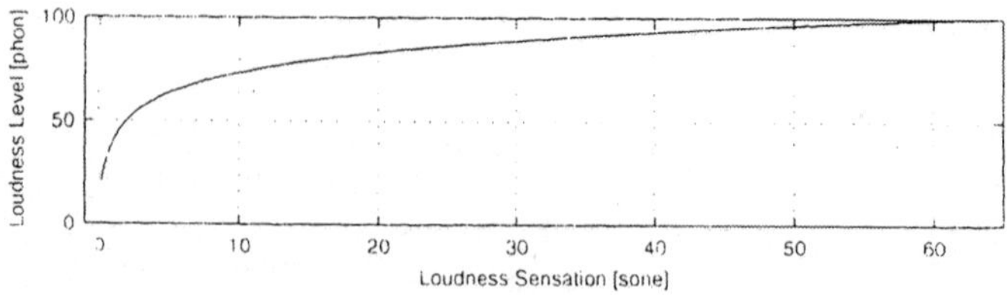

Figure 6. The relationship between the loudness level and the loudness sensation.

We are most sensitive to frequencies around 2kHz to 5kHz. The hearing threshold rapidly rises around the lower and upper frequency limits, which are respectively about 20Hz and 16kHz. Although the equal loudness contours are obtained from experiments with pure tones, they are frequently applied to calculate the specific loudness of the criticalband rate spectrum. The loudness matrix in phon, L_{phon}, can be calculated usingthe equal loudness contour matrix C_{elc} and the corresponding phone values to eachc contour cphon = [3, 20, 40, 60, 80 100]. $C_{elc}(i, j)$ contains the decibel values of the j-th loudness contour at the i-th critical-band. Values in between two equal loudness contours are Loudness Level [phon] interpolated linearly, as follows

$$
\begin{aligned}
\mathbf{L}'_{dB}(i,t) &= \max(\mathbf{L}_{dB}(i,t), \mathbf{C}_{elc}(i,1)), \\
level_{i,t} &= \operatorname*{argmin}_{j}(\mathbf{L}'_{dB}(i,t) < \mathbf{C}_{elc}(i,j)), \\
r_{i,t} &= \frac{\mathbf{L}'_{dB}(i,t) - \mathbf{C}_{elc}(i, level_{i,t}-1)}{\mathbf{C}_{elc}(i, level_{i,t}) - \mathbf{C}_{elc}(i, level_{i,t}-1)}, \quad \text{and} \\
\mathbf{L}_{phon}(i,t) &= \mathbf{c}_{phon}(level_{i,t}-1) + r_{i,t}\,\mathbf{c}_{phon}(level_{i,t}).
\end{aligned}
\tag{14}
$$

Note that $L_{phon}(i, t)$ can only be calculated if there exists an equal loudness contour j in $C_{elc}(i, j)$ so that $c_{phon}(j) > L_{phon}(i, t)$. The highest decibel level used here is 100dB and $p0$ is adjusted manually so all sounds are below this limit.

Sone

Finally, from the loudness level L_{phon} the specific loudness sensation L_{sone} per criticalband, following, is calculated as,

$$\mathbf{L}_{sone}(i,t) = \begin{cases} 2^{\frac{1}{10}(\mathbf{L}_{phon}(i,t)-40)} & \text{if } \mathbf{L}_{phon}(i,t) > 40 \\ \left(\frac{1}{40}\mathbf{L}_{phon}(i,t)\right)^{2.642} & \text{otherwise.} \end{cases} \quad (15)$$

The relationship between phon and sone can be seen in Figure 6. For low values up to 40 phon the sensation rises slowly until it reaches 1 sone at 40 phon. Beyond 40 phon the sensation increases at a faster rate. The highest values that occurred in the experiments conducted are below 60 sone, due to the adjustment of the threshold in quiet $p0$.

Examples

The methods applied so far have mainly been developed based on experiments with very simple sounds. Alternative ways to calculate L_{sone} include models which simulate each part of the ear, from the deflections of the outer ear to the activations of the neurons in the auditory nerve. A Matlab toolbox, namely HUTear[2], which implements such models has been developed at the Helsinki University of Technology.

On the other hand, the methods described in the previous sections have successfully been applied several times, for example, in. Similar methods are frequently used especially in the speech processing community. However, this is not a guarantee that these methods work in this context. It is important to fully understand what this series of transformations has done with the data, and what exactly the data "looks like" before the data-mining process is continued and further feature extraction steps are applied. A distorted voice articulates strange sounds while instruments including drums and probably at least one electric guitar play a scratchy theme, all in all a very interesting and unusual sound experience.

PCM Audio Signal

Although the amplitude cannot be directly expressed as a physical unit, the amplitude values correspond to sound pressure values. While Fur Elise hardly reaches 5% of the maximum amplitude at its highest sound pressure intensities, the amplitude of Freak on a Leash comes close to the maximum several times. This is also reflected in the subsequent plots and can be seen from the color-bars to the right of each plot. The intensities reach a maximum of about 60dB or 6 sone on the left, and about 80dB or 25 sone on the right side.

As part of the experiments conducted, the PCM data was originally scaled so that the maximum value of a piece of music equals the maximum possible amplitude. This was later dismissed since it showed no significant positive effects on the final results. Intuitively, it can be argued that the volume settings of the speakers are usually not changed while listening to different pieces of music. If there are significant differences in the sound intensities, then these might be important characteristics of the respective pieces of music.

Power Spectrum

The feature extraction steps from the 11kHz PCM audio signal to the specific loudness per critical-band preceding and half of the succeeding time frame. The pure power spectrum would not reveal much information, which is why the decibel values are used. The values displayed P′ have the following relationship to P

$$\mathrm{P}'(i, t) = 10 \log_{10} \frac{1}{p_0} \min(p_0, \mathrm{P}(i, t)). \tag{16}$$

On the left side the harmonics are very clearly visible as the equidistant, parallel, horizontal lines, which become weaker at higher frequencies. With a higher frequency resolution, for example, by increasing the sampling frequency or using a wider time frame, it would be possible to determine the exact pitch of the piano tones played. However, the exact pitch is not relevant for the genre of a piece of music.

The harmonics of Fur Elise can also be used to estimate the intensities of the tones played. The further up on the frequency scale the harmonics are still visible, the more intense the keynote has been played.

The power spectrum of Freak on a Leash suggests that there is not much variation in the music sequence. The main characteristic seems to be a texture of vertical lines, indicating the beats. However, there are also some harmonics visible as vertical lines. Very typical is how the whole spectrum is active and that the power intensities are highest in the lower frequencies.

The main active frequencies of Fur Elise are contained within this spectrum which corresponds to what can be seen in the subplot. On the other side Freak on a Leash contains high frequencies that are not within the spectrum, as the subplot suggests the texture continues over the entire audible spectrum. However, simple tests using average PC speakers revealed no difference in the sound sensation of Freak on a Leash at 11kHz or 44kHz sampling rate. Notice how the average specific loudness sensation decreases from bark 17 to bark 20. Thus, the limit of 5.5kHz is suitable for Freak on a Leash.

Critical-Band Rate Spectrum

The values of the critical-band rate spectrum B have been transformed to decibel just as those of the power spectrum, and all subsequent are, expect for the specific loudness sensation. Notice that the decibel range slightly increases as the frequencies are bundled together into critical-bands.

Generally it appears that the data has become fuzzy. The harmonics of Fur Elise are hardly recognizable while some diffuse activities have become more apparent. On the other hand the keynotes of Fur Elise are still clearly recognizable. Notice that a deficiency has become more apparent as well. When listening to the sequence there is no bass noticeable, however, the subplot shows a significant activity at bark 1, it is present in the power spectrum, but being limited to the lowest frequencies it is hardly visible. This seems to be some error in the recording but does not influence the perceived sound quality.

The critical-band rate spectrum of Freak on a Leash reveals an effect caused by low-pass filtering the music up to 5.5Hz. While throughout bark 1 to 19 the intensities are rather continuous, at bark 20 there is a discontinuity. The values of the 20th critical-band are clearly lower compared to the 19th. The answer to this can be found looking at Table 1. The 20th critical-band is defined from 5.3kHz to 6.4kHz. Despite this apparent discontinuity the information necessary to determine the genre is still contained in the data, in the same way, as the genre can be determined listening to the low-pass filtered music.

Spread Critical-Band Rate Spectrum

The spreading function is asymmetric with a stronger influence on the bands above than on those below the one it is centered on. It is also important that the spreading function does not influence the temporal resolution. Post-masking effects, which smoothen the temporal dimension, have been ignored since they showed negative influences on the determination of the exact beat intervals.

Looking at the spread critical-band rate spectrum it is not possible to recognize the harmonics of the tones. While the harmonics influence our sensation an untrained listener is not able to identify them exactly. Instead, an untrained listener might perceive the harmonics as shadows of the keynote that add to tones richness. Wonho Yang mentions that spreading the critical-bands might not have a positive impact when trying to measure the objective speech quality. Generally some perhaps very typical and important features might be lost through the smoothing.

Specific Loudness Level - Phon

The effects of the equal loudness level transformation for the critical-bands. While the intensities in the lower frequencies are reduced the intensities around bark 18 are increased. Für Elise does not use the frequencies around 4kHz (which corresponds to the 18th critical-band). The constant activity in the background, which becomes apparent, is another deficiency in the recording.

This deficiency seems to be caused by the generally very quiet recording, which enables broadband noise to become noticeable, especially in the frequency spectrum we are most sensible too, which is around 4kHz. However, in the same way as this deficiency does not appear to be significant in the illustrated specific loudness level images, it does not influence the perceived genre when listening to the recording of Fur Elise.

On the other side Freak on a Leash uses the frequencies around 4kHz frequently. Some not recognizable instruments and some parts of the distorted male voice are active in that area.

Specific Loudness Sensation - Sone

The sound of Freak on a Leash is far more complex and cannot be analyzed in a similar way. Although there is something like a melody, which is played throughout the sequence, it is hard to localize it in the specific loudness sensation plot. The melody is not the main characteristic of this sequence, whereas the strange sounding soundscape definitely is. Something that can be noticed is the recurrent pattern at the low frequencies. Three times there is a larger pause with a specific pattern right before it. Between these there are two smaller pauses. These are followed immediately by a sound running down the frequencies from about bark 5 to 2. And these again, are followed every time in the same distance, by a sound running down the frequencies from bark 5 to 2, although not as intense.

Dynamics

So far each song is represented by several 6-second sequences of the specific loudness sensation per critical-band, $L_{sone}(i, t)$. It would be possible to use $L_{sone}(i, t)$ to calculate similarities between the data. One option would be to compare two sequences L^{a}_{sone} and L^{b}_{sone} point-wise, i.e. comparing $L^{a}_{sone}(i, t)$ and $L^{b}_{sone}(i, t)$ for all i and t. The result might be quite surprising. For example, shifting Rock DJ by only 40ms would result in a huge difference to the un-shifted sequences - although they sound the same.

Thus, the final representation of the data must be invariant to time shifts. Weil and Fruhwirth have used the Fourier transforms of the activities in the frequency bands, which are also used here. Ellis has shown that using a similar concept it is possible to predict the pitch of a sound. Ellis analyzed periodically recurring peeks in the loudness of a frequency band by calculating the autocorrelation. The main difference between Weil, Fruwirth and Ellis is the frequency ranges they analyze. While Ellis analyzes patterns with periods of about one millisecond (which corresponds to frequencies up to 1kHz), Fruhwirth limits his investigation to frequencies up to 25Hz. Weil uses a similar spectrum as Fruhwirth, though limits his analysis to 15Hz.

Amplitude Modulated Loudness

The loudness of a critical-band usually rises and falls several times. Often there is a periodical pattern, also known as the rhythm. At every beat the loudness sensation rises, and the beats are usually very accurately timed. The loudness values of a critical-band over a certain time period can be regarded as a signal that has been sampled at discrete points in time. The periodical patterns of this signal can then be assumed to originate from a mixture of sinuids. These sinuids modulate the amplitude of the loudness, and can be calculated by a Fourier transform. An example might illustrate this. To add a strong and deep bass with 120 beats per minute (bpm) to a piece of music, a good start would be to set the first critical-band (bark 1) to a constant noise sensation of 10 sone. Then one could modulate the loudness using a sine wave with a period of 2Hz and an amplitude of 10 sone. The modulation frequencies, which can be analyzed using the 6-second sequences and time quanta of 12ms, are in the range from 0 to 43Hz with an accuracy of 0.17Hz.

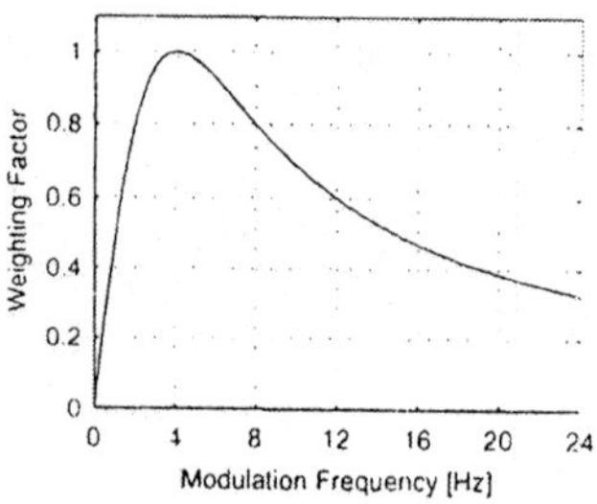

Figure 7. The relationship between fluctuation strength and the modulation frequency.

The modulation amplitude $\Delta L_i(n)$ with the frequency f_{res} (n, 512, 256/11025=2) (Equation 5) of the *i*-th critical-band is calculated as follows,

$$\Delta \mathbf{L}_i = \text{fft}(\mathbf{L}_{sone}(i, 1 \ldots 511)), \qquad (17)$$

where $L_{sone}(i, 1 \ldots 511)$ is a 6-second sequence of the the i-th critical-band of any piece of music. The *fft* function is the same as in Equation 8. Since there are only 511 values for the FFT, the signal is padded with one zero.

Fluctuation Strength

The amplitude modulation of the loudness has different effects on the sensation depending on the frequency. The sensation of fluctuation strength is most intense around 4Hz and gradually decreases up to a modulation frequency of 15Hz (Figure 7). At 15Hz the sensation of roughness starts to increase, reaches its maximum at about 70Hz, and starts to decreases at about 150Hz. Above 150Hz the sensation of hearing three separately audible tones increases.

The fluctuation strength of a tone with the loudness ΔL, which is 100% amplitude modulated with the frequency f_{mod} can be expressed by,

$$f_{flux}(\Delta L . f_{mod}) \propto \frac{\Delta L}{(f_{mod}/4\text{Hz}) + (4\text{Hz}/f_{mod})}. \tag{18}$$

The modulation amplitudes F(i, n) of the i-th critical-band and the modulation frequency f_{res} (n, 512, 128/11025) (cf. Equation 5) are weighted according to the fluctuation strength sensation as follows,

$$\mathbf{F}(i, n) = f_{flux}(|\Delta \mathbf{L}_i(n+1)|. f_{res}(n)). \tag{19}$$

Notice that ΔL(0), with f_{res}(0, 512, 128/11025) = 0Hz, is ignored since it does not influence the fluctuation.

The modulation amplitudes are highest at the lowest modulation frequencies. All other frequencies would play a minor role in calculating the distances between two sequences.

The fluctuation strength is spread out more evenly across the spectrum. Notice that the standard deviation shows clear patterns of vertical lines, which are caused by sequences with a strong beat at the corresponding modulation frequencies. Around bark 1 to 3 there are some highlights, these are typical bass 30 patterns.

As mentioned above the highest modulation frequency which can be calculated is about 43Hz. However, music will usually not show much fluctuation at frequencies beyond 10Hz (600bpm). The standard deviation of the fluctuation strength rapidly decreases after about 5Hz and there is hardly any fluctuation around 15Hz. The mean, median, and maximum values of the fluctuation strength confirm that there is not much activity beyond 10Hz. To reduce the amount of data only the frequency values up to 10Hz are used, which are the first 60 values.

Modified Fluctuation Strength

The fluctuation strength can be used for point-wise comparison of two music sequences. Each $F(i, n)$ has a meaning which does not depend on time shifts. For example, the value at F(1, 8) describes the fluctuation strength at the first critical-band (bark 1) with the modulation frequency of 1Hz, which corresponds to a bass with 6Cbpm.

The 3-dimensional matrices F can be treated as images. Individual characteristics of these images can be emphasized or suppressed using image processing methods. A similar approach where image processing techniques are applied to music data was presented by Mellinger. There are two basic types of fluctuation patterns. Classical music does not tend to have one dominant periodical beat pattern. It usually has a lot of variation in its tempo. On the other hand contemporary rock music usually contains at least one strong specific beat. This is reflected in the specific fluctuation strength in such a way that rock music has sharp vertical lines. These often range over all the critical-bands, sometimes only in the lower frequencies, sometimes only in the higher frequencies. On the contrary, for example, F¨ur Elise or similar music will have a more spread fluctuation over several frequencies close to each other. To distinguish these two types of patterns more clearly a gradient filter is used to emphasize sharp vertical lines.

After emphasizing vertical lines it is necessary to suppress irrelevant characteristics, in particular the exact location of peeks. This can be illustrated, for example, using three 6-second music sequences given as F^a, F^b, and F^c. For simplicity they shall contain all zeros except for $F^a(2, 8)$ = 10 sone and $F^b(1, 9)$ = 10 sone. The sequences F^a and F^b both have a bass beat, with almost the same frequency. However, using for example the Euclidian vector norm, the sequences F^a and F^b would be double as far apart from each other as they are from F^c.

More intuitive would be if F^a and F^b would be much closer to each other than they are to F^c. To be able to use the Euclidean vector norm and recognize such similarities some spreading is applied. In the above example F^a is smoothened so that, for example, the peek at $F^a(2, 08)$ is spread first over the critical-bands up and down 4 bands and then over the modulation frequencies with 31 Gaussian weighting factors. The same is done for the peek at $F^b(1, 9)$ resulting in the desired effects regarding their Euclidean distances.

The modified fluctuation strength (MFS) F_{mod} is calculated as follows.

$$\mathbf{F}'(i,n) = |\mathbf{F}(i,n) - \mathbf{F}(i,n+1)|, \text{ and} \qquad (20)$$
$$\mathbf{F}_{mod} = \mathbf{S}_i \mathbf{F}' \mathbf{S}_n.$$

The first part of this equation calculates the difference between two adjacent modulation frequencies n and $n + 1$, this emphasizes the vertical lines, which correspond to specific beats. S_i is a 20 by 20 matrix, defining how the values of F′ are spread over the critical-bands. S_n is a 60 by 60 matrix, with the spreading values for the modulation frequencies. The index n only runs from 1 to 60, ignoring the modulation frequencies beyond 10Hz. The main difference is the range of the maximum and standard deviation values. Since high peeks are spread across the neighboring modulation frequencies and critical-bands, their peek values decrease, and so does the standard deviation. The main characteristics, such as the vertical lines, which can be seen in the maximum and standard deviation statistics, are not significantly modified.

Examples

Korn, Freak on a Leash and Beethoven, Fur Elise are used to demonstrate the relationship between the specific loudness given by L_{sone} and the MFS F_{mod}. Only the first 60 values (excluding the 0Hz value) are used, which corresponds to the frequencies up to 10Hz. Notice the difference in the ranges of the values. The application of the gradient filter reduces the fluctuation strength of Fur Elise, while the main vertical line a little below 7Hz in Freak on a Leash is emphasized.

The rhythmic event plot indicates that there are several rhythmic events with the average frequency of about 3.6Hz. In the fluctuation strength subplot the modulation frequencies around 4Hz are emphasized more. There are no clear vertical lines though, since there are no periodic beats recurring with the exact distance in between. On the other side Freak on a Leash has a very clear vertical line, corresponding to the sound of drums which add periodical beats to the music.

Model of Rhythm

To compare the results obtained using the fluctuation strength with models based on the overall loudness, the model of rhythm presented in is used. A rhythmic event is defined as a maximum in the loudness-time function. More specifically the model postulates that only maxima above a value of $0.43N_m$ are used, where N_m represents the loudness of the highest maximum within a relevant time, which is assumed to be the interval of 6 seconds here. A second condition is that only relative maxima of sufficient height are considered. If $\Delta N < 0{:}12N_m$ then the maxima are ignored, where ΔN is the difference in loudness between the last minimum and the respective maximum. As a final condition, only maxima which are separated more than 120ms are considered to be separate rhythmic events. If there are several maxima within this time frame, only the highest maxima is selected.

Computational Efficiency

One aspect of good features representing music is that they should be computationally efficient as music collections grow large in size rapidly. In this section some practical issues are summarized related to the feature extraction process. All time statements refer a P2 350MHz with 256MB RAM using Matlab 6and compiled Matlab functions.

The original 359 MP3 files, which are used for the experiments, occupy about 1.3GB on the hard disc and

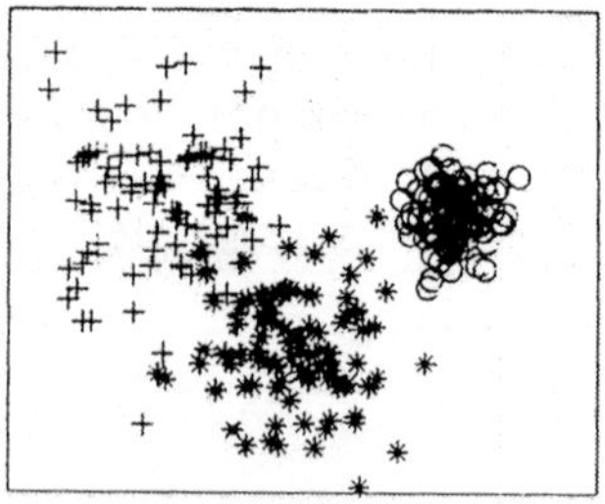

(a) Dataset

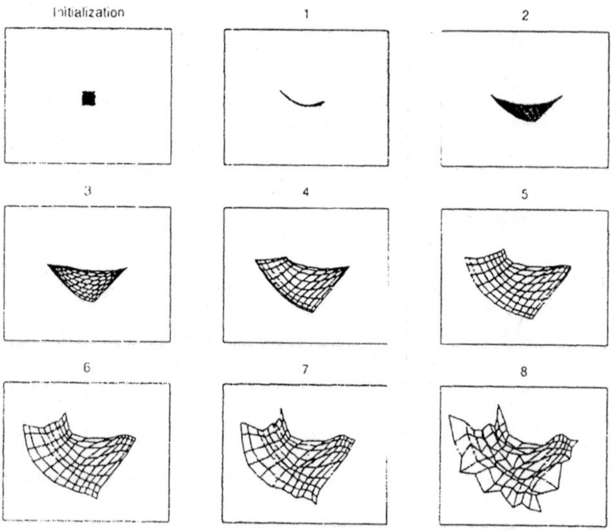

(b) Training

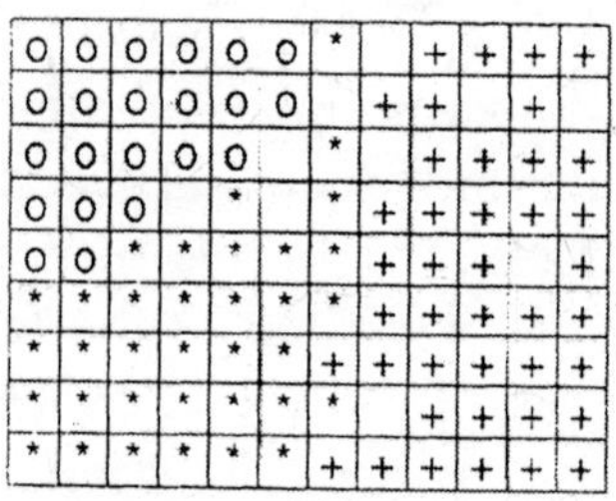

(c) Map

Figure 8. The batch SOM algorithm

represent about 23 hours of music. Winamp3 was used to convert the MP3 format to the 11kHz mono PCM format. The PCM data is known as WAV in Microsoft systems and as AU in Unix systems. The PCM data occupies about 1.7GB. The conversion only takes a few minutes.

The PCM data is then read by Matlab and the results of the intermediate steps are saved to the disk. The 3940 selected 6-second sequences, stored as PCM data, occupy about 490MB of storage. The specific loudness values are stored for each piece of music separately in the Matlab MAT format. Together they occupy 150MB of storage. The fluctuation strength data matrix with all 256 modulation frequencies has (stored in single precision) about 80MB. Matlab takes about 2 hours for a complete feature extraction run.

CLUSTERING

The music collection is organized based on these features. The main tool used for this is the self-organizing map (SOM) algorithm, which is a clustering method with intuitive visualization capabilities. SOM has been applied several times to support the evaluation of the feature extraction process and the SOM is the basis of the final user interface to the music collection.

Self-Organizing Maps

The goal of clustering data is to find groups (clusters) of data items that are similar to each other and different from the rest of the dataset. Clustering is a method to summarize the main characteristics of a dataset. For example, a music collection could be summarized by describing the groups (genres) it consists of. Each group could be described, for example, by the number and variation of its members. It might also be interesting to know the relationship between these groups. For example, a genre might have several sub-genres.

For the purpose of clustering data several algorithms have been developed. One very frequently employed clustering algorithm is the SOM. The SOM was developed 1981 as an artificial neural network, which models biological brain functions. Since then it has undergone thorough analysis. The algorithm and its variations have been employed several times in domains such as machine vision, image analysis, optical character recognition, speech analysis, and engineering applications in general, see for example. The SOM is a powerful tool that can be used in most data-mining processes especially in data exploration. Moreover, the SOM is very efficient compared to other non-linear alternatives such as the Generative Topographic Mapping, Sammon's Mapping, or generally Multi Dimensional Scaling. An example for the efficiency of the SOM is the WebSOM1 project.

The Batch SOM Algorithm

One of the variations of the original SOM is the batch SOM algorithm, which is significantly faster and has one parameter less to adjust. Although the algorithm is different the architecture of the map is the same. The map consists of map units, which are ordered on a grid. Usually this grid is rectangular and 2-dimensional and is used to visualize the data. An example can be seen in Figure 8(c). Each of the map units is assigned to a reference vector, also known as model or prototype vector. This vector lies in the data space and represents the data items that are closest to it. Units, which are close to each other on the grid, also have similar model vectors and thus represent similar data.

The batch SOM algorithm consists of two steps that are iteratively repeated until no more significant changes occur. First the distance between all data items x_i and the model vectors m_j is computed and each data item i is assigned to the unit that represents it best c_i. V_j denotes the Vernoi set of data items which are best represented by unit m_i.

In the second step each model vector is adapted to better fit the data it represents. To ensure that each unit j represents similar data items as its neighbors, the model vector m_j is adapted not only according to V_j but also in regard to the Vernoi sets of the units in the neighborhood. Which units are considered to be neighbors and how much influence they have on the unit j is defined by a neighborhood function.

A common choice for the neighborhood function $h_t(j, k)$ is a Gaussian function which is centered on mj and has a standard deviation σt which decreases with each iteration t. Assuming a Euclidean vector space, the two steps of the batch SOM algorithm can be formulated as

$$c_i = \operatorname*{argmin}_j \|\mathbf{x}_i - \mathbf{m}_j\|^2, \quad \text{and}$$
$$\mathbf{m}_j^* = \frac{\sum_i h_t(j, c_i)\, \mathbf{x}_i}{\sum_{i'} h_t(j, c_{i'})}, \tag{21}$$

where m_j^* is the updated model vector. Although it is usually very unlikely it might occur that a data vector x_i is equally closest to two or more model vectors. In this case randomly one of these model vectors should be chosen to be c_i. An efficient way to implement this is to first calculate the sum s_j of all data vectors in a Vernoi set Vj and then use them to calculate the weighted average,

$$
\begin{aligned}
\mathbf{V}_j &= \{\mathbf{x}_i \mid c_i = j\}, \\
\mathbf{s}_j &= \sum_{\mathbf{x}_i \in \mathbf{V}_k} \mathbf{x}_i, \quad \text{and} \\
\mathbf{m}_j^* &= \frac{\sum_k h_t(j,k)\, \mathbf{s}_j}{\sum_{k'} h_t(j,k')\, |\mathbf{V}_{k'}|}
\end{aligned} \tag{22}
$$

Parameters

Basically there are two parameters to adjust when using the batch SOM with a rectangular grid and a Gaussian neighborhood function, namely the map size and σ_t. Usually it is not difficult to find good parameter settings, and there are some basic rules of thumb that are helpful. The number of map units should be somewhere in the range of √(n), where *n* is the number of data items. The map size is usually rectangular. Depending on the display used, often a ratio between the width and the breadth of, for example, 4 to 3 is chosen. The number of units defines the resolution of the map. More units will lead to a higher resolution of the mapping.

However, the SOM algorithm scales approximately $O(m^2)$, in regard to the number of units m. The second parameter σ_t is also know as the neighborhood radius, since it defines in which radius of a unit other units are considered to be neighbors. In wellestablished schedules are published which define at which iteration the radius should have which value. If the map is initialized well (e.g. using Principal Component Analysis) the initial radius can be set to about $c/8$, where c is either breadth or width of the map, choosing the bigger value. If a random initialization is chosen then a good initial radius is c/4. The radius then quickly decreases to ¼ of this initial value. This is known as the rough training phase.

The actual number of iterations depends on the ratio between data items and units. The next and final phase is the fine tuning phase. Starting with the radius set to the value where the rough training ended the radius is slowly decreased to 0. When the neighborhood radius is 0 the SOM algorithm is the same as the k-means algorithm. With 0 neighborhood radius the units are only updated in regard to the data they best fit, ignoring surrounding units, and thus representing the data mapped to them as well as possible.

Simple Example

The algorithm is illustrated using Figure 8. The dataset (Figure 8(a)) is 2-dimensional and contains three groups each represented by 100 members and normally distributed around their centers. Figure 8 (b) depicts the form of the map in the data space. Starting with a random initialization, 8 subsequent training iterations are shown. After these 8 iterations the map fits the data rather well (Figure 8 (c)). There are several interesting aspects of the SOM that can be seen.

First of all the SOM does not map the data linearly. A linear mapping could be achieved using, for example, a Principle Component Analysis (PCA). The SOM uses its units efficiently, as few units as possible are wasted not representing any data. Furthermore, areas in the data space with a high density of data items are represented by more units than areas with a lower density. This is also known as magnification.

In figure 8, the batch SOM algorithm illustrated with a simple 2-dimensional toy dataset. Starting with a random initialization 8 training iterations are calculated and the position of the model vectors in the data space visualized. Finally the units are labeled with the most frequent class they represent.

The model vectors are most dense in the area of the 'o' class (Figure 8(b), 8th iteration). Interesting is also the training itself. Notice how the map slowly unfolds to fit the 40 data. When the neighborhood radius is high initially, each map unit represents a large amount of data and thus the model vectors of the units tend to be around the mean of the whole dataset.

As the neighborhood radius decreases the units become more flexible and are able to fit the data better. Notice also how the smoothness decreases drastically in the last two training iterations. These are the final steps of the fine tuning phase, regardless of the neighbors the units try to match their data as well as possible.

Music Sequences

Generally, the sequences of one piece of music have similar characteristics. For example, one characteristic of the 9 sequences of Fur Elise is that they have very low MFS values, while those of Rock DJ are about 10 times higher. Another rather typical characteristic is the beat pattern. For example, Fur Elise hardly has any vertical lines, while Rock DJ has a few lines that are present in almost all of its 12 sequences. Another characteristic of Rock DJ is the strong but rather slow bass, which can be seen in most of its sequences in the lowest 2 frequency bands at a low modulation frequency (1.7Hz).

Pieces of Music

This section deals with the question of how to represent a piece of music based on its 6-second sequences. This is necessary to obtain the final map of the whole pieces of music and not their sequences as in the previous section. The representations should be in a vector space and the metric, which defines the distance between the vectors of the pieces of music, should correspond to their perceived similarity.

One straightforward approach would be to use the average of the sequences to represent to corresponding piece of music. On the other hand it seems to be very intuitive that most pieces of music will contain different types of sequences. For example, a piece of music might include some slower sequences and some faster sequences. Also the instruments used and the existence of vocals may alternate between the different sequences of one piece of music. It is questionable if the average of a slow and a fast sequence would be a good representation for such a piece of music. To decide how to combine the sequences four methods are evaluated using the SOM. The following sub-sections start with a description of Principal Component Analysis, which is used throughout this section. Then the different methods are described and evaluated. The methods are Gaussian Mixture Models, Fuzzy C-Means, k-means with a simple response measure, and finally the simplest approach, the median of the sequences.

Principal Component Analysis

In many data analysis applications such as image recognition, e.g., it is common to use Principal Components Analysis (PCA) to reduce the dimensionality of the data. Especially, when the data is highly correlated, such as the

MFS representations of the music sequences, the d-dimensional data can be compressed very efficiently using PCA and resulting in a much lower m-dimensional eigenspace.

The PCA is a linear projection, and it guarantees that the m-dimensional eigenspace best preserves the variance of the data in the d-dimensional space. This is equivalent to preserving the sum of the squared distances between the data points in the d-dimensional space in the m-dimensional space as well as possible. Often this is referred to as minimizing the reconstruction error or minimizing the empirical risk.

The MFS data is represented in 1200 dimensions, corresponding to first 20 criticalbands and 60 levels of the modulation frequency in the range from 0-10Hz. These 1200 dimension can be reduced significantly using PCA while preserving most of the information.

The main characteristics are preserved, for example, it is clear that the values are very low and there are no vertical lines in Fur Elise, while the values of Freak on a Leash are much higher and there is a significant vertical line below 7Hz. Using 80 dimensions sharpens the images so that most details become apparent, for example the low valued, vertical lines of Freak on a Leash around 2Hz to 4Hz.

There are several advantages when using low-dimensional representations. Obviously, less storage is required and the clustering algorithms need fewer computations to find solutions. Furthermore, clustering algorithms which use random elements, for example for initialization, will more likely produce similar results in different runs, since the number of possible solutions and the number of variables which need to be determined are decreased significantly.

The linear projection x^* into the low-dimensional eigenspace of a vector x is calculated as

$$x^* = (x - c)V \tag{23}$$

where V is a d by *m* matrix with orthonormal columns and c is the mean of all vectors in the dataset. The vector x is reconstructed from x^* with

$$x = x^*V^T + c \tag{24}$$

The *m* columns of the matrix V are the first *m* eigenvectors of the covariance matrix Q sorted descending according to their eigenvalues. The *d* by *d* matrix Q is calculated from the dataset after c has been deducted, so that the data has zero mean. The space spanned by the *m* orthonormal eigenvectors is referred to as the eigenspace. The matrix V can be computed efficiently based on Singular Value Decomposition (SVD).

Gaussian Mixture Models

As stated previously, the goal is to represent the pieces of music based on their sequences. One possibility is to assume that the music sequences represent only a fraction of all available music sequences. Furthermore, it is straightforward to assume that there are different clusters of sequences and that most sequences cannot clearly be assigned to one specific cluster but rather have a certain probability of belonging to each cluster. A piece of music can then be defined by the average probability by which its sequences belong to the clusters. Finally it is necessary to make some assumptions regarding the shape of the clusters.

It is very common to assume Gaussian clusters so that each cluster is defined through a center and a covariance matrix.

These assumptions lead to Gaussian mixture models. The GMM models the density function that generates the dataset from a mixture of Gaussian basis functions (clusters). The (posterior) probability P(i | x) that a data item x is generated by a cluster i is

$$P(i|\mathbf{x}) = \frac{P(\mathbf{x}|i)P(i)}{P(\mathbf{x})}. \tag{25}$$

where P(i) is the prior probability of the cluster i and $\Sigma_i P(i) = 1$. The normalization factor $P(x) = \Sigma_i P(x \mid i)$ ensures that $\Sigma_i P(i \mid x) = 1$. The likelihood P(x | i) to observe a data item x in a cluster i is given by the multi-dimensional normal distribution

$$P(\mathbf{x}|i) = \frac{1}{(2\pi)^{d/2}\det(\Sigma_i)^{1/2}} \exp\left(-\frac{1}{2}(\mathbf{x}-\mu_i)^T \Sigma_i^{-1}(\mathbf{x}-\mu_i)\right) \tag{26}$$

where d is the dimensionality of the data space. For a cluster i the center is denoted by μ_i, Σ_i denotes the covariance matrix and det(Σ_i) its determinant. The likelihood to observe the dataset X given the GMM defined by the set of parameters θ is

$$\ell(\theta) \equiv P(\mathbf{X}|\theta) = \prod_{n=1}^{N} P(\mathbf{x}_n|\theta). \tag{27}$$

The parameters of a GMM can efficiently be estimated iteratively using the EM algorithm. The EM algorithm consists of two steps, namely the expectation and the maximization step which are repeated iteratively until the likelihood function converges to a local maximum. For the experiments with the music collection the GMM-EM functions of the Matlab Netlabtoolbox were used. Due to numerical problems the eigenspace with only 20 eigenvectors was used and the number of clusters was limited to 30.

To allow the clusters to fit the data better the full covariance matrix was estimated, which means that the clusters could be any form of ellipsoid rotated in any direction. To initialize the covariance matrices and the centers of the basis functions 5 iterations of k-means were used. And a few GMM-EM runs were made from which the model with the best likelihood was selected. The 30-dimensional vector u representing a piece of music with the indices of its sequences given by M is calculated as

$$\mathrm{u}(i) = \frac{1}{|M|} \sum_{m \in M} P(i|x_m), \quad \text{for } i = 1 \ldots 30. \tag{28}$$

Note that $\sum_i \mathrm{u}(i) = 1$.

Typical results of training a SOM based on vectors of pieces of music combined from their sequences by GMM-EM The map unit, which represents elise, usually always represents the same pieces of music which are adagio, air, kidscene, and mond. All of these are slower, playful, peaceful, classical pieces of music with few instruments, for example, kidscene is a piano solo, and air includes only a few string instruments.

Generally, all classic music in the collection on the map is located around the lower left to the center left. Not as clear as the mapping of elise is the mapping of korn-freak. The song is usually not located together with exactly the same but always around limp-pollution, limp-nobodyloves and other songs from Limp Bizkit. Sometimes the perceptually very different songs deepisyourlove, and wildwildwest are mapped near by too. The map does not seem to distinguish very well between songs like korn-freak, and Limp Bizkik, Papa Roaches, New Model Army songs in general on one side, and songs like lastchristmas and deepisyourlove on the other side. This might be caused by the limitations regarding the dimensionality of the eigenspace and the limited number of clusters used to represent the sequences.

The song rockdj is always around limp-counterfeit, limp-nookie and other Limp Bizkit songs and usually also next to cocojambo. All these songs have stronger beats at about the same frequency as Rock DJ and vocals. However, there seems to be a significant perceptual difference between the rather aggressive Limp Bizkit songs and Rock DJ.

All in all the results are not completely satisfactory, which might be related to the limitations caused by the numerical problems of the statistically sound GMM-EM.

Fuzzy C-Means

An alternative to the GMM is Fuzzy C-Means (FCM), which basically offers the same solution in regard to combining sequences of a piece of music to one vector. The goal of FCM is to find the fuzzy cluster centers and the values of fuzzy membership of the data items to the clusters, minimizing the following error function,

$$E = \sum_{i=1}^{C} \sum_{n=1}^{N} \gamma(i, \mathbf{x}_n)^b \, \|\mathbf{x}_n - \mu_i\|^2 . \qquad (29)$$

where the C is the number of clusters, N is the number of data items (music sequences), μ_i is the center of the i-th cluster, x_n is the n-th data vector and the paramter b > 1 is a fixed value, which needs to be specified. When b $\rightarrow \infty$ the error function is equivilant to the error function of k-means. For $b \rightarrow \infty$ all cluster centers converge to the centroid of the training dataset. In other words, the clusters become completely fuzzy so that each data point belongs to every cluster to the same degree. Typically the value b is chosen around 2.

Additionally to the error function FCM uses the following constraints,

$$\sum_{i=1}^{C} \rho(i, \mathbf{x}_n) = 1, \quad \text{for } i = 1, \ldots, N, \tag{30}$$

which ensures that the membership of any data item to all clusters adds up to 1. The FCM algorithm minimizes the error function (Equation 29) subject to the constraints (Equation 30). The iterative algorithm consists of two steps which are repeated until the error function converges. First the memberships are (re-)estimated based on some estimation for the cluster centers, and then the cluster centers are re-estimated based on the new values for the membership. The respective calculations are,

$$\begin{aligned} \mu_i &= \frac{\sum_i \rho(i, \mathbf{x}_n)^b \mathbf{x}_n}{\sum_i \rho(i, \mathbf{x}_n)^b}, \quad \text{and} \\ \rho(i, \mathbf{x}_n) &= \frac{z_{in}}{\sum_{k=1}^{C} z_{kn}}, \quad \text{where } z_{in} = \|\mathbf{x}_n - \mu_i\|^{2/(1-b)}. \end{aligned} \tag{31}$$

For the experiments with the music collection the 80 dimensional eigenspace of the music sequences was used, the centers of the FCM were initialized using a few iterations of the faster kmeans algorithm, the number of clusters was set to 120 and the parameter b was set to 1.1 which is rather low. The reason for the low value of b is that higher values yielded very similar cluster centers which did not represent the variations in the data appropriately.

The higher dimensionality of the eigenspace and the higher number of clusters dramatically increases the number of possible solutions to the clustering problem. Due to the random initialization of the FCM cluster centers (more accurately, the random initialization of the k-means centers, which are used to initialize the FCM centers) there is a greater variation between different FCM results then between the GMM-EM results.

The unit, which represents elise, usually also represents kidscene and mond and is always near merry, adadio, air, fortuna, funeral, and other similar classical pieces of music. Generally, all classic music in the collection on the map is located around the lower right to the lower center.

For korn-freak the FCM results are slightly better compared to those using GMM-EM, because the 4 times higher number of eigenvectors and clusters allows a higher resolution. Frequently similar songs by Papa Roaches (such as pr-revenge and pr-deathcell) and several songs by Limp Bizkit are located around korn-freak, however, the song wildwildwest is still in the immediate vicinity.

The unit representing rockdj (Rock DJ by Robbie Williams) is usually always located together with different pieces of music when comparing two FCM runs with the same parameters but different random initialization.

k-means

The k-means algorithm basically does the same (crisp clustering) as the SOM, with the significant difference that there is no neighborhood defined between two clusters (map units). Practically, k-means is equivalent to the SOM when the neighborhood radius of the SOM is set to zero.

The k-means algorithm can be used in the same way as the FCM and GMM-EM algorithms, however, each music sequence will not have a fuzzy membership or probability of belonging to several cluster but instead will be assigned to one cluster only.

The error function the k-means algorithm minimizes is

$$E = \sum_{n=1}^{N} \|\mathbf{x}_n - \mu_{c(n)}\|^2. \tag{32}$$

where $\mu_c(n)$ is the centroid of the cluster closest to the data vector x_n.

The centers of the clusters are initialized randomly, for example, by selecting C random data items. Then two steps are repeated iteratively until the error function (Equation 32) converges. The first step is to find $\mu_c(n)$ for all $n = 1, \ldots, N$ and in the second step for each cluster the new center is calculated as the mean of all data items belonging to it.

The experiments with the music collection were conducted setting the number of clusters to 120. Several runs were made and based on the error function the best clustering was chosen. Since each piece of music is usually represented by more than one sequence counting the average number of sequences per cluster would yield fuzzy results. The degree of fuzziness can be increased, for example, using a very simple method such as giving the best matching cluster for a sequence 3 points, the second best 2 points and the third best 1 point. Then the average points of all clusters can be calculated for each piece of music.

FCM results depend on the random initialization and thus two runs might produce different results. However, the classical music cluster is usually always the same. Especially, elise is always around the same group, which is basically the same as the group which can be seen in the GMM-EM or FCM results. Interesting though is that the mountainking is mapped to the same unit as elise. The two and a half minutes of mountainking are represented by 6-second sequences.

While the first 5 sequences are well comparable to elise, the 6th sequence is perceptually very different. The reason why mountainking and elise are mapped together lies in the ranking method used, which is very robust in respect to outliers. The unit representing korn usually also represents pr-revenge, pr-deathcell, limpnobodyloves, pr-binge, and other songs by Papa Roaches and Limp Bizkit, which match rather well. A song which does not seem to match too well is rem-endoftheworld (Its the end of the World by REM). The songs of REM in general seem to be much less aggressive then those of Papa Roaches or Limp Bizkit, however, the specific song Its the end of the world, is more aggressive then the usual REM songs.

Median

So far the approaches assumed that the sequences of a piece of music might have perceptually significant differences. Alternatively, it is possible to assume that the differences between the sequences of a song are perceptually insignificant and that only the parts they have in common are significant. To obtain a common representation of several sequences the mean of all characteristics can be calculated.

However, the mean is sensitive to outliers and thus the median seems to be more appropriate, especially considering that less then 1/3 of all available sequences are used to represent a piece of music. For example, In the hall of the mountainking by Grieg is represented by 5 rather quite and one very powerful sequence. The one powerful sequence would dominate the mean, while it has practically no influence on the median. For the experiments with the music collection the median is calculated from the 1200-dimensional MFS values, and then represented in the 80-dimensional eigenspace.

The median of Fur Elise summarizes the sequences very well. The median indicates that there are activities in the range of 3-10 bark and with a modulation frequency of up to 5Hz. However, the values of these activities are very low. The single sequences of Fur Elise have many more details, for example, the first sequence has a minor peek around bark 5 and 5Hz modulation frequency.

The median of Yesterday is a good summary as well. There are several activities in lower and some in the upper critical-bands and there is no significant vertical line that Critical-band [bark]. Some of the sequences of Rock DJ seem to have very different patterns. However, detailed analysis shows that they all have something in common, and this is revealed by the median. Although this analysis might suggest that the median is a good solution this is only partially the case.

Many pieces of music might be confined to one genre, even if this genre might be between two other genres, however, especially modern music tends to combine different MFS patterns. On the other hand the dynamic usually does not completely change.

Another advantage of using the median is that the random initializations (GMMEM, FCM, k-means) are no longer needed and thus the results are very stable and different runs will yield the same results, unlike the previous approaches. Although this approach is much simpler than the others and can be computed significantly faster, the quality is comparable.

The map unit in the lower left, which represents elise (Fur Elise by Beethoven) contains similar classical music such as air, adagio, kidscene, and mond. It is interesting to see that just as with the k-means approach the mountainking is mapped together with elise. The unit is surrounded by classical music such as merry, jurassicpark, branden, forelle, and walzer.

Generally, the music with lower fluctuation strength is in the lower left and the highest values are around the upper right. Strong beat patterns can be seen especially in the upper left, around the upper right including the area to the lower right. When using GMM-EM and FCM the model vectors are linear combinations of MFS vectors and thus can be reconstructed easily. When using the k-means approach with the ranking it is not possible to reconstruct exact MFS representations from the model vectors, but it is possible to calculate the MFS of a model vector from the mean of the MFS vectors of the pieces of music mapped to it. The MFS of model vectors to which no pieces of music are mapped can be interpolated from surrounding map units.

2

Ascetic/Aesthetic Visual Music

Real art isn't translating an already existing concept into the visual, but is the discovery of the Idea. The question remains how the artist or, for Schopenhauer, the genius moves beyond the concept, the imitative, the mere representation of a phenomenon. Cage and Kandinsky used silence and abstraction in their move away from the representational art and the norms of traditional notated art. For Schopenhauer it is a person of genius who is able to get beyond the representation to the will to become the "pure subject of knowing."

> Now according to our explanation, genius consists in the ability to know, independently of the principle of sufficient reason, not individual things which have their existence only in the relation, but the Ideas of such things, and in the ability to be, in face of these, the correlative of the Idea, and hence no longer individual, but pure subject of knowing. Yet this ability must be inherent in all men in a lesser and different degree, as otherwise they would be just as incapable of enjoying works of art as of producing them. Generally they would have no susceptibility at all to the beautiful and sublime; indeed, these words could have no meaning for them. We must therefore assume as existing in all men that power of recognizing in things their Ideas, of divesting themselves for a moment of their personality,

> unless indeed there are some who are not capable of any aesthetic pleasure at all. The man of genius excels them only in the far higher degree and more continuous duration of this kind of knowledge. These enable him to retain that thoughtful contemplation necessary for him to repeat what is thus known in a voluntary and intentional work, such repetition being the work of art. Through this he communicates to others the Idea he has grasped. Therefore this Idea remains unchanged and the same, whether it is called forth by a work of art or directly by contemplation of nature and life. (The World as Will and Representation, Volume1)

If all willing springs from a lack or deficiency, from suffering, we will discover that, any "attained object of willing" will give only temporary satisfaction. Schopenhauer-as if he knew what was coming in the electrate era-recognized the endless cycle of desire and disappointment that can fill an image-based form of communication. This endless cycle describes the temporary respites offered by-but rarely delivered-the advertising consumptive culture. While these consumer goods promise a brief reprieve from suffering they have no long lasting effect.

In this electrate era the images are designed to offer beauty with one hand while encouraging more desires of the will with the other. Lasting peace and happiness can never be achieved by a fulfilling of the will. To reach this state requires being raised up from the "endless stream of willing." When we reach "pure, will-less knowing," we will be unaffected by everything that moves our will. When we move into this liberated state we are no longer an individual, but are "pure subject of knowing. We are only that one eye of the world which looks out from all knowing creatures."

Vertov and the Kino-Eye

Dziga Vertov attempted to be the eye that "captured life unawares." Rather than starting with a script or other narrative structure he attempted to capture life. While Vertov had a strongly socialist agenda, he was experimenting with getting into the actual visual and sound textures of life. He experimented with recording street noises and editing them but the equipment of his time was not up to it. He describes the day that led to this experiment, "I was returning from the railway station. In my ears, there remained the chugs and bursts of steam from a departing train...someone swearing...a kiss...somebody's exclamation... laughter, a whistle, voices, the ringing of the station bell, the puffing of a locomotive...whispers, shouts, farewells."

He was stymied in his ideas for this audio collage. At the suggestion of some filmmakers he decided to try his vision on film instead of in the collection of sound. The Man with the Movie Camera, the resulting film, Vertov called a "visual symphony." In the proposal for the film we see how far Vertov hoped to take this. "The Man with the Movie Camera constitutes an experiment in the cinematic transmission of visual phenomena without the aid of intertitles (a film with no intertitles), a script (a film with no script), theatre (a film with neither actors nor sets)." Vertov saw the need to take film beyond the mere representation of what the eye could see.

> Until now we have violated the movie camera and forced it to copy the work of our eye. The better the copy, the better the shooting was thought to be. Starting today we are liberating the camera and making it work in the opposite direction-away from copying. The weakness of the human eye is manifest. We affirm the Cine-Eye, discovering the chaos of movement: the result of Cine-Eye's own movement; we affirm the

> Cine-Eye with its own dimensions of time and space, growing in strength and potential to the point of self-affirmation.

Vertov takes the viewer into the mechanics of the film so that it looses its power of representation. The films shows us the camera and the operator, the film editor, getting the theater ready for the show, and the projectionist-leaving no question in the mind of the viewers that they are watching a construct. Vertov in creating this visual symphony, captured the activity of people-getting up, working, playing, being intoxicated (with religion), being destroyed by capitalism (with the people rushing into the marketplace) and moving about the city with many forms of transportation. Vertov envisioned his whole effort as creating a montage, not just within the edit.

To make a montage is to organize pieces of film, which we call the frames, into a cine-thing. It means to write something cinematic with the recorded shots. It does not mean to select pieces, to make `scenes' (deviations of a theatrical character), nor does it mean to arrange pieces according to subtitles (deviations of a literary character). Every Kino-Eye production is mounted on the very day that the subject (theme) is chosen, and this work ends only with the launching of the film into circulation in its definitive form. In other words, montage takes place from the beginning to the end of the production.

Vertov took seriously his own mandate-to separate from the language of theater and literature. He keeps the viewer constantly aware that he is looking at a screen, and they are repeatedly reminded of his intervention with speed change, direction change and split screens. This pushes the viewer to go beyond the representation and enter into the art at a deeper level.

Schopenhauer believes that most people will never be able to attain this state-of experiencing the Idea-for they seek objects only in relation to their will. Their interface with objects is arranged around a system of desires, attainment, and the lack of fulfillment, which starts the cycle all over again. The question is; how can the individual will be frustrated in such a way as to allow us to find true art? Schopenhauer takes us on the first step of discovering two of these ways with a discussion of beauty and the sublime.

> Thus what distinguishes the feeling of the sublime from that of the beautiful is that, with the beautiful, pure knowledge has gained the upper hand without a struggle, since the beauty of the object, in other words that quality of it which facilitates knowledge of its Idea, has removed from consciousness, without resistance and hence imperceptibly, the will and knowledge of relations that slavishly serve this will. What is then left is pure subject of knowing, and not even a recollection of the will remains. On the other hand, with the sublime, that state of pure knowing is obtained first of all by a conscious and violent tearing away from the relations of the same object to the will which are recognized as unfavourable, by a free exaltation, accompanied by consciousness, beyond the will and the knowledge related to it. This exaltation must not only be won with consciousness, but also be maintained, and it is therefore accompanied by a constant recollection of the will, yet not of a single individual willing, such as fear or desire, but of human willing in general.

The difference is primarily related to how this state of "pure will-less knowing" is achieved. Does it appear with opposition by a "disappearance of the will from consciousness" or is it achieved by a "conscious exaltation above the will." Schopenhauer is clear that beauty and the sublime are not opposites but are two ways of going beyond the will. The opposite of the sublime is that which appears "charming or attractive." These charming objects stimulate the will by offering "satisfaction and fulfillment."

This stirring of will draws the viewer "down from pure contemplation." What Schopenhauer is seeking to avoid is art that stirs the will through representations that cause desire or whet the appetites. The purpose of art is the opposite of this-to enable the viewer to enter into a will suppressed state of contemplation. This state is similar-although less intense-to that of the artist creating the work. The sublime arises when something that is unfavourable to the will "becomes the object of pure contemplation."

If we are beyond the will, when we call something beautiful we are no longer speaking in terms of desire or in terms of the individual object.

> By calling an object beautiful, we thereby assert that it is an object of our aesthetic contemplation, and this implies two different things. On the one hand, the sight of the thing makes us objective, that is to say, in contemplating it we are no longer conscious of ourselves as individuals, but as pure, will-less subjects of knowing. On the other hand, we recognize in the object not the individual thing, but an Idea; and this can happen only in so far as our contemplation of the object is not given up to the principle of sufficient reason, does not follow the relation of the object to something outside it (which is ultimately always connected with relations to our own willing), but rests on the object itself.

When contemplation recognizes the beautiful-but without individual desire to possess or control-it moves beyond the realm of the advertising based image to a place of will-less knowing.

The images and the connections made by advertising images-which attempt to define the beautiful life-attempt to reach the viewer in their emotional centre while avoiding any foray into logic. While logical reflection will deflate most advertising claims and hinted connections, Schopenhauer does not suggest that we can find the true beauty by reason and logical reflection. He suggests that art must go beyond the scientific reason and beyond the symbolic attachment or relationship.

> What kind of knowledge is it that considers what continues to exist outside and independently of all relations, but which alone is really essential to the world, the true content of its phenomena, that which is subject to no change, and is therefore known with equal truth for all time, in 'a word, the Ideas that are the immediate and adequate objectivity of the thing-in-itself, of the will? It is art, the work of genius. It repeats the eternal Ideas apprehended through pure contemplation, the essential and abiding element in all the phenomena of the world. According to the material in which it repeats, it is sculpture, painting, poetry, or music. Its only source is knowledge of the Ideas; its sole aim is communication of this knowledge...art...plucks the object of its contemplation from the stream of the world's course, and holds it isolated before it.

This contemplation is the opposite of science, which follows reason and can't find complete satisfaction. Art considers things without the rational method of the principle of sufficient reason. This, according to Schopenhauer, is the form of true genius-the ability to do "pure contemplation." "Accordingly genius is the capacity to remain in a state of pure perception, to lose oneself in perception, to remove from the service of the will the knowledge which originally existed only for this service...to discard entirely our own personality for a time, in order to remain pure knowing subject, the clear eye of the world." The true genius is animated and restless because the present can't fill their consciousness. The true genius requires imagination to see, not what nature has formed, but the intended form within the Will. The logic of mathematics and science obscure this insight rather than assist it.

Building musical instruments requires the usage of mathematical formulas, and construction techniques informed by science. The builder must understand the physics of form and strength, and the relations of length and size to tone. However to create instruments that go beyond the average the builder must be in touch with less scientific things as well.

Sobell, the builder of the instruments in the Visual Music 8/8 Project, imagines the beauty found in a raw piece of wood, imagines the shape of that wood carrying the opportunity for sound and visual contemplation. He can hear in his mind how particular wood grains will vibrate with sound when the instrument is completed and the attached strings are struck. Many of the formulas for building an instrument involve science and math, in terms of mechanical strength, string length and fret placement. These qualities alone however will not make a fine instrument. To make a fine instrument requires the ability to see into the wood-to see the form hidden in the wood, to hear the vibrations inherent within the wood.

In Stefan E-V, Sobell is choosing the grain patterns and placement for the back of a large-body bouzouki. The tighter grains of the Cocobolo wood will provide deep clear tone with good separation in the final instrument. Stefan A-IV shows Sobell trimming the bracing to the shape and thickness that maintains structure strength but allows full toned vibrations. The builder must function in both ways to build instruments of true beauty. Sobell's instruments, for those who recognize it, holds the eternal Ideas apprehendable through contemplation.

Schopenhauer identifies the challenge for the artist-to go beyond the will, beyond the representation to the Idea. The artist must become the knower. Jacquette suggests,

> The artist suffers extraordinarily, according to Schopenhauer, because genius experiences the greatest frustrations of creative activity in its compulsion to represent nonrepresentational knowledge...The artist, then, is first and foremost a knower, someone with a distinctive albeit nonrepresentational imagination-enhanced knowledge of Platonic Ideas acquired by sensory experience of the world as idea.

Schopenhauer considers how one reaches this state of pure knowing. He has already given us a hint in the discussion of beauty and the sublime, with the struggle-free feeling of the beautiful and the "conscious and violent tearing" exaltation of the sublime. It should come as no surprise that Schopenhauer suggests suffering as a way that can lead an understanding of the world without the will. While the one path, aesthetic contemplation, is similar to the effect of beauty, the other leads to more struggle. Ascetic suffering, self-denial, is the other path to a suppressed individual will, which will reveal the "pure knowledge." For the artist, who is called to suffer, the frustration and repression of the will opens the way for the art to come forth.

Ascetic

Schopenhauer describes ascetic suffering, in a constellation of words which circle around the themes of suffering and denial within a deliberate course of life. Ascetic suffering is: saintly self denial, nonrepresentational, denial of the will to live (not to be confused with a desire for suicide-which is often driven by the individual will), disciplined self-denial, a deliberate suppressing and breaking of the will, deprivation of the will's longing for bodily needs-often seen in chastity and voluntary and intentional poverty. This suffering is a form of freedom, freedom as resignation, or freedom from the will altogether.

The person chooses suffering, "therefore, every suffering that comes to him from outside through chance or the wickedness of others is welcome to him; every injury, every ignominy, every outrage." For the person who has achieved this state, ecstasy and other intense emotions lose their effectiveness for they are simply signs of the will's attachment to objects. The experience is a loss of individuality.

> His will turns about; it no longer affirms its own inner nature, mirrored in the phenomenon, but denies it. The phenomenon by which this becomes manifest is the transition from virtue to asceticism. In other words, it is no longer enough for him to love others like himself, and to do as much for them as for himself, but there arises in him a strong aversion to the inner nature whose expression is his own phenomenon, to the will-to-live, the kernel and essence of that world recognized as full of misery. He therefore renounces precisely this inner nature, which appears in him and is expressed already by his body, and his action gives the lie to his phenomenon, and appears in open contradiction thereto...he ceases to will anything...thereby denies the affirmation of the will that goes beyond the individual and thus announces that the will, whose phenomenon is the body, ceases with the life of this body.

Schopenhauer twists us around lest we all become "desert fathers" in a quest to become an artist. We can't deliberately choose this life from our will, with the desire to create art that comes from "pure knowledge."

Now since, as we have seen, that self-suppression of the will comes from knowledge, but all knowledge and insight as such are independent of free choice, that denial of willing, that entrance into freedom, is not to be forcibly arrived at by intention or design, but comes from the innermost relation of knowing and willing man; hence it comes suddenly, as if flying in from without. Suffering doesn't leap forth as a new subject to readers of Schopenhauer-suffering is one of the essential experiences of human existence-what becomes new is the relationship of self-denial to the creation of art. Documentary film-makers and photographers often focus on the pain and humiliation of humanity.

Documenting suffering as art

Documentary film has been used as a vehicle to bring the subject of human suffering into the consciousness of society for years. We must determine if they remain in the individual experience or move beyond it to the Idea. Paula Rabinowitz claims that, "The invention of the individual witness whose personal story serves as a template for history has been crucial to twentieth-century Western accounts of atrocity and war." The accounts of mass destruction have assumed a sense of urgency in our culture and the individual narrative serves as a universal truth. Claude Lanzmann is one of the witnesses to the Holocaust-one of the most atrocious events of the last century.

Lanzmann, who has tried to bring forth the unspeakable holocaust, works much like Kandinsky with the abstract visual, or with an aesthetic visual approach rather than trying to use historical artifacts from the holocaust. Rabinowitz describes his style,

> Shoah reimagines the relationship of viewer to film, and of history to documentary, by producing a historical document without references. Lanzmann makes visible the unseen, the witnessing of an event

> without witness, through speech: the purpose of the extermination camp was not only to annihilate a people, but to erase the evidence of its existence, to deny the power of looking and telling.

Lanzmann pushes his witnesses to recount painful memories. They must reenter a place of suffering for the crafting of this film. The film forces us to resign ourselves to the pain, to give up the desired explanation, the desired happy resolution of the traditional Hollywood film including Steven Spielberg's Schindler's List.

Shoah, by Lanzmann, is made up of testimonies and visuals relating to place and movement. It is not an historical document but is about the "relation between art and witnessing." Shoshana Felman suggests in relation to Shoah that, "Knowledge is shown by the film to be absolutely necessary in the ongoing struggle to resist the blinding impact of the event, to counteract the splitting of eyewitnessing. But knowledge is not, in and of itself, a sufficiently active and sufficiently effective act of seeing." This is an echo of Schopenhauer who refuses to consider that art could come out of reason, but says instead that pure knowledge comes out of art. Lanzmann had few rules when he set out to produce Shoah, but was clear in his determination not to answer the question of why. He says, "Not to understand was my iron law during all eleven years of the production of Shoah." You can't start from a rational position of truth and get to what is truly there. Lanzmann describes the results if he hadn't followed this rule,

> You can imagine a conversation between the SS of Treblinka, for instance, and me about their life, about how did they come to this point, how did they arrive there. This has been attempted already. They talk very much about their parents, about their childhood, about their schooltime. And there is a gap, and they know perfectly well that they cannot bridge it.

Lanzmann himself reports his own difficult experience of making the film. "My problem was to transmit. To do that one cannot allow oneself to be overwhelmed by emotion. You must remain detached. This work has plunged me into an immense solitude... But it was essential not to be crushed. Or to crush others. I tried rather to reach people through their intelligence."

Documentary photographs have been used in equally gripping ways. In the thirties, the Farm Security Administration sent photographers across America to document the economic disaster. Rabinowitz explains the purpose, the "team needed to provide evidence of the brutalizing conditions of rural poverty to ensure that the programs instituted by the New Deal would continue; but they also needed to create arresting images, icons that could enter and alter cultural memory." Dorothea Lange became famous for many photographs taken during this time-Migrant Mother is possibly the most iconic of these. Rabinowitz reports on Lange's experience of this photograph,

> Dorothea Lange recalled her encounter with Migrant Mother Florence Thompson as an exchange: she claimed they both understood that each woman could do something for the other. This exchange was hardly an equal one: Lange received material and career benefits from the portrait of Thompson and her children; perhaps she and her children eventually benefited from the migrant camps which the government set up after the plight of these hungry families became a national outrage, spurred in part by the wide circulation of Lange's photographs.

Although Migrant Mother has become iconic, the original viewers of the image were moved not by the particular emotion of the woman but by the larger sense of suffering it contained. The current viewer, however, may be more attracted to the beauty of the image-and the technique-then they are grabbed by the universal Idea.

Felman suggests that these documents of suffering do not bring as to a complete statement of knowledge.

> What the testimony does not offer is, however, a completed statement, a totalizable account of those events. In the testimony, language is in process and in trial, it does not possess itself as a conclusion, as the constatation of a verdict or the self-transparency of knowledge. Testimony is, in other words, a discursive practice as opposed to a pure theory.

Testimony stays away from being conceptually based, which Schopenhauer discounts, but goes beyond the individual will toward the universal Idea of pain. For photographers, like Lange, it is an entering into the suffering that allows the creation of the art that functions at a deeper level. To move to the general makes the voice echo the Idea that is exposed in the testimony of a particular event.

For some writers and artists the experience of suffering is not their choice. Felman states that poet Paul Celan's "witness is not that of an 'invited,' but rather that of an evicted, traveler: one whose journey has originated in the constraint of deportation, in the throes of an ejection from his native country." The challenge for many documentary artists is choosing, consciously, to enter into the suffering of an event or an individual's experience. To enter is to leave behind the desire for simple easy constructs or to leave behind the basic desire for happiness. Choosing to enter into the suffering is to deny the will, to put aside the desire for a quick and easy solution, to accept the experience of pain. Avital Ronell speaks to this breaking of the will, "We have a blind urge to stop the question, the desire to snatch a quick answer, an answer that will kill the question." She suggests that,

> Philosophy has to stop testifying for the defense team but must go into the emotion. It must abandon its traditional pursuit of conciliation. Philosophy can't be detached, but needs to stay with the untamable ravages of horror. They must stop making sense of something that can't be resolved...Art must make a choice, while knowing whatever you have done may not be right.

The documentary artist may not live in a state of total denial, but the act of stepping into this pain-not a private personal pain, but a universal pain of humanity-brings the same possibility of the ascetic experience. Many times the most difficult denial-is to deny that you can fix something, that you can make the situation better, that you can create this art without causing more pain.

Some artists would choose to avoid working with these issues because it runs the risk of re- traumatizing the subject. To choose to be the instrument of any pain is not an easy decision, but the true artist also recognizes that they are bound by an equally painful-if not more painful-option of being silent. To be silent in the face of this pain is to deny the witness, is to acquiesce to the desire for silence of those who committed the atrocity, to give in to the will and ignore the Idea.

Journey Toward Forgiveness, produced for ABC television release, is an example of this difficult decision. Wilma Derksen, whose daughter had been abducted and killed more than 10 years before, confessed that she had been unable to watch the home movies of her daughter since that brutal event. During the hour and a half long interview, she cried for more than fifteen minutes. The act of production though allowed her to reflect on the person that she had become, to again view this family footage, to recognize the strength of her support group. The producer had to enter into this intense experience of pain, had to live within the tension of this pain, had to allow the pain to sit there unresolved, to find the Idea that is contained in the art.

Near the end of the production, the family survivors group-that Derksen was part of-invited the producer to sit with them since they recognized the same effects of trauma within him as they had experienced. The task of this documentary production style required the entering into of pain, suffering, and a loss of the sense of control. Derksen and the other subjects chose to re-enter their own pain, invited the producer to walk with them into the pain, because they were committed to the documentary work that would come out of that interaction. "Barb"-one of the subjects-in the documentary video, Beyond the News: Sexual Abuse, entered into her personal pain as a way of letting the "truth" be brought into view.

During the production "Barb" was able to tell her story but when the camera was shut off let out a primal scream and wept for an extended period of time. Neither of these shows suggest easy answers or quick resolutions-in fact they invite the viewers to also enter the pain. Artists could create these works without stepping into the pain, by reflecting on the sublime in a detached way, but they would be tempted to stay on the surface, to fulfill the willful desire for an aesthetic resolution that doesn't muck in the pain. To enter the pain, to expose oneself to the chance of opening up more pain, of refusing to offer quick answers can be the entry point into the creation of art that reaches the Idea. Dori Laub talks about the experience of one who listens to another human who has experienced suffering.

The listener can no longer ignore the question of facing death; of facing time and its passage; of the meaning and purpose of living; of the limits of one's omnipotence; of losing the ones that are close to us; the great question of our ultimate aloneness; our otherness from any other; our responsibility to and for our destiny; the question of loving and its limits; of parents and children; and so on. This is the pain of the documentary artist who chooses to leave the natural longing of the will behind and pursue the course of denial in the construction of their art.

John Atwell suggests what an artist, who has chosen to enter into this suffering, offers to the viewer.

> The genius, through his extraordinary insight into the fact that life is essentially suffering, reaches the point at which the great question of life stands out most vividly-whether to affirm life or deny it-and he chooses to affirm life, knowing full well what his choice involves...sacrificing himself, as it were, for the good of humankind by creating artworks that facilitate apprehension of the Platonic Ideas by others and that, equally, offer others the now-and-again consolation of aesthetic serenity.

Most commentators on Schopenhauer seem bound to the traditional ideas about the ascetic path. Jacquette's comments illustrate this,

> The best route through suffering to an understanding of the world as Will for Schopenhauer is therefore more specifically suffering induced through deliberate efforts at suppressing the will. This involves the disciplined self-denial of ascetism, leading by degrees from deprivation of the will's longing for such bodily necessities as food, water, companionship, and sleep, to the experience of a mystical loss of individuality and dissolution of the subject-object distinction.

These commentators, by sticking to traditional definitions of the ascetic life miss the rich possibilities that come to artists who make themselves available to the pain of the world around them. How Can I Sing a Glad Song, from the album *But Until Then*, illustrates a musicians struggle with the experience of pain. The song written after a trip to Liberia, where six political/ethnic factions were destroying the people and the country with a civil war, demonstrates the desire to let that suffering be expressed in music. The author did experience during this trip not only the suffering of others but the deprivation of food, water and rest. In spite of a return to a more normal physical life, the composer chose to remain in the pain seeking the Idea. Few if any artists master fully the denial of the will, according to Schopenhauer, but the documentary artist can enter into the suffering of others, denying their individual will and creating an artistic work. However, Schopenhauer suggests that the aesthetic path is the more normal path for the artist.

For Schopenhauer the aesthetic path involves contemplation, with an overwhelming experience of beauty and the liberation temporarily from suffering. The genius suffers more than all others and this aesthetic experience is a temporary liberation from that suffering. The aesthetic pleasure delivers knowledge from service of the will, causes a forgetting of oneself as an individual and is an enhancement of consciousness. It leads to the pure will-less, timeless freedom of pure knowing. The aesthetic experience frees one from the world as representation and becomes the intuitive apprehension of the Platonic Idea.

While Schopenhauer seems unclear about the effort the person makes in relation to this aesthetic experience it is clear that this path involves little or less denial of the will. Aesthetic contemplations are moments where the will is suppressed as opposed to the ascetic path, which implies a more constant denial of will. Just as the experience of beauty requires less effort to set aside the ordinary concerns of the will than does the experience of the sublime, so too does the aesthetic path require a less continual denial of the will. The aesthetic experience as Jacquette explains,

> Involves a brief but pregnant suppression of the individual will. What Schopenhauer means by this is that in contemplating nature or art, the aesthetic genius stands so enraptured in an encounter with beauty or the sublime that there occurs something like a mystical union of the subject with the object in a dissolving of the subject-object distinction. The desires of the individual will are overruled by absorption in the moment of aesthetic appreciation.

Lucian Krukowski extends this moment into the art itself, suggesting that within it is the momentary separation from will. "Artworks, even the arts of time-music, drama-are about stillness, when stillness is understood in its metaphysical sense as completeness and perfection." Having stillness within the arts of time-music and video-challenges artists to create still motion. In the Visual Music 8/8 Project, Terry D-III captures the motion of the player within the portrait.

In Keith D-III the heads and bodies begin to disappear melting into the instruments, into the enveloping music making-the rational mind is removed as the mood of the music takes over. Both of these images work to bring completeness by capturing more than just a moment, but the deeper essence of what is happening. Visual Composition I (see next page) contains slow mostly abstract motion that brings a sense of completeness like sitting by slowing flowing water. Visual Composition VII, also abstract, moves at a much faster pace but also gives a sense of completeness within the motion.

If the artwork carries this momentary suppression of the will within itself, that does not mean that the whole process of the completion of the artistic piece is carried out in this moment. For Schopenhauer there are three stages in the aesthetic creative process. First you have the sensory reception of the Platonic Ideas. The artist may seek out the moment by cognitive activity, but it usually happens in the midst of contemplation. Secondly, the artist will complete or perfect the Ideas and find a vehicle for the communication of the Idea. Thirdly, the production of the work requires an act of the will, creating a non-discursive expression as intelligible form in an artistic medium.

Schopenhauer sums up, "In the aesthetic method of consideration we found two inseparable constituent parts: namely, knowledge of the object not as individual thing, but as Platonic Idea, in other words, as persistent form of this whole species of things; and the self consciousness of the knower, not as individual, but as pure will-less subject of knowledge." Schopenhauer's theory is a major alternative to the more respected scientific method of knowing and the corollary of expert technique. The artist-and the visual composer in particular-must not get tied up in the scientific enquiries and into the obsession with creating the next computer technique if they want to create art. The aesthetic process leads to Schopenhauer's discussion of genius in the creation and reception of art.

Composition I

Visual Composition I -the most simply composed of the eight-uses five images and a total of eight layers. No loops were created for this composition-which keeps the transfer modes and opacity set at a constant amount but uses changing anchor points to create the visual motion. The resulting interaction of the layers creates the predominately abstract final visual composition. Many of the layers move completely off of the viewing area and back in at various points in the changing time. A directional blur adds a sense of unity to the whole.

Visual Composition I has a limited color palette and transforms slowly as the color forms move horizontally back and forth. The images have some artifacts of the human face and occasional bright landscape backgrounds come to the fore. Musical Composition I, the resulting musical composition, uses two instruments-a mandolin and a bouzouki. All of the portraits correspond to a mandolin, but the coding process-due to the stacked repeating layers-adds notes an octave lower on a bouzouki. The movement causes the speed and duration of notes to change-especially as the image uses less than 30% of the screen area. The notes move in and out of apparent sync with each other based on the direction of movement-left to right moves the notes out of the traditional beat location.

Composition VIII

Visual Composition VIII used five visual loops to create the final composition. Each visual loop is created from multiple layers of one image. The portrait Anna G-II is the visual base for three of the five loops. Tim Bowman-unlike many of the other visual composers-did not use any transfer modes but created most of this look using movement and scale. Many of the layers were used at over 200% scale-which added pixelization to the final composition. The usage of scale created abstraction in two ways for Bowman: using only small parts of the image and the degradation caused by the pixelization. This composition has long cross over opacity changes, sudden panning motions and occasional vertical bumps which define and interrupt the visual tempo.

The resulting Musical Composition VIII uses two instruments-octave mandolin and mandola-with three foundation notes and the additional notes added due the large percentages used in the scale parameter. The music is sparse with repetitive sounds giving way to occasional variations and additions.

Composition IV

Visual Composition IV starts with a base of loops. Composition IV-terry-used twenty-four times in the final visual composition-is created from images of Terry playing the bouzouki layered on top of themselves with a difference transfer mode along with changing opacities and anchor points. The base built from these loops is unified with a gaussian-blur. Above this is a visual loop made from one Photoshop file containing eight layers-portrait Mel D-VII-which adds the images of the girl dancing as the image layers slides across the screen. This visual composition is the only one of the eight to effectively use any of the layered Photoshop files to create movement. (Visual Composition 11 did use two layers, of image Anna G-I, to create a sense of motion with a rotating instrument.) This visual loop also uses a variety of motion and radial blurs that vary each time this loop is used within the final visual composition. Terry D-VII follows each of the Mel D-VII visual loops acting like a visual bridge back to the main movement.

Another loop, Composition IV-instr, is created from Terry D-V111 and Geoff D-II, which move back and forth horizontally over each other (anchor point and difference transfer mode). After all of these visual loops are implemented a wavy-motion adds fluidity to the project and unifies the base. At random intervals a portrait of Keith and the Flying Toads playing in a pub move back and forth blending with what is already there.

Musically this composition creates a looping layer upon which the other instruments build. (Listen to Composition IV-terry MIDI file to hear the base created by Composition IV-terry Visual.) Musical Composition IV uses a mandolin, mandola, octave mandolin and bouzouki-but requires six instruments to be able to play the complex parts of the composition. The Composition IV-688 creates the most melody-like part of this composition because the added images create a descending musical run at the intervals it used in the composition. (Listen to Composition IV-688 MIDI file to hear this progression.)

Composition VII

Shawn Hunter started the composition process by creating eight visual loops-each using eight to fourteen layers of images from within one instrument/performer set. These visual loops are either fifteen or thirty seconds long. Of these eight visual loops Hunter used five-in paired stacks of ten layers-to create six different visual movements. These movements give visual priority to different of the five visual loops-using the screen and overlay transfer-modes, a variety of positions, opacities and motion movements-creating six similar but varied movements. These six movements were then arranged in order-with some overlapping-to create the final visual composition.

An evaluation of the individual instrument loops offers insight into the compositional style of Hunter. Composition VII-100-one of the three loops not used in the final composition-offers the clearest fragments of information from the original portraits used to create this loop. Although it has changed everything to black and white-the instrument shape, frets, and neck are apparent at many places and has more crisp edges than do any of the other instrument loops. Composition VII-200 also has vestiges of the instrument images from which it was created-but in this case the changing color forms do not appear to follow the information in the portraits as clearly. Composition VII-400 maintains some reference to the facial shapes from which it is constructed, but is primarily large areas of black and white interacting with each other. The lighter values tend to draw the attention while the black is backgrounded.

Composition VII-800 is the only one of the five instrument loops that is not mono-toned in character-the others accomplish this by adjusting the hue of the whole instrument loop. Composition VII-800 uses three-dimensional camera angles and movement along the z-plane to create vivid colors-that evolve and change-within the deep engulfing areas of black. All of these visual compositions use multiple image layers, a variety of transfer modes, and movement to create these largely abstract loops. Composition VII-600 has the banding-associated with polarization-in the transitional areas between the light and dark values. All of the instrument loops are formatted closer to a square shape than is the final composition-which means only part of the visual loop is used as they become part of the final composition.

Each of the six movements gives visual preference to different of the instrument loops-although each movement does use each of the five instrument loops twice. The instrument loops are layered on top of each other and use the screen and overlay transfer modes with no changes in opacity, scale or movement. Within the visual composition, visual content can be obscured by what is layered above it-dependent of course on the opacity and transfer mode.

Musical compositions however are capable of playing all the notes-which don't obscure the sound by elimination but by creating such a large pool of sound that the individual sounds cannot be separated out-the sound looses any sense of definition.

Hunter's visual composition-when decoded following the standard set of rules puts all the looping music on top of each other creating a large pool of sound. This does not give the upper sound loops any preference, unlike the way the visual loops are used. When this preference is taken into account by giving preference to the higher-layered loops the music begins to have six more discrete movements. This pays closer attention to what Hunter is doing with the usage of the these loops and allows some of the loops that are lower and more obscured-possibly totally obscured visually-to disappear behind the other sounds. This version of the musical composition-the one used by the Visual Music 8/8 Project-has more variety and vitality as the loops trade back and forth their dominance and the listener can hear the variations that Hunter has created visually.

The music coded by the individual instrument loops creates a very repetitive sound-the mandolin loop (Listen to Composition VII-400 MIDI file.) is the closest to resembling music with a traditional melody. In the Composition VII-400 the viewer is drawn to the lighter shades that move gracefully through the image-the instrument loop corresponds to a mandolin and results in the higher notes in the final composition. These higher notes also grab attention in the final music composition. Composition VII-200, on the mandola, is very repetitive but contains one of the least complex loops created by Hunter.

Composition VII-300, also on mandola, has three discrete variations within the loop that repeats five times.

Composition VII-800 has slow repetitions with occasional tempo changes to offer variety. Composition VII-600 is the most densely layered music-with occasional breaks in the relentless pace. The six movements give preference to different of these loops in pairs: 400/300, 800/200, 400/300, 300/600, 800/200, and 300/800. These preferences of Hunter-all based on his visual aesthetic preferences-create a varied piece of music with discrete movements that flow through the final composition.

The Role of the Genius

The reception of art has lower requirements than does the production. Paul Guyer points out this difference in referring to Schopenhauer's writings.

> The production of art through genius clearly requires the highest degree of activity; the reception or appreciation of art produced by others, however, requires not only a lower degree of activity than such production of art, but even a lower degree of activity than aesthetic response to nature. This is because in a work of art the Platonic. Ideas have already been isolated out by the artist.

In spite of the work of art bringing the Idea closer to the viewer, it does not mean that most people experience it. Schopenhauer says, even "the most excellent works of art, the noblest productions of genius, must eternally remain sealed books to the dull majority of men, and are just inaccessible to them. " It does not even mean that the artists, themselves, can explain, interpret, or fully understand their own art-or that they can articulate with words the Idea that is coming out of the art.

The artistic activity is to bring to completion the Will-not by seeing what nature has formed but the intent of that formation. "But it is perception above all to which the real and true nature of things discloses and reveals itself," says Schopenhauer,

> although still in a limited way... But if our perception were always tied to the real presence of things, its material would be entirely under the dominion of chance, which rarely produces things at the right time, seldom arranges them appropriately... For this reason imagination is needed, in order to complete, arrange, amplify, fix, retain, and repeat at pleasure all the significant pictures of life, according as the aims of a profoundly penetrating knowledge and of the significant work by which it is to be communicated may require.

What all of this means for the artist-who listens to Schopenhauer-is that art is not constructed by reference to myth, culture or belief, but by the direct portrayal of the Will. This eliminates the codified symbolism that would make art easy to interpret with one-to-one correspondences.

Already here in the discussion of genius we find Schopenhauer discriminating between music and the other arts-and as expected suggesting that the creation of the melody requires the most genius. Lydia Goehr stresses Schopenhauer's view that music requires more genius for its composition than do any other forms of art.

> Music is the product of genius, Schopenhauer explains, but it requires more genius than does the production of the other arts. The same dualism Which separates the Will from representation, the universal from the particular, the metaphysical from the physical, music from the plastic and literary fine arts also separates the composer-genius from the embodying (phenomenal) person.

Goehr reminds us though that music has the most to offer those who listen or experience the music. The experience of music, as the highest form of aesthetic experience, is "remote from pain" because it is without phenomenal reality. Unlike in our everyday existence, in music we experience the life of the Will without bearing the full pessimistic brunt of its associated frustrations. Music offers us, therefore, even if for just a brief moment, a redemption from our perpetual suffering.

The artistic dilemma

What is an artist to do? The artist can choose-if you can really choose-the path with the self-denial of asceticism, following in the footsteps of the mystics and desert fathers. This is a full denial, or suppression of the will. The artist can also choose to enter fully into the suffering of world as a listener-walking alongside in the suffering-during the production of documentary works. The artist must leave behind the will that asks for tranquility and happy endings. Alternatively the artist can be open to the momentary liberations from the individual will of the aesthetic path.

In either case the artist is at a risk to experience at a deeper level the suffering that Schopenhauer claims is a major component of the human experience. It appears that the artist must pay the price for the revealing of the Idea, for the artist as Lucian Krukowski points out can never stay fully in the moment or life where the will is suppressed.

> The lessons contained in art, those glimpses of the possibility-and rewards-of a contemplative life, may secure art's philosophical value, but they place the artist in a dilemma that is as personally insoluble as it is vocationally necessary. The dilemma is this: artists, like philosophers, must face the "true nature" of will in order to reveal it; but unlike philosophers, artists cannot escape the will by withdrawing from its imperatives, for artistic creativity is action in the world., Schopenhauer's philosopher has good reasons to deny

> the value of action: Ambitions are never fully realized; happiness is a chimera just beyond reach; progress is a coercive illusion; and there is no God to help along. The artist's product-the artwork-shows us the tranquil alternative to the will through images of the world of forms, a world where there is no inadequacy to instigate action. Yet the completeness of art's content must take shape-be created-within the world of will, and here we find the dilemma Schopenhauer gives to creativity. Artists cannot deny ambition or the hope of progress if they are to fashion the images that, viewed philosophically, provide good reasons for just such denials. In this sense, the didactic import of art's content cannot be applied to the actions that lead to its creation-nor can it inform the lives of its artists.

The pleasure the genius gets from everything beautiful is the return for the artist-the reward for accepting the task and the suffering. As Schopenhauer explains,

> The pleasure of everything beautiful, the consolation afforded by art, the enthusiasm of the artist which enables him to forget the cares of life, this one advantage of the genius over other men alone compensating him for the suffering that is heightened in proportion to the clearness of consciousness, and for the desert loneliness among a different race of men...This purely knowable side of the world and its repetition in any art is the element of the artist. He is captivated by a consideration of the spectacle of the will's objectification. He sticks to this, and does not get tired of contemplating it, and of repeating it in his descriptions. Meanwhile, he himself bears the cost of producing that play; in other words, he himself is the will objectifying itself and remaining in constant suffering.

While this begins to sound like the self-denial of the ascetic path previously described by Schopehhauer, for the artist it does not contain the "resignation" of the saint and deliver him from life forever-it is only a temporary reprieve. Unlike the way of the mystic, the artist does not leave life and experiences only a temporary moment of contemplation.

Sobell, the instrument builder from the Visual Music 8/8 Project, finds the sensuous beauty in the grains of the various woods that he carefully shapes, scrapes, smoothes, bends, carves into the intricate details of an instrument. He carefully chooses each piece of wood, examining it closely so that he can hear the silent sound contained in the fiber that will another day be part of an instrument making delightful sounds for the player and listener to hear. Even the crafting that Sobell does involves his ability to perceive something different than the average person does in the piece of wood. This returns us once again to the importance that Schopenhauer has for all artists.

> The world can appear in its true color and form, in its complete and correct significance, only when the intellect, freed from willing, moves freely over objects, and yet is energetically active without being spurred on by the will...the intellect of the genius is detached from the will and so from the person, and what concerns these does not conceal from him the world and things themselves; on the contrary, he becomes distinctly conscious of them, and apprehends them in objective perception in and by themselves; in this sense he is reflective.

Wolfgang Schirmacher summarizes our challenge,

> Schopenhauer perceived in art a realm in which this entirely different world lived by us for moments all too rare, lived by creative artists as well as by neocreative viewers, by writers and empathetic readers. Through its transition to ethics Schopenhauer's "gnostically tinted aesthetics or world lessness," as found in his philosophy of art, becomes an "aesthetics of aliveness" that in the "experience of otherness" overcomes the stagnation of the given world. But in "pure knowing" as well, in the work of philosophical genius, we can

> become "the clear eye of the world." Compassion is a way of life enabling us to put into practice the "turning" of the will, and thus achieve its suspension.

Schopenhauer is not advocating that artists choose to be ascetic, in fact suggesting that few can master that self-denial-but artists should not abandon the idea too rapidly especially as we work within the rapid pace of the electrate age. Artists can at least consider the possibility of entering more fully into the pain of others, especially in the field of documentary art. It is unlikely that many artists will go so far as to follow Schopenhauer's suggestion of avoiding images of desire-food and nudes-which lead to desire and a breaking of the desired contemplation. The artist must pay attention to what gets in the way of their contemplation-of what calls to their individual will.

Schopenhauer placed a high value on aesthetic contemplation, which is a needed correction to the tendency of modern artists to get so enamored by the electronic tools available that they no longer experience the momentary times of the "suppression of the will." The visual composer-often working solely with digital tools-must find ways to stay connected to the suffering world-not getting lost in their electronic cave which rarely functions as the desert hermits cave did, Technique must not get in the way of following the ascetic and aesthetic paths that Schopenhauer has delineated. Schopenhauer moves us beyond an obsession with technique, beyond the imitative representational arts, as we reach for the "pure knowledge"

3

Consonance/Dissonance in Visual Music

Schopenhauer writes from a context, which assumes a literate or mathematical approach to music-in both the composition and performance of music. This literate approach is dependent on a written or notation system of documenting music. This notation system-even the idea of creating a notation system-is a practice of Western culture. In many cultures music is transmitted person to person, remaining primarily in an oral tradition. Alison Knowles evaluates the effect of using a notation system,

> Western notations brought about the preservation of "music," but in doing so encouraged the development not only of standards of composition and performance but also the enjoyment of music that was more or less independent of its sound, placing the qualities of its organization and expressivity above sound itself,. . until recently, notation was the unquestioned path to the experience of music.

Knowles may be overly optimistic about the listeners experience of music, which has much less to do with the notation system and much more emphasis placed on the value of the sound produced. Listeners, while often concerned that musical pieces be played correctly, especially with pop music define correctness not based on a notation of the music but by a previous listening experience of the music-either in a concert or from a recording.

Pop musicians have to be aware of their need to replicate in a concert setting the music that they create in the recording studio-which affects the choices they make during the recording process. The listeners concerns about correctness of music performance are more concerned with how something sounds than they are about the matching of a literate notation system. The notation system retains its position of predominance in "classical music" or with the highly trained musician.

The introduction of electronic technology has returned music back to a form of the oral culture-although one that is mediated electronically rather than face-to-face. Many people now learn music from recordings-rather than from a person or from notated scores. Musicians use the recording technology to create new music and sounds but remain firmly bound by the auditory experience of this music. This electronic oral culture though does not require the total forms of memory recall-as does the traditional oral culture-to pass on the musical traditions. The recorded music provides the mnemonic device to pass on music from one musician/composer to the next. The recording technology is also used to document new works in progress and to track the development of experimental forms of composition.

Trevor Wishart considers this electronic-oral system to still be based on the notation system developed in the literate era. "The fundamental thesis of this (analytic notation) system is that music is ultimately reducible to a small, finite number of elementary constituents with a finite number of elementary constituents with a finite number of `parameters', out of which all sounds possibly required in musical praxis can be notated by combination. "

In folk music-which has remained in the oral age-musicians without any ability to function in a literate sense-are still bound by a similar set of notes and rhythms. The main parameters of this system were pitch and rhythm, which appear to create a two-dimensional "lattice. " In addition to the notation system, the other foundation of the notated-Western music was instrument technology-which may explain the way that folk music has some of the same boundaries. This technology contributed to the system by creating families of instruments with a stable timbre and a system of variable pitches. The piano/keyboard is the ultimate representation of the "lattice" based system.

Stringed instruments have a greater variability of timbre because of more player variability. Wishart claims this system gives precedence to the score over the vision or experience of the player and creates within the listener expectations of a particular type of sound. His view-while containing elements of truth-ignores the large variety of instruments available to musicians and composers, especially with the inclusion of numerous ethnic instruments from around the world. In addition to this large pool of instruments are those that are being changed and developed by modern instrument builders.

Sobell-the builder of the instruments used to organize the Visual Music 8/8 Project-has been instrumental in revitalizing the usage of several of these instruments. Sobell built his first cittern in 1973 and developed his bouzoukis and mandolins from that original design. Niall O Callanain and Tommy Walsh highlight Sobell's importance to the development of these instruments, "The English cittern was recently revived by Stefan Sobell of Northumberland in

England, who makes them to suit the more modern folk music, usually with four or five courses of double strings. The bouzouki that is generally played in Ireland today, takes it's shape from the cittern and is often referred to as such. " Paul Kotapish points out Sobell's motivation,

> Stefan Sobell, probably the best-known of the British Isles luthiers, was the first to experiment with carved tops and backs on a bouzouki-like instrument. Ironically, it was a Portuguese guitarra, not a bouzouki that got him started. "'I didn't know what to do with it until I strung it mandolin style: GDAE," he recalls. "When I met Andy Irvine in the late `60's, he tuned it GDAD, and that open tuning lent itself to accompanying songs and playing tunes. It made a lovely sound but without much projection. About the same time I got hold of an old Martin C-3 (round-hole archtop), which I got by trading a concertina and a car engine to some American kids. I thought if I could combine the big projecting clanging tone of the Martin with the shape, feel, and tuning of the Portuguese guitar, then I'd really have something. "

The traditional Greek bouzouki was bowl-shaped and had six strings, "but when it became integrated with Sobell's newly revived cittern, a new instrument was created. It sounded like a bouzouki but looked like a cittern. . . and is now accepted as part of the Irish musical tradition. " Sobell uses this body shape to build bouzoukis and mandolins with different body sizes and neck lengths. These instruments have played a role in the resurgence of the interest in acoustic Irish music.

Inside the System

Schopenhauer-in this literate context-chose the theories of Rameau to structure his musical understanding around. Lawrence Ferrara describes and critiques this choice,

> Rameau's Traite de I'Harmonie is symptomatic of the Age of Reason in its presentation of a rationally based, logical harmonic disposition rather than the more empirically based practice of the realization of chords over a `figured bass' and species counterpoint codified in the music theory of Fux (Johann). Rameau advocated a `vertical' (harmonic) method; Fux championed a blending of `vertical' (through realization of `figured bass') with `horizontal' (through `species counterpoint') approaches in the teaching and analysis of music composition. In a C chord the constituent notes are C, E and G: C is the root, E is the third and G is the fifth. Any one of these three notes could be the bass or lowest note of this chord on a piano, in a choral piece for four parts, or in an orchestral piece for twenty parts. Distinctive in Rameau's approach is that the bass note is always understood in terms of the root (in this case, C) and music is conceived as a progression of vertical states that imply a `functional harmony'. . . In this century, especially through the work of Heinrich Schenker and his students, a theory of free composition developed from the eighteenth century Fuxian contrapuntal theory of the sort that was actually practiced by the masters of Western music,. . Schenker' concludes that Rameau's harmonically based approach misses the linear, in contrapuntally directed lines which combine and express harmony. . . Recognizing Schopenhauer's partiality for melody over harmony,. . it is exceedingly unpropitious that Schopenhauer embraced the non-linear, harmonic approach of Rameau.

The most important feature Schopenhauer took from Rameau deals with the way a scale is created. As you shorten or lengthen a string, the frequency (speed of vibration) is in inverse proportion to the length that is vibrating. This structure is based on, Pythagoras, who noted that there is a relationship between the length of a vibrating string and the musical sound. If you take two strings of the same material and the same amount of tension and stop one of them at the halfway point, it will produce a note that sounds an octave higher then the full-length string-just as the octave mandolin (with double the length strings) sounds an octave lower than the mandolin.

From divisions-using simple numerical numbers-of the length of the string came the foundations of the Pythagorean interval theory upon which western music and instrument technology is built. Western music however uses a "tempered" scale-rather than one that is accurate mathematically-which only preserves the octave. All other intervals such as the fifth, major third and minor third are merely approximations. The intervals which are based on the relationship of small numbers-the third, the fourth, the fifth and the octave-are the "consonant" intervals. "'Dissonant" intervals are based on larger correlative numbers. Schopenhauer based his understanding of consonance and dissonance on this theory.

Wishart reminds us that the predominate instruments and the notation system dominate the way music is created and evaluated.

> A musical instrument is a device used to stabilize, through its resonancestructures, the pitch and timbral dimensions of a sound-event. The morphological structure of the sound-event is thus dominated by the characteristics of the natural phenomenon of resonance. The typical instrumental musical object is of the attack-resonance type. The gestural input from the performer, especially in the highly technologically developed Western instrumentarium, is thus subordinated to this particular natural phenomenon structure.

Wishart wishes to blame codification/notation on those who want to control music and keep it in the literate world. "Committed verbalists will not be convinced by anything

I have to say about the separation between `meaning' and `signification'. For the linguistic philosopher all problems are reducible to problems of signification within language and such a philosopher will merely deny the validity of our problem. " Wishart seems to ignore, or be unaware of Schopenhauer's theory that music goes beyond the concept, beyond the word, beyond the representational, to the Will. Wishart understands that music goes deeper-this is a given for any musician that is part of an oral tradition-but seems most concerned with the structure around which music is built.

Music in an oral, pre-notation, era is monitored by the ear and responded to immediately by the receiver. Wishart suggests that what is most important about this oral practice is the gesture, as opposed to the more literate, western, approach that deals with the properties of sound found on a "lattice" notation system. These gestures include timbre modulation, amplitude, frequency modulation versus the more narrow "lattice parameters" of pitch and duration. The essence of what is important for the oral performer-especially in the folk presentation-is the emotional communication aided by rhythm. The emotional response of the oral tradition would align it closely with the theory of Schopenhauer.

Melody: Rhythm and Harmony

Schopenhauer gives a superior value to the melody-which carries the "sequence and continuity of progress", moves with more speed than other parts, leads the whole, and is the "highest grade of the will's objectification. " Melody, according to Schopenhauer, has two elements: rhythm and harmony. Rhythm is related to the duration of the note, the meter, and is the quantitative element. Rhythm is created by a repeated division of sound-division into equal parts corresponding to one another-first into larger parts, which are then divisible into smaller parts. These durations hold everything together in the music with their similar measures of time. Analogies can be made to math with relationships of lengths and to symmetry in architecture. For rhythm to happen, points of time must be measurable and measured.

While rhythm is related to duration or the quantitative, harmony is interested in the qualitative-the pitch and depth of the notes. The measurement is the rapidity of vibrations as opposed to the duration of sound. Harmony requires certain notes, notes that come from the key the melody is structured around. The music form, or structure, is the alternation of `discord and reconciliation'-progress from consonance to dissonance and resolution back to consonance.

This progression moves from the original key center to a competing key center and back to the original key center, back to the fundamental note of the composition. For the visual musician the movement between consonance and dissonance is usually based on the interactions of color and form and the movement from the dark to light-which correspond to the harmony part of Schopenhauer's discussion of melody. For the visual musician to effectively add rhythm will require the duration-based parameter of movement.

Hans Richter, who respected greatly the abstract work of Kandinsky, wanted to use motion in addition to form and color. Working with Viking Eggeling, he chose the form of a scroll to get away from the static nature of the easel.

> I consider the scroll as a new art form which, despite "sociological difficulties" that it might encounter (such

> as being despised by art dealers as too difficult to sell, or finding no room for its display over a potential purchaser's fireplace) ought to become a modern medium of expression. It must in fact, as there are sensations to be derived from it which can be experienced in no other way, either in easel painting or in film,. . After each of us in 1919 had finished his first scroll, we began to understand that we had gotten more than we asked for: the necessity to release this accumulated "energy" into actual movement! Never during our collaboration had we dreamt of that. But there it was. And movement implied film!

Richter produced his first film "Rhythm 21" in 1921, to go beyond the limits of the scroll. "We were in a new medium altogether. It was not only the orchestration of form but also of time-relationship that we were facing in film. The single image disappeared in a flow of images. . . We realized that the `orchestration' of time was the esthetic basis of this new art form."

Richter by his usage of film does not mean most of what film stands for today. He saw it much more closely related to the idea of visual poetry with the rhythm that Schopenhauer valued. Film means visual rhythm and movement-which becomes the unifying structure-much like music or his chosen word "poetry. " Richter created this rhythm with such divergent images as; moving eyeballs rolling around the screen, human faces moving through the frame, rectangles moving around the screen and lights flashing around until the whole screen washes to white. Another piece shows; people walking in precise steps, feet going up and down a ladder, a clock turning rapidly, all the while employing the ability to alter the speed of movement. In yet another piece he uses pulsing boxes, which change sizes, to create a sense of three-dimensional space with overlapping and changing positions.

Richter dreamed of a new art form called "film poetry" which would become an accepted part of modern art. Siegfried Zielinski continues to analyze the historical urges for creating time-based media. The artists are driven by the urge to make the art sensitive for the other-the scientists use the time-based media with the desire to make something transparent and to explain it for the other. While Richter experienced some success with his usage of the scroll and even more with the usage of film, as Zielinski points out it is only with the invention of electricity that time-based media becomes a reality-even film is only the illusion of movement.

The progression of the Visual Music 8/8 Project demonstrates the same movement. The portraits have some of the qualities of the scrolls that Richter worked with-they require the eye to move to see the whole, have a large ratio between height and width dimensions, and add a sense of temporality to a static image. The eight sets of portraits-when viewed in a line hanging on a wall-also function like a scroll as the eye moves along the extended line of images. The visual compositions function more like the film that Richter worked with-incorporating movement and change over time. These compositions as Zielinski noted are dependent on technology for their creation and technology to make them accessible to the viewer.

Overtones and Sympathetic Vibrations

When the melody sounds, or the bass adds the lower note, there are added vibrations to each "pure" note. If a D note is played the ear hears faint overtones-which are multiples of frequency of the D-that make up a D chord. Stringed instruments also have sympathetic vibrations where one vibrating note may cause another to vibrate based on its length and string tension. This mirrors Schopenhauer's understanding of the nature of overtones. "With the sounding of the low note, the high notes always sound faintly at the same time, and it is a law of harmony that a bass-note may be accompanied only by those high notes that actually sound automatically and simultaneously with it through the accompanying vibrations."

In the Visual Music 8/8 Project, five of the portraits in the Stefan set have harmonics, where two images are composited into the final portrait. Stefan D-11 and Stefan E-V function similar to musical harmonics. A wide angle view of Sobell working is merged with another more close-up image-the different focal lengths offer octave separated pitches as harmonics do in music. Anna A-VI has two images layered on top of each other-these function more like sympathetic vibrations or faint overtones as the second image is dimly seen laying on top of the other one.

Within the visual compositions of the Visual Music 8/8 Project, these overtones of faint sound become common as the composers use images at low opacity and lay them in on top of other images. The visual composers have at their disposal a number of tools to make these overtones function within the visual realm. In Adobe After Effects different layers of images can be combined using transfer modes-which calculate the resulting look by combining the layers. Several of these transfer modes: lighten-compares the two layers and uses the lighter information, darken-compares the layers and uses the darker information, overlay-lighter areas in the top layer will lighten and darker areas will darken, hard light-increases the shadows, contrast and saturation, work together to create a blend of the images that usually gives predominance to one image while using faint parts of the other image.

Zielinski states that vibrations are a part of the total world, "Johan Wilhelm Ritter wanted to show that all materials are vibrating,. . everything exists in a tension between the plus and the minus. . . in fact the whole universe is vibrating. " It is these vibrations that are part of the suffering world and part of creating the temporary respites offered by music and the other arts.

The Purpose of Dissonance

Consonance and dissonance, for Schopenhauer, are about the mathematical relationship of notes,

> all harmony of the tones rests on the coincidence of the vibrations,. . so long as the vibrations of two tones have a rational relation to one another, expressible in small numbers, they can be taken together in our apprehension through their constantly recurring coincidence; the tones are blended and are thus in harmony. On the other hand, if that relation is an irrational one, or one expressible only in large numbers, no intelligible coincidence of vibrations occurs. . . and accordingly are called a dissonance. As a result of this theory, music is a means of making intelligible rational and irrational numerical relations. "

Alongside this mathematical construct, in Schopenhauer, is an element of mysticism-which an exploration of the ascetic-aesthetic paradigm has revealed. Schopenhauer suggests that dissonance-going beyond the numerical understanding-actually functions to reveal consonance. Schopenhauer views life as full of suffering and strife, where music serves as an aesthetic experience that brings a brief respite from this situation. The movement from dissonance to consonance offers a temporary break from suffering just as aesthetic reflection does.

Ferrara characterizes the split of dissonance and consonance as resistance and satisfaction. "Harmonic dissonance in music strikes discord in our consciousness because of its numerical relations to large number vibrations as calibrated in acoustics. Dissonance is resisted by the will. " If we consider the ascetic way of knowing, dissonance-like pain is resisted by the will--finds aesthetic resolution in consonance. The back and forth construction serves to move us beyond the conscious will into the experience of the Will. Within this relationship of vibrations music becomes

> the material in which all the movements of the human heart, i. e. , of the will, movement whose essential nature is always satisfaction and dissatisfaction, although in innumerable degrees, can be faithfully portrayed and reproduced in all their finest shades and modifications; and this takes place by means of the invention of the melody.

A binary construction-like consonance and dissonance-can be carried into a variety of fields. In the Visual Music 8/8 Project, lightness and darkness function in similar ways as do consonance and dissonance in sound. Visual Composition VII (see chapter 3) moves through heavily saturated dark moments to resolve into a brighter resolution-and then plunges into the same cycle again and again. Visual Composition IV has swirling dark moments from the dark pub that resolve into visual bridges of lightly-colored mandola tops and the outdoor brightness of the concert with the dancing girl.

Zielinski points out the binaries that Athanasius Kircherus experimented with-light/shadow and light/music-and his attempts to bring the binary world into harmony.

> Kircherus, experimented with light and music, as well as composition. . . He worked on the musurgia

> universalis where he proposed that sound waves worked like light waves, and if reflected they would become stronger. . . He built a sequencer, scala musica, which was able to compose harmonious music by using fragments of sound. . . His goal was not to substitute for composers but for people who could not compose He worked at disharmonious unison, which brings together what cannot come together. . . He worked at bringing the binary construction, light and shadow, of the world together in a harmonious relationship,. . This binary construction in acoustics leads to dissonance and consonance.

As Schopenhauer states, music without either consonance or dissonance would be of no purpose.

> Accordingly the harmonious progress of notes consists of the alternation of dissonance and consonance that conforms to the rules of art. A sequence of merely consonant chords would be satiating, tedious, and empty, like the languor produced by the satisfaction of all desires. Therefore, although dissonances are disquieting and have an almost painful effect, they must be introduced, but only in order to be resolved again into consonances with proper preparation,. . This is precisely in keeping with the fact that there are for the will at bottom only dissatisfaction and satisfaction,. . so music has two- general keys, the major and the minor, corresponding to those moods, and it must always be found in the one or the other.

The Visual Music 8/8 Project maintains an openness to using a variety of notes, or combination of notes, in fact even solitary notes within the compositions. The project by its design does not require either a melody-at least not what listeners would consider a melody-or harmony. The system allows dissonance, combinations of dissonance and consonance, a strong repetitive consonance, totally dissonant pieces with no resolution, or a piece that alternates between them.

The musical compositions exemplify this range from the minimal note usage of Musical Composition 1 to Musical Composition IV with clear moments of melody playing out above the more repetitive drone-like lower notes. Visual Composition 1 is composed of just five images-which means that Musical Composition I has only five different notes used over and over to build the sound experience. The visual composition is primarily consonant with only minimal changes in the color palette and in the shapes-the musical composition however with a strong droning sound borders on being dissonant throughout.

Visual Composition II has extreme moments of dissonant colors and movements that are resolved with the textures of the vertically moving instrument at measured interludes. The composers do not have either traditional music composition method-the mathematically formulated literate method described by Schopenhauer or the oral method used by many composers-available to them to guide the outcome of their compositions. Their choices are limited solely to the visual aesthetic and the experience that they get visually from the composition.

4

Visualisation of Music: Emerging Trends

According to famous musician Schopenhauer: "music is the answer to the mystery of life. The most profound of all the arts, it expresses the deepest thoughts of life." He places the arts onto a continuum from the lowest to the highest-architecture rarely if ever undertaken purely for art but has a special relation to light and is not a copy-sculpture, painting, literature, poetry and music. This continuum matches his objectification of the will: from lowest to highest. Music is more like mathematics-more abstract and independent of the phenomenal world.

Music, since it passes over the Ideas, is also quite independent of the phenomenal world, positively ignores it, and, to a certain extent, could still exist even if there were no world at all, which cannot be said of the other arts. Thus music is as immediate an objectification and copy of the whole will as the world itself is, indeed as the Ideas are, the multiplied phenomenon of which constitutes the world of individual things. Therefore music is by no means like the other arts, namely a copy of the Ideas, but a copy of the will itself, the objectivity of which are the Ideas. For this reason the effect of music is so very much more powerful and penetrating than is that of the other arts, for these others speak only of the shadow, but music of the essence.

Since Schopenhauer claims that music is a copy of the Will, he rejects the suggestion that music is-or should be-imitative of natural sounds like thunder, birds or running water. Just as music does not imitate the sounds of water, music does not represent individual occurrences, feelings or emotions but the universal occurrences. Schopenhauer leaves a fissures open in his theory for the visual composer to squeeze through in the quest to bring the visual into the place of music.

First, music is a language of feelings and emotions-that goes into the realm of the universal. Second-and related to the first-music is valued for the abstract way in which it functions. A look at Kandinsky's compositions suggests that a high level of abstraction without recourse to the physical world is possible in the visual arts. The visual compositions are not intended to represent the playing of music-even though the portraits start with images of the construction of the instruments and their being played-but are to function in two ways-as a visual music experience and as a method of composing music allowing the composer to use only the visual aesthetic. Third-visual compositions do not need to start from the position of the idea-or the concept that comes from contact with the world-they are fully capable of coming from the deeper sense of the Will. Fourth-music is more closely related to time than to space-the visual compositions are closely tied to a sense of time-more so than to a static space.

Artistic Visualisation of Music

History is full of artists and theorists who have created systems that bring colour-or light-and music together.

Attempts have been made for hundreds of years to find a correlation between sound and light-or to force the two into a comparative analogy. Goethe, for some time, embraced the idea that there was a correlation between the vibration frequencies of sound and of light. Kenneth Peacock states that, "Sir Isaac Newton was the first to observe a correspondence between the proportionate width of the seven prismatic rays and the string lengths required to produce the musical scale D, E, F, G, A, B, C."

Niels Hutchison suggests that Newton forced his colour theory to match the music theory. "Newton felt obliged to divide the naturally-occurring spectrum into seven colours, one for each note of a musical scale. In this way the phenomena of light and sound were united in one mathematical matrix." These seven colors, chosen by Newton, are still used to describe the rainbow.

Newton's schema has been challenged by new discoveries in the science of light. Hermann von Helmholtz supplemented the traditional set of primary colors with the additives of red, green and blue. Hutchison demonstrates how Helmholtz moves into the colour-music analogy.

> The tonal range, from the darkest colour to the lightest, became more clearly defined. Particularly, pairs of complementary colours, such as red and blue-green, were isolated in the spectrum; it was eventually demonstrated that any pair of its own could reconstitute white light, if painted on a spinning disc. Helmholtz was very taken by the colour-music analogy... He personally preferred an A scale, so that his additive primaries of red, green and blue-violet would most closely match a major chord - in this case, A, C# and E. Spacing was all important to Helmholtz: closer colours were not so harmonious, nor did they give as pure an impression in his view. The complementaries, such as red and blue-green, satisfied

> him more, and he likened them to the satisfying musical intervals of the fourth and the major third.

Willard Wright, in The Future of Painting, predicted that the art of colour, which in his time was expressing itself in painting, would need a new medium. He expected that light would be this new medium for the artistry of colour.

> What, one asks, will be the ultimate medium of this new art of colour? There can be little doubt concerning the answer. Already the future of the art of colour is evident. The medium of this new art will be light, namely: colour in its purest, most intense form, and with determinable vibrations. That light is the logical means for the expression of colour is obvious, for colour is light; and only through light (that is: the heliotropic aspect of colour) can colour be made to function most effectively. Pigments are merely colors by proxy, without purity, and low in vibration.

Measurable vibrations of colour were important to Wright's theory. These vibrations, according to Wright, act on the optic nerve in a similar way to the action of sound vibrations act on the ear.

Tom DeWitt suggests that visual music must look for its own aesthetic-that is in touch with the psychology of sight. DeWitt starts with aural research by Helmholtz, "Helmholtz concluded that we appreciate the geometric progression in sound frequencies because our ears seem to produce these overtones even in the absence of their physical presence. In other words, we enjoy the art born from the subtle manipulation of our aural psychology."

DeWitt appropriates this methodology and employs it to study sight. He exposes several discoveries: First, the eyes respond differently to black and white than they do to colour from colour. He suggests this is due to the difference in light sensitivity between the rods and cones. The change between them may trigger an emotional release. Second, the aesthetic of symmetry comes from the "bilateral symmetry" structure of the human optic system. Third, sight is tied to a time based cycling.

The persistence of vision closely matches our aural perception, that is, discrete sound events become continuous tones at about 20 cycles per second. Like the reduction of a score into beats and measures, films are made of frames and shots. The film medium invites artists to become visual musicians, dividing up time according to a sense of change. Hence one aesthetic that music can teach visual artists is that of tempo... it might be advisable to continue this formalism further, so that the exact duration of time between cuts would be based on a set beat frequency either subdivided by rational fractions or lengthened by integral multiples. Certainly, music has shown that this simple scheme appeals to an innate rhythmic sensibility in our psychology.

This rhythm can be created by other methods than cuts, such as pulses, jumps, and moving objects. The motion can be used to express emotion, from excitement to calm. Fourth, the brain is able to finish only partially seen objects.

> The brain is capable of recognizing images that are partially blocked or occluded from view by opaque foreground objects. Contrast this visual mechanism with hearing. The ear may be exposed to the summation of many simultaneous sounds, but the brain extracts coherent information from subsets of the total sound environment. This is a process of subtracting from our immediate awareness unwanted elements of a complex audio waveform. However, when the eye sees an occluded object, the brain fills in the missing elements, completing the process of recognition by adding pieces.

Schopenhauer also theorizes about the senses and ranks them. Sight gets the nod over hearing. He states, "Sight has the highest rank, inasmuch as its sphere is the most far-reaching, and its receptivity and susceptibility the keenest. This is due to the fact that what stimulates it is an imponderable, in other words, something hardly corporeal, something quasi-spiritual. Hearing has the second place, corresponding to air." The ranking continues on to the lowest senses of smell and taste. These senses are the most likely to be objective and subject to the will. Schopenhauer suggests that the perceptual boundaries of hearing contribute to the nature of music.

> Perceptions through hearing are exclusively in time; hence the whole nature of music consists in the measure of time, and on this depends not only the quality or pitch of tones by means of vibrations, but also their quantity or duration by means of the beat or time. The perceptions of sight, on the other hand, are primarily and predominantly in space; but secondarily, through their duration, they are also in time also. Sight is the sense of the understanding that perceives; hearing is the sense of the faculty of reason that thinks and comprehends.

For visual musicians to be successful, given these parameter would require a strong temporal sense and a decrease in the reliance on the spatial perceptions. Movement and rhythm work well because they combine the spatial and temporal perceptions.

The passive nature of hearing leads to the power it exerts on the mind. Schopenhauer suggests why the visual musician-one attempting to do visually what music is capable of-may fail in their effort.

> The effect of music on the mind, so penetrating, so immediate, so unfailing, and also the aftereffect that sometimes follows it, consisting in a specially sublime

> frame of mind, are explained by the passive nature of hearing just described. The vibrations of the tones following in combined, rational, numerical relations, set the brain-fibres themselves vibrating in a similar way. On the other hand, from the active nature of vision, the very opposite of hearing, we can understand why for the eye there can be nothing analogous to music, and why the colour-organ was a ludicrous error.

Colour Organ

Louis-Betrand Castel developed a clavecin oculaire, a "harpsichord for the eyes", in 1734. He describes his inspiration,

> The idea for a clavecin oculaire was stimulated by writings of Athanasius Kircher, who had experimented with the magic lantern-an invention that became the slide projector. In his first article on the subject, Castel asked: "Why not make ocular as well as auricular harpsichords? It is again to our good friend (Kircher] that I owe the birth of such a delightful idea. Two years ago I was reading his Musurgia: there I found that if during a beautiful concert we could see the air which is agitated by all the various tremors of the voice and instruments, we would be astonished to see it sown with the most vivid colors."

Castel describes an instrument of five octaves, with each note having a colour associated with it. For instance C was blue and had white or black mixed with it to go up and down the scale. During the nineteenth century there were a number of experiments to bring together sound and colour; from Frederick Kastner using gas jets, D.D. Jameson using oil lamps and bottles full of colored liquid, and William Schooling using vacuum tubes. Alexander Wallace Rimington patented his Colour-Organ-which became the name for many other colour light instruments-in 1893. Peacock describes the instrument,

> Rimington was convinced that physical analogies of some kind existed between sound and colour. In his book, he repeatedly compared the two phenomena, claiming that both 'are due to vibrations which stimulate the optic and aural nerve respectively'... Rather than attempting to show an exact parallel between vibration frequencies of light and sound, he divided the spectrum into intervals of the same proportions as occur in a musical octave. Thus the ratio between two light waves approximated that for a corresponding interval in sound. Each octave contained the same colors; and registral placement of colors was directly proportional to saturation, i.e. higher octaves contained more white light. The Colour-Organ stood over 10 feet high. A complex apparatus, it employed 14 arc lamps and many filters varnished with aniline dye. It also required a power supply capable of providing 150 amps. The five-octave keyboard resembled that of an ordinary organ and was connected by a series of trackers to a corresponding set of diaphragms in front of special lenses. Stops were furnished to control the three variables of colour perception: hue, luminosity, and chroma (colour purity). One stop allowed the performer to spread the spectrum band over the entire keyboard instead of over one octave-proof of Rimington's flexible attitude concerning the analogy between particular colors and tones.

Rimington's "instrument" only produced colour and was not capable of making sound. His instrument used traditional notation, playing the same notes on the keyboard as with a "sound" based instrument. It was his expectation that his instrument would be played simultaneously with a sound-producing one. Rimington's C note corresponded to deep red-unlike Helmholtz who gave this colour to the G note and Castel who gave the C to blue. The various theorists and builders did not have a consistent relationship of colors and notes.

Thomas Wilfred, who built the Clavilux in 1922, rejected theories that created a correspondence between light and sound. Peacock comments on his commitment to light and the Clavilux,

Light alone was the principal feature of a new art form he named "Lumia"... He considered the term "colour-music" a metaphor; yet his art resembled music by including factors of time and rhythm in live performance. Wilfred first used light in a purely abstract manner, but he later decided form and movement were essential. These he achieved via filters which permitted the projection of moving geometrical shapes onto a screen... Wilfred's main instrument, employing six projectors, was controlled from a "keyboard" consisting of banks of sliders. An elaborate arrangement of prisms could be inclined or twisted in any plane in front of each light source. Colour intensity was varied by six separate rheostats which Wilfred operated delicately with his fingers. Selection of geometric patterns was effected via an ingenious system of counterbalanced disks.

Wilfred, in Light and the Artist, lays out his framework for creating what he considered to be the eighth fine art-named Lumia-using the medium of light. The parameters around which Wilfred worked lay an interesting conceptual framework to compare to the visual music experiment-form, colour and motion. He assigned the most importance to form and motion-allowed for static compositions deeming them less important-but suggested that eye required form and so that motion and colour could not function independently of form.

> Form has four sub-factors: LOCATION-Where is it? VOLUME-How big? SHAPE-What is it? CHARACTER-What is there about it?...Color also has four sub-factors: HUE-What colour is it-red, green, blue? CHROMA-How much gray has been mixed with

> the pure hue? VALUE-How much white in that gray? INTENSITY-How strong is the light it sheds?... In lumia the term motion applies to all phenomena in the time dimension. Motion may therefore occur in a static form, with changes in volume, shape, character, hue, chroma, value and intensity. Like form and colour, motion has four sub-factors: ORBIT-Where is it going? TEMPO-How fast? Speeding up? Slowing down? RHYTHM-Does it repeat anything? FIELD-Is it constantly visible, or does any part of its orbit carry it beyond the range of vision?

The visual arts are easier for Schopenhauer, and other theorists, to explain. He suggests that all people recognize human beauty when it is seen, but the artist sees this with more clearness. The artist in fact with his presentation exceeds that of nature. Schopenhauer disputes those who try to limit the subjects of painting to special events or people. He discusses historical painting, and suggests that no event in human life should be left out of the possibilities for painting.

These paintings should include everyday life as well as significant historical events. This becomes apparent when exploring the significance of painting for art versus that of history. "The outward significance is the importance of an action in relation to its consequences for and in the actual world ...The inward significance is the depth of insight into the Idea of mankind which it discloses... In art only the inward significance is of importance; in history the outward."

It is this distinction between the inward and the outward that suggests some of what is special about music.

> The truth which lies at the foundation of all the remarks we have so far made is that the object of art, the depiction of which is the aim of the artist, and the knowledge of which must be consequently precede his

> work as its germ and source, is an Idea in Plato's sense, and absolutely nothing else; not the particular thing, the object of common apprehension, and not the concept, the object of rational thought and of science.

Cheryl Foster suggests several types of art that don't fit into Schopenhauer's schema. The "degenerate mode of allegory known as symbolism, for in its practice, art veers entirely of course from perceptual contemplation into territory through which one must be guided by concepts alone." Schopenhauer offers a corrective to any art theory that overemphasizes conventions, concepts and categories of artistic creation. The task of visual music is full of attempts to break with conventions-but in breaking with the conventions these artists often remained closely aligned with scientific concepts and techniques-which Schopenhauer demonstrates is just as dangerous.

Artistic Expression of Music

For Schopenhauer the artistic endeavour is always a temporary respite. The artistic expression gives a glimpse of real life-the innermost nature of life-but doesn't offer total satisfaction. All art speaks the language of perception, but not the language of reflection, so they do not offer a permanent universal knowledge. While art can be employed by either-the concept or the Idea-it is clear where Schopenhauer sees genuine art coming from.

> The concept is abstract, discursive, wholly undetermined within its sphere, determined only by its limits, attainable and intelligible only to him who has the faculty of reason, communicable by words without further assistance, entirely exhausted by its definition. The Idea, on the other hand, definable perhaps as the adequate representative of concept, is absolutely perceptive, and although representing an infinite number of individual things, is yet thoroughly definite.

> It is never known by the individual as such, but only by him who has raised himself above all willing and all individuality to the pure subject of knowing... For this reason the most excellent works of art, the noblest productions of genius, must eternally remain sealed books to the dull majority of men, and are inaccessible to them... Now it follows from all that has been said that the concept, useful as it is in life, serviceable, necessary, and productive as it is in science, is eternally barren and unproductive in art. The apprehended Idea, on the contrary, is the true and only source of every genuine work of art.

Unfortunately many artists are only imitators. Imitators-in contrast to the genius who grasps the Idea-observe what has an affect in genuine works. They take this observation, turn it into a concept-or technique-and of course destroy any possibility of creating genuine art. These artists birth their work from the concept and "like parasitic plants, they suck their nourishment from the works of others."

Schopenhauer links the usage of allegory and symbolism to the conceptual arts-as a "mistaken effort" which does not serve the purpose of art. He rejects allegory, since the art must go through some decoding effort, or matching interpretive effort to arrive at the meaning. This is more of a scientific exercise than the artistic effort Schopenhauer has been describing. The viewer also must not engage in this kind of analogy or symbolic interpretation method.

A viewer must stand before a piece of art and wait to see if it "speaks" to her. They must not address the art, which means they would only hear themselves talking-but their imagination must be excited. It is the fact that art, at least the best art does not speak directly to the mind or senses, but directly to the inner being, for "the very best in art is too spiritual tc be given directly to the senses; it must be born in the beholder's imagination, though it must be begotten by the work of art."

Schopenhauer suggests that the artistic medium may be a better place tc explore the issues-of the medium of visual music-than is the place of discourse.

> The communication of such a thing can therefore take place only on the path of perception, which is that of art. Therefore, whoever is imbued with the apprehension of an idea is justified when he chooses art as the medium of his communicatior.. The mere concept, on the other hand, is something completely determinable, hence something to be exhausted, something distir.ctly thought, which can be, according to its whole content, communicated coldly and dispassionately bywords.

If a work of art attempts to convey a concept instead of an Idea it gives up the "innermost kernel" and leaves the viewer unsatisfied. True art can't be reduced to a distinct concept. Schopenhauer does not see music as a vehicle to carry the lyric-but it is an independent art and does not require words to give it meaning. The voice is foremost an instrument of tone, and should have little concern for expressing the often inconsequentiεl lyrics. For Schopenhauer the words are too closely tied to the conceptual. If a composer writes music for the text then he will respond to the "affections of the will" that the words are based on. The words connect with the direct ways of knowledge.

However if we look at music that is purely instrumental we see that it speaks directly to the inner essence. Schopenhauer speaking of a Beethoven symphony says, "all the human passions and emotions speak from this symphony; joy grief, love, hatred, terror, hope, and so on in innumerable shades, yet all, as it were, only in the abstract and without any particularization; it is their mere form without the material, like a mere spirit world without matter." Composers cannot by conscious intention seek to communicate concepts without giving up the true significance, the "innermost kernel" of the music.

Feelings, Emotions, Passions

Schopenhauer always separates music from the other arts in his discussion,

> It stands quite apart from all the others. In it we do not recognize the copy, the repetition, of any Idea of the inner nature of the world... its effect on man's innermost nature is so powerful, and it is so completely and profoundly understood by him in his innermost being as an entirely universal language, whose distinctiveness surpasses even that of the world of perception itself ...Therefore, from our standpoint, where the aesthetic effect is the thing we have in mind, we must attribute to music a far more serious and profound significance that refers to the innermost being of the world and of our own self... its imitative reference to the world must be very profound, infinitely true, and really striking, since it is instantly understood by everyone, and presents a certain infallibility by the fact that its form can be reduced to quite definite rules expressible in numbers, from which it cannot possibly depart without entirely ceasing to be music.

Music does not use the language of reason, words, but the language of passion-music acts directly on the passions or emotions, not on the individual will. The emotions and passions that music goes directly to are not specific ones but to the "essential nature" of those emotions. Music "never expresses the phenomenon, but only the inner nature, the in-itself, of every phenomenon, the will itself."

Music offers the secrets contained in many scenes and events, and brings an enhanced commentary on the visual information. Movies and television use music to grab attention, to guide the emotional response, to proclaim special events, to infuse with adrenaline-this music is meant to bypass the reasoning and grab people in their emotions. Much of this music is formulaic and imitative-observing what works in real artistic works-it works on the emotions but lacks the power beyond the first body response. Since music is not a copy of the phenomenon, or "of the will's adequate objectivity"-but is a "copy of the will itself'-it expresses the "thing-in-itself' of the phenomenon.

> We could just as well call the world embodied music as embodied will; this is the reason why music makes every picture, indeed every scene from real life and from the world, at once appear in enhanced significance, and this is of course, all the greater, the more analogous its melody is to the inner spirit of the given phenomenon."

Just as music is superior in all the arts, for Schopenhauer the melody is the pinnacle of music. He suggests that the melody needs the bass to produce the maximum effect, but that it is the most important part of the music. "The invention of melody, the disclosure in it of all the deepest secrets of human willing and feeling, is the work of genius, whose effect is more apparent here than anywhere else, is far removed from all the reflection and conscious intention, and might be called an inspiration." The melody is in the superior position because it just as music compared to the other arts-gets the closest to the Will.

Orality to Visual Music

Godfrey Reggio-producer of the "Qatsi" series, which uses only images and music for feature length movies-states that the image has become the dominant form of communication in our culture. He argues that we live within the image, that the image has an overwhelming power in our culture. Greg Ulmer defines this current era as electracy-a secondary orality that combines features of the oral and literate cultures mediated and networked by electronic technology. The image becomes the mode of logic ushering in new ways of thinking. Ulmer's mandate is to reform the way of structuring thought and societal organization as we move into this era of electracy.

> The "apparatus" theory that guides the heuretic project to invent electracy suggests that the nation state as the collective form of identity in the print era will eventually be replaced by some other yet to be determined collective order. The apparatus as a matrix of technology, institutions, and identity formation also suggests that the individuals gathered together within this new political arrangement will not experience their identity as "self' ("selfhood" being specifically a literate experience and behavior). It is possible to point to what is happening to individual identity experience, at least, but more difficult to say at this point what is happening collectively. In an image based apparatus people experience themselves as a surface look (just as in literacy they experienced themselves as a separate interiority). It is not a matter of one replacing the other, but of being as look supplementing and displacing interior "character.

This shift into image-based electracy, brings with it changes to all forms of communication, to social constructs, even to political formations.

Music-especially composition, and to a lesser degree performance-remains solidly in the oral age. The composition of music in popular and folk genres is created in an oral style-where the ears and the evaluation of sound is constantly referred to in the process. Music composed in the classical style is created in a literate or mathematically reasoned style-where the composer has a firm understanding of the relationships of notes, instruments and technique to the resulting sound.

Both compositional styles are solidly based on the understanding or experience of the sound associated with the created forms. For the orally created pieces the sound is made concurrently with the composition. For the literate style, the composers understand the sound relationships in their mind without actually hearing the sound at the time of composition. Both methods compose with an awareness of what the final composition will sound like and can accurately predict what a performance or recording will produce. Toward a Poetic of Visual Music sets out to challenge the composer to consider the possibility of composing with a visual aesthetic rather than the customary aural one.

Entering electracy

In orality, thinking was a voice from outside ones head. In literacy, the idea was contained in the word, usually the printed word. Within electracy, people see/experience their own unique image of life. Oral peoples who experienced thought as spirit were organized collectively in tribes; literate people who experience thought as self are organized collectively in nation states. The heuretic principle suggests that electrate peoples who experience thought as virtual image will organize collectively in some new way that as yet has not come fully into view (but perhaps is glimpsed in multinational corporations).

The forms of music have changed with the continuing. experiments into the electronic production of music, however the composition of music still has not given priority to the image. The music industry has become multinational and would warrant exploration based on Ulmer's theories. Derrick De Kerckhove considers how people have used these changing media. "Written words are concepts in isolation, until they are combined into images by the reader".

In the literate era readers produced their own images within their own imagination-based on the word constructs and their own collection of experiences. Television, however, provides the images in the electrate age. "Instead of scanning text to create and store images, children who watch TV must quickly generate from loosely connected fragments and reconstitute the object vision. This is very different from labeling objects and stringing them together in coherent sentences." De Kerckhove sees this primarily in negative ways-but the case can be made that television requires viewers to assemble images, impressions and emotional impulses into a set of understanding. The viewer assembles meaning, not in coherent literate sentences as De Kerckhove desires, but in another less reasoned way-which highlights the fact that television and text speak to very different aspects of the human being. Text speaks primarily to the mind while the image starts at the emotion.

De Kerckhove claims that the effect of this difference is that the viewer is already receiving the information fully processed. "If the video screen has such a direct impact on my nervous system and my emotions, and so little effect on my mind, then most of the information-processing was actually being performed by the screen." An alternate to this view is to understand the brain being asked to process information in a different way that does not use the same word based logic that De Kerckhove considers superior.

De Kerckhove follows in the footsteps of his mentor, Marshall McCluhan, who stated, "Printed books, themselves the first uniform, repeatable, and mass-produced items in the world, provided endless paradigms of uniform commodity culture for sixteenth and succeeding centuries." The images continue or amplify the mass-produced quality of this commodity culture. Guy Debord talks about the commodity fetishism where consumers make fetishes out of products-and the associated images of happiness, success and satisfaction-that offer a shortcut to happiness and the solution to other manufactured needs.

Like De Kerckhove, Debord sees the images used as a form of mind/viewer control. For De Kerckhove it was a replacement for thinking while Debord considers the breakup of community and ensuing isolation. "With the advent of long-distance mass communication, the isolation of the population has become a much more effective means of control." Debord suggests that this also leads to the downfall of art as it breaks away from its community role of myth maintenance and the common language of the literate era.

> As soon as art-which constituted that former common language of social inaction-establishes itself as independent in the modern sense, emerging from its first, religious universe to become the individual production of separate works, it becomes subject, as one instance among others, to the movement governing the history of the whole culture as a separated realm. Art's declaration of independence is thus the beginning of the end of art.

These controlling images lead to unthinking behavior-where the person actually lives within the image mediated life.

The spectator's alienation from and submission to the contemplated object (which is the outcome of his unthinking activity) works like this: the more he contemplates, the less he lives; the more readily he recognizes his own needs in the images of need proposed by the dominant system, the less he understands his own existence and his own desires. The spectacle's externality with respect to the acting subject is demonstrated by the fact that the individual's own gestures are no longer his own, but rather those of someone else who represents them to him. The spectator feels at home nowhere, for the spectacle is everywhere.

For those who remain intellectually in the literate age, the image culture appears to be unthinking-even a major step backwards. Those who are fully part of this era process information in very different ways and are not interested in the text based conceptual signification. They become more intuitive and eclectic in the complex of image-based signification.

Debord describes the electrate era as one dominated by the spectacle. "The spectacle is not a collection of images; rather, it is a social relationship between people that is mediated by images." Ulmer would give the imagebased era a much richer matrix of meaning than do either Debord or De Kerckhove-who are more committed to a literate sense of identity. Debord suggests that all of life becomes an illusion.

> The spectacle erases the diving line between self and world, in that the self, under siege by the presence/absence of the world, is eventually overwhelmed; it likewise erases the dividing line between true and false, repressing all directly lived truth beneath the real presence of the falsehood maintained by the organization of appearances. The individual, though condemned to the passive acceptance of an alien

> everyday reality, is thus driven into a form of madness in which, by resorting to magical devices, he entertains the illusion that he is reacting to this fate.

Roland Barthes discusses three meanings contained in images: first, studium which is the predictable denotation and what we know it is; second, the culturally understood meaning, third, the punctum or obtuse which has details that sting the viewer evoking a memory that could be wild, personal and is not codified. (Barthes) It is this third meaning that becomes important when considering the electrate age. Ulmer suggests,

> The meanings that are namable in a photograph are called "studium" (constituted by the public encyclopedia of concepts) and the obtuse meaning "punctum"-that which stings or pricks one emotionally. The photograph produces a feeling that we associate with the experience of recognition and epiphany... Nor is there anything esoteric about third meanings. The punctum juxtaposes to ideological (mis) recognition an alternative, a personal memory based not on the public archive but a private repertoire. The subversiveness of this move is not in the content but just in the effect of having two databases to call upon, to slow the fixation of meaning, to interrupt the exchange... Here is the key to reasoning in the electronic digital apparatus. The language apparatus is a prosthetic memory-an artificial memory that augments and extends the power of living organic human memory. And each apparatus has its own way of performing this supporting function. The power of the photograph to stimulate involuntary personal memory is the point of departure for an electrate institutional practice.

In this image-based culture music functions in a congruent role-working in collusion with the television and movie image, energizing the advertising sting, and assisting in the evoking of involuntary memories. Barthes worked with the third meaning primarily in regard to film and photography; but music also functions in the third meaning stinging the emotion as much or more than do photographic images. Music evokes memories, feelings, moods-a whole range of emotions.

Music has and continues to play a major role in the formation of belief systems-in the advertised product of happiness, in the mystical union with the popular culture icon, with the claim of the political person wrapping themselves in an iconic image or label, with the power of the sporting hero to elicit loyalty, with the religious invocation of exclusion and correctness. While recognizing the decline of traditional religiosity-which has strong attachments to the literate text-based era-Slavoj Zizek identifies an new embodiment of spirituality. This new spirituality offers people another fetish, which allows them to accept life in this spectacle driven modality-in spite of their arguments that they have left behind the religiosity of the literate age.

> Although "Western Buddhism" presents itself as the remedy against the stressful tension of capitalist dynamics, allowing us to uncouple and retain inner peace and Gelasenheit, it actually functions as its perfect ideological supplement... "Western Buddhism" thus perfectly fits the fetishist mode of ideology in our allegedly `post ideological' era.

This spirituality, rather than functioning outside of or in contrast to the ideology of global capitalism, actually accommodates the capitalistic urge and the age of "unbelief."

So, when we are bombarded by claims that in our post-ideological cynical era nobody believes in the proclaimed ideals, when we encounter a person who claims he is cured of any beliefs, accepting social reality the way it really is, one should always counter such claims with the question: Ok, but where is the fetish which enables you to (pretend to) accept reality "`the way it is"? The function of the image, fetish, spectacle continues to require exploration-especially in regard to the way it is used in musical performance and the parade of ever changing pop stars who push the consumption of fashion, music and entertainment news.

Music Visualisation in Electrate Age

When we consider the place that image has in our culture we are not surprised by the change in communication and societal organization. While most forms of communication have increasingly moved to a predominance of the "image", music especially when it comes to composition is still in orality or literacy. If you look at the performance of music a strong visual/image component has become normal with choreographed dance moves, lavish costuming, elaborate staging, designed sets, and image projections.

With performance music becomes more an image-based spectacle-moving substantially into the electrate age. Music performers also become part of the spectacle carrying much of the fagade demanded of the popular culture icon. The influence of music videos has been felt throughout the electronic media industry-ironically affecting the production of television, movies and advertising-with the usage of visual styles and preference for image communication over that of the word. Ulmer suggests that performance may be the most important part of music in the electrate age, "performance may be to electracy what definition was to literacy."

In popular music the image has become more important than the actual production of the music. This has changed the very criteria of who gets chosen by the labels to promote-often elevating the image over the quality of musicianship. The performance is what gives them their signification which may be more about declassification-where the dictionary text-based method is about classification. Ulmer elucidates,

> Walter Ong and other grammatologists have shown, for example, that school with all its practices such as concept formation and method is the institutionalization of alphabetic writing. Once the move was made from manuscript to print, at least two foundational practices of medieval schooling were abandoned: mnemonic training and scholastic logic ...While the entire administrative superstructure of literate specialized knowledge will be translated into cyberspace, once there much of it will evaporate ...The history of literacy shows that we may expect profound changes to result from the changes in the language apparatus of our civilization that have been underway at least since the invention of photography in the early nineteenth century.

De Kerckhove notes how these same changes have affected music.

> From the Renaissance up to the recent reversal provoked by electronic technologies, the writing down of music has amounted to mastering sound and reducing to second class status all spontaneous popular forms of traditional folkloric rhythms. The opposition between writing and music is almost a biological one, as writing takes control of the brain while organized sound takes control of the whole body.

An interesting trend with the move into the electrate age has been a renewed interest in the oral heritage of music-roots music in the United States has made a resurgence with films such as O Brother Where Art Thou?; Irish, Celtic, and Scottish music have festivals and dedicated radio shows; and builders of ethnic acoustic instruments are experiencing a greater demand. Music in the electrate age is getting closer to its emotional roots. The invention of the audio recorder assists in both the resurgence of oral roots music, the continued oral composition style and in the commoditization of the musical product. Later sections will explore the role of the audio recorder particularly with Brian Eno and John Cage and their usage of found sounds.

The composition of music, especially in the popular arena has remained in the oral age. Composers work with the sounds and put them together with a constant reference to what is heard. Patterns and sounds are memorized and recycled into the next composition. Musicians then memorize these compositions for their performance, or lip sync to already recorded music. DJ's use the sounds found on records to create new sonic mixes from these found already recorded sounds. Composers who have been more traditionally trained often compose in a more literate manner, with a formal understanding of the mathematical relationships of different notes, sounds and instruments.

This knowledge allows them to compose based on a mental understanding of how to put these different sounds together. Their knowledge is still rooted firmly in an aesthetic that is based on the auditory process. From the written score trained musicians play the repeatable music forms previously composed. Few, if any, composers use the visual/image as the driving aesthetic in the composition task of music. Ulmer challenges us to think about our ways of knowing, our ways of creating and the process of getting there.

> It turns out, however, that the practice most relevant to the obtuse order of meaning, most revealing of mood and atmosphere as categorical states of mind, is music. The point for electracy is not the music as such, or does not stop with the music but the mood it supports and evokes... In literacy it is possible to write concepts

> directly (justice); in electracy it is possible to image moods directly.

Music has been associated with mood and emotion for centuries. Schopenhauer associated music with abstraction and emotion-but not specific emotions. It was natural for music to play an important part in the formation of an image culture in spite of it not being apprehended by the eye-because of this close tie to the emotional part of being. The problem Toward a Poetic of Visual Music explores is whether music can be composed in this image/ electrate era using the image and its associated aesthetic instead of resorting to the auditory process-where music is primarily composed with an oral or literate manner.

Ulmer details the way patterns change with a movement from one era to the next. "When the oral narratives were recorded or written down in the alphabet, it became possible to discern a pattern, a ,repetition of signifiers that was not perceptible in spoken discourse." Following the path suggested by the theory of Ulmer we will explore what happens when music is composed with a visual aesthetic. The exploration will start from three points; the philosophy of Arthur Schopenhauer, the practice and thought of eight experimental artists, and the artistic endeavor-the Visual Music 8/8 Project-which combines the visual, hidden codes and the composition of sound. What will we discover in this era of a second orality-that combines features of the oral and literate while giving predominance to the image?

Toward a Poetic of Visual Music

If in this era of electracy the image or visual becomes the dominant aesthetic-then how do we bring music fully into this aesthetic? Toward a Poetic of Visual Music will put forward a poetic philosophy-a form of knowledge about the shaping of a material or the artistic method of creating a work. The Visual Music 8/8 Project, will explore two ways of creating visual music. The first is creating visuals that have the character of music and which viewers may respond to in ways that are similar to how they respond to music.

The Visual Music 8/8 Project will challenge viewers to respond to images in the same way that they respond to music-with the portrait sets and visual compositions created from the portraits. The challenge is to create images that elicit the same kinds of associations and emotional connections that listening to music does. The second and more difficult will be to find ways to compose, produce, and play music using a visual aesthetic. The visual compositions will include a hidden code that will lead to the creation of musical compositions. These musical compositions will allow the viewers to experience the sound created via a visual aesthetic.

Music composers bring the visual together with music primarily in two current practices. Composers create music while watching a visual track-they attempt to bring congruence to the music-visual mix by matching the emotional or action qualities of the visual: The composition is carried out in an oral or literate manner with composer interpreting the significance of the visual and matching the tone and quality to that of the music. The Godfrey Reggio and Phil Glass collaborations begin to break out of this method-it is unclear in some instances which comes first in the process, the visual or the aural.

The second way is to take a piece of music and create a set of visuals which may match the narrative content (lyrics), the rhythm, the emotional content of the music, or simply be a stylized performance of the music. This approach uses a visual aesthetic that responds to the content of the music but the visual aesthetic does not influence the composition of the music. A third, but less frequent, attempt would be the usage of computer-generated systems that match a set of visuals with pre-existing music. These often work with colors or geometric shapes and are usually independent of any human judgment based oral or visual aesthetic. Human judgment and control is minimized once the system has been created.

Toward a Poetic of Visual Music and the Visual Music 8/8 Project will demonstrate artistically and philosophically the following five things. First, visual music compositions/ experiences can be created that will elicit responses in the viewers that are similar to the responses of those who listen to music. These responses will mirror what the essence of music carries-the deeper emotional connections, the energy, the meditative possibilities, or the engrossing enveloping character of music. These explorations will include the troublesome issues of rhythm, musical sound decay, repeatability, melody and harmony-attempting to bridge the divide between the aural and the visual. This task will require some definitions of the essence of music emphasizing its emotion, connections, energy, and meditative qualities.

Second, it is possible to compose music using a visual aesthetic-rather than the customary aural one-and listeners will recognize the resulting sounds as music. For this to be fully realized the visual composers must have no awareness, during the compositional activity, of what the resulting "music" will sound like. The visual composer must be focused fully on the visual content of their compositions-ignoring the possible auditory connections that might be made.

Third, this visual music can overcome the challenge to maintain human contact-with the accompanying levels of imperfections and the variability of aesthetic taste-throughout the visual music composition process. Many of the current attempts to create visual music use a computer generation process, where a software designer create algorithms that generate the visuals or the music based on these principles. Many of these compositions flounder in the traps of geometric shapes and primary colors.

Fourth, these visual compositions can attain the same position as that held by music in the philosophy of Arthur Schopenhauer-superior to all of the other arts. This effort will question the stratification he has laid out, especially the stratification within music-that assigns melody a superior position over the bass.

Fifth, further experiments will be suggested that will continue the journey toward this poetic and raise several more issues that would warrant historical analysis and philosophic reflection. These experiments will only touch the surface of the musical match with light and color, or the role of vibration in sight and hearing.

Other approaches would be appropriate for the challenge set forth by this poetic. Exploring the use of dance and choreograph, as in several Merce Cunningham productions, or dancers attached to motion capture software, as Troika Ranch does, which then creates music via a real-time MIDI engine leads to fascinating interplays of image and music. The dancers body appears to have a memory of rhythm which is closely related to the aural experience of music. This experiment works at the separation from this aural experience, choosing to focus on attaining the visual music using only a visual aesthetic.

Synesthesia where perceptions in one sense are accompanied by perceptions in another sense, could make the claim to offer rich insight into the quest for a poetic of visual music. Richard Cytowic suggests that,

> Synesthesia is the involuntary physical experience of a cross-modal association. That is, the stimulation of one sensory modality reliably causes a perception in one or more different senses. Its phenomenology clearly distinguishes it from metaphor, literary tropes, sound symbolism, and deliberate artistic contrivances that sometimes employ the term "synesthesia" to describe their multisensory joinings.

Toward a Poetic of Visual Music, is attempting to deliberately use one aesthetic-visual-in place of another-aural. With synesthesia being an involuntary experience it proves to have less value to this particular project. We will study the compositional philosopy of Vasily Kandinsky-who Cretien van Campen claims had synesthesia.

Peter Greenaway often organizes his films around sets of numbers, letters, or even drawings. This method allows him to structure his work without the traditional narrative structure, which he tries to avoid. Draughtsman's Contract is organized around 12 drawings, The Belly of the Architect uses the number seven, Drowning by Numbers counts from one to a hundred, 8 1/2 Women works with the number of women, The Cook, the Thief, His Wife and Her Lover is organized with various palettes of color.

John Cage, an experimental composer, has used the I Ching many times as a tool to create his music. Ulmer explains, "the I Ching, the Chinese Book of Changes, expressing the wisdom of tradition that shaped Japanese culture, has a similar combinatorial arrangement, representing all human experience in 64 hexagrams or archetypal situations." 4'33'; the famous "silent" piece, was built using the I Ching tables to give it a solid structure without Cage needing to make the choices in traditional ways.

The organizing principle chosen for this dissertation and artistic experiment are a set of instruments in the mandolin and bouzouki family-mandolin, mandola, octave mandolin, cittern, bouzouki-where the predominant design of the instrument is an eight-stringed acoustic instrument. The eight strings are in pairs-tuned alike or one-octave apart from each other. These instruments, the number eight, and pairs will serve as the organizing principle of both the philosophical and artistic explorations. The philosophical part, Toward a Poetic of Visual Music, is paired with the artistic experiment, the Visual Music 8/8 Project.

The philosophical writing itself is organized into pairs of movements; the philosophical writings of Arthur Schopenhauer are joined with explorations into the compositional methods of experimental composers and visual artists. Pairings of words-like Consonance and Dissonance-are used to structure the four Schopenhauer sections-which move like a four movement symphony with its themes, variations and conclusion. Each Schopenhauer section is paired with a section exploring artists/composers. The four artist/composer sections bring together a pair of artists-one visual and one musical-in the discourse about composition.

The Visual Music 8/8 Project

The Visual Music 8/8 Project explores the same issues in an image based composition enquiry. The project starts with images of a set of instruments all built by the innovative luthier, Stefan Sobell, in his Northumberland shop. Eight sets of portraits will be created of Sobell building musical instruments, seven people playing the instruments, and the instruments themselves. For each person/instrument combination there will be eight finished portraits. These portraits will be used to create eight visual compositions. The visual composers will use Adobe After Effects to animate the still images into a two to four minute piece of "visual music". After Effects, a two-dimensional animation program, allows extensive changes in position, opacity, rotation, and scale and a limited set of three-dimensional work including lighting and camera angle changes.

The eight visual compositions will lead to the composition of eight pieces of music created with visual aesthetic-by a hidden code to decode the programming that is done by the visual music composers. Four other animators will be invited to each do one of the visual animations so that several visual aesthetics and perspectives can be experienced.

The Visual Music 8/8 Project progresses by a series of stages to produce the full final project:

Photographing the instruments.

Photographing the creation of and playing of the instruments.

Creating the pairs in eight groups of eight images.

Creating a larger group of 330 images that will be used in the animation process. The original eight portraits will represent the strings of the instruments-the additional images represent the changing tone of a string as it is fretted (shortening the string length). 42 of these images contain multiple Adobe Photoshop layers-which allow for eight images per string on each of the eight instrument/people combinations.

Creating a secret code/notation system for the correspondence between image and sound.

Creating the visual music, from the collected images, using Adobe After Effects-which will also be done by four other animators/visual composers.

Decoding/notating the visual music with the key into a notated form.

Recording/ Performing the created music

The completed Visual Music 8/8 Project will be ready for a gallery exhibition including the following components:

64 images-shown in groups of 8 (These will be named with the first name of the person, the letter corresponding to the tuning of the string, and Roman numerals going from I to VIII to define the order. For example, Anna G-II-from an octave mandolin-or Stefan A-IV-from a mandola.)

Eight visual compositions ready to show on some form of monitors. (These will be named Visual Composition with roman numerals from I to VIII.

Eight music compositions-created by the visual composers-ready to play on an audio system. (These are named Musical Composition with the Roman numeral from the corresponding Visual Composition.)

Flusser: Image and the Work of Photography

The base of the Visual Music 8/8 Project is accomplished with the use of photography. The photograph has played an important role in the change from literacy to electracy and the creation of an image-based culture. Debord suggests that the elevation of'sight brings about the elevation of abstraction and "it is inevitable that it should elevate the human sense of sight to the special place once occupied by touch; the most abstract of the senses, and the most easily deceived, sight is naturally the most readily adaptable to present-day society's generalized abstraction."

Abstraction joins emotion as an attribute that causes Schopenhauer to elevate music to a superior position among the arts-and will of course be a part of the effort to bring the visual into the realm of music. Vilem Flusser goes further in suggesting that the camera, the image-maker, is closely tied to the eye. "Tools in the usual sense are extensions of human organs... Is the camera then a machine because it appears to simulate the eye and in the process reaches back to the theory of optics?"

Flusser in Philosophy of Photography. works with the apparatus of the camera and how images are created.

> Photographers, it is true, do not work but they do do something: They create, process and store symbols ...one sees that the camera produces symbols: symbolic surfaces that have in a certain way been prescribed for it. The camera is programmed to produce photographs, and every photograph is a realization of one of the possibilities contained within the program of the camera.

Flusser suggests that the camera is doing a similar task as written language, storing or using symbols. As Ulmer and others have suggested the writing of language limited what was communicated by what the written language was able to contain. In like fashion the photographic image is limited by what can be captured through the lens by the film-the digital photographic process does expand the breadth of what can be contained in the photographic image. Just as writers prefer certain forms of writing because they come closer to "true" signification, Flusser asserts that many photographers

> prefer black-and-white photographs to colour photographs because they more clearly reveal the actual significance of the photography, i.e. the world of concepts ...the colours of photographs are at least as theoretical as black and white. The green of a

> photographed field, for example, is an image of the concept `green'... The more genuine the colours of the photograph become, the more untruthful they are, the more they conceal their theoretical origin.

We will come back to similar issues with Schopenhauer and the occasional effort by musical composers to bring symbols of other sounds into their music so people would hear the rain or cannon. The Visual Music 8/8 Project has chosen the limits of two types of lenses-wide angle and macro-in the acquisition of the portraits and base materials for the visual compositions. These lenses do not match the traditional lens length that is used in the acquisition of portraiture.

Flusser goes beyond discussing the apparatus of the camera by discussing the importance of images.

> Images are significant surfaces. Images signify-mainly-something "out there" in space and time that they have to make comprehensible to us as abstractions (as reductions of the four dimensions of space and time to the two surface dimensions). This specific ability to abstract surfaces out of space and time and to project them back into space and time is what is known as "imagination." It is the precondition for the production and decoding of images ...The significance of the image as revealed in the process of scanning therefore represents a synthesis of two intentions: one manifested in the image and the other belonging to the observer.

Flusser understands that images and texts often function together in an era that straddles literacy and electracy. "Texts admittedly explain images in order to explain them away, but images also illustrate texts in order to make them comprehensible." To suggest that image and text have a similar discourse would be to ignore the gulf that separates them. As filmmaker, Richard Fenwick suggests,

> Words have a linear, discrete, successive order ...Visual forms-lines, colours, proportions etc ...are just as capable of articulation, or complex combinations as words, but ...the most radical difference is that visual forms are not discursive. They do not present their constituents successively but simultaneously.

This is the tension that will remain throughout this document as it attempts carry the discourse both philosophically and visually.

Flusser was concerned with how images could hide the reality and how they can function as signifiers of something else. The movement in the Visual Music 8/8 Project from the visual composition to the musical composition is based on a secret set of codes which decide how the usage of a particular image within the composition will result in a particular note or series of notes to be played-based on it's scale, position, opacity, etc..

Siegfried Zielinski reports that, cryptology, the use of hidden codes, has a long history, within the media sciences, from substitution codes, to systems of transpositions, to very complex forms of encoding all designed to maintain the secrecy of the message. From the notation codes, which are hidden from the visual composers, assignments of instruments, strings, pitches and durations will be made. A more traditional notation will be created from which the music can be recorded or performed. This notation will employ a system of tablature, which suggests what should happen to each string of a particular instrument at anytime within the musical composition.

Wassily Kandinsky offers a caution to those who enter the philosophical discussion of aesthetic issues.

> There are also philosophers of aesthetic who write profound books about an art which was yesterday condemned as nonsense. In writing these books they

remove the barriers over which art has most recently stepped and set up new ones which are to remain for ever in places they have chosen. They do not notice that they are busy erecting barriers, not in front of art, but behind it. And if they do notice this, on the morrow they merely write fresh books and hastily set their barriers a little further on. This performance will go on unaltered until it is realized that the most extreme principle of aesthetic can never be of value to the future, but only to the past. No such theory of principle can be laid down for those things which lie beyond, in the realm of the immaterial. That which has no material existence cannot be subjected to a material classification. That which belongs to the spirit of the future can only be realized in feeling, and to this feeling the talent of the artist is the only road. Theory is the lamp which shed light on the petrified ideas of yesterday and of the more distant past.

5

Theoretical Basis of Different Musical Forms

The term musical form is used in two related ways:

1. a generic type of composition such as the symphony or concerto
2. the structure of a particular piece, how its parts are put together to make the whole; this too can be generic, such as binary form or sonata form

Musical form (the whole or structure) is contrasted with content (the parts) or with surface (the detail), but there is no clear line between the two. In most cases, the form of a piece should produce a balance between statement and restatement, unity and variety, contrast and connection. There is some overlap between musical form and musical genre. The latter term is more likely to be used when referring to particular styles of music (such as classical music or rock music) as determined by things such as harmonic language, typical rhythms, types of musical instrument used and geographical origin.

The phrase musical form is typically used when talking about a particular type or structure within those genres. For example, the twelve bar blues is a specific form often found in the genres of blues and rock and roll music. Forms and formal detail may be described as sectional or developemental, developemental or variational, syntactical/ embodied/extensional or processual/engendered/ intensional, and associational or hierarchical. Form may also be described according to symmetries or lack thereof and repetition. A common idea is formal "depth", necessary for complexity, in which foregrounded "detail" events occur against a more structural background.

For example: Schenkerian analysis. Fred Lerdahl, among others, claims that popular music lacks the structural complexity for multiple structural layers, and thus much depth. However, Lerdahl's theories exclude "associational" or intensional details which are used to help articulate form in popular music. Allen Forte's book The American Popular Ballad of the Golden Era 1924-1950 analyses popular music with traditional Schenkerian techniques, but this is only possible because pre-rock popular ballads are the genre most accesible similar to the Romantic music those theories were designed to analyse.

Extensional music is, "produced by starting with small components - rhythmic or melodic motifs, perhaps - and then 'developing' these through techniques of modification and combination." Intensional music "stars with a framework - a chord sequence, a melodic outline,m a rhythmic pattern - and then extends itself by repeating the framework with perpetually varied inflections to the details filling it in." Middleton also describes form, presumably after Gilles Deleuze's Difference and Repetition, through repetition and difference. Difference is the distance moved from a repeat and a repeat being the smallest difference. Difference is qualitative and quantitative, how far different and what type of difference.

In classical music, there are many labels applied to forms, abstract formal designs, as contrasted with the principals and procedures of combining materials: form. Typical structures used to shape a single movement include:

1. Sectional forms, the larger unit (form) is built from various smaller clear-cut units (sections), combinational, sort of like stacking legos:
   — Strophic form (AA...)
   — Binary form (AB)
   — Ternary form, less often tertiary (ABA)
   — Arch form, (ABCBA)
2. Developmental forms, larger unit (form) is built from small bits of material given different presentations and combinations, usually progressive:
   — Sonata form, also called sonata-allegro
3. Variational forms, larger unit (form) is built from sections treated to one type of presentation at a time, but varying succesively:
   — Rondo (ABACADA...)
   — Variation form, sometimes theme and variation (AA'A"A'"...)
   — Passacaglia and Chaconne

These structures are defined by the distribution of different thematic material, melodies, key centres, and other materials used. While many of the above forms are partly defined by their tonal schemes these forms may be applied to music which has a differing or no tonal scheme. More than one formal method may be used, including in-between types, and music which is not composed with the above or any other model is called through composed.

Especially recently, more segmented approaches have been taken through the use of stratification, superimposition, juxtaposition, interpolation, and other interruptions and simultaneities. Examples include the postmodern "block" technique used by composers such as John Zorn, where rather than organic development one follows separate units in various combinations. These techniques may be used to create contrast to the point of disjointed chaotic textures, or, through repetition and return and transitional procedures such as dissolution, amalgamation, and gradation, may create connectedness and unity.

Composers have also made more use of open forms such as produced by aleatoric devices and other chance procedures, improvisation, and some processes. (ibid) Types of piece which may or may not incorporate one or more of the above structures as part of their overall makeup include:

- Ballet, larger musical composition intended for Ballet dance form
- Cantata
- Chorale
- Concerto

Dance, smaller musical composition intended for presentation of a dance, either as accompaniment for dancing or as music as such

- Duet
- Etude or study
- Fantasia
- Fugue
- Mass
- Opera

— Oratorio
— Prelude
— Requiem
— Rhapsody
— Sonata
— Suite
— Symphonic poem
— Symphony

Forms of chamber music are defined by instrumentation (string quartet, piano quintet and so on). The structure of a chamber work is typically similar to a sonata.

Metre (music)

Metre is the measurement of a musical line into measures of stressed and unstressed beats, indicated in Western notation by a symbol called a time signature. Properly, "metre" describes the whole concept of measuring rhythmic units, but it can also be used as a specific descriptor for a measurement of an individual piece as represented by the time signature—for example, "This piece is in 4/4 metre" is equivalent to "This piece is in 4/4 time" or "This piece has a 4/4 time signature."

A measure has two purposes in Western traditions of music, the first is to block out a series of beats, and the second is to form the building block of larger sections of music, such as a phrase. Time signatures imply strongly accented beats, and others that are less accented, changing time signature changes the pattern of emphasizing notes, either by playing certain notes louder, or by sustaining them as in swing or rubato. A measure is similar to a metrical foot in poetry.

There are four different types of metre in common use:

— simple duple (ex. 4/4)
— simple triple (ex. 3/4)
— compound duple (ex. 6/8)
— compound triple (ex. 9/8).

If each beat in a measure is divided into two parts, it is simple metre, and if divided into three it is compound. If each measure is divided into two beats, it is duple metre, and if three it is triple. Some people also label quadruple, while some consider it as two duples. The latter is more consistent with the above labelling system, as any other division above triple, such as quintuple, is considered as duple+triple (12123) or triple+duple (12312), depending on the accents in the musical example. However, in some music a quintuple may be treated and perceived as one unit of five, especially at faster tempos.

Table 1

	Duple:	Triple:
Simple:	beats divided in two; two beats per measure	beats divided in three; two beats per measure
Compound:	beats divided in two; three beats per measure	beats divided in three; three beats per measure

Table 2

	Beats divided in two:	Beats divided in three:
Two beats per measure:	simple duple	simple triple
Three beats per measure:	compound duple	compound triple

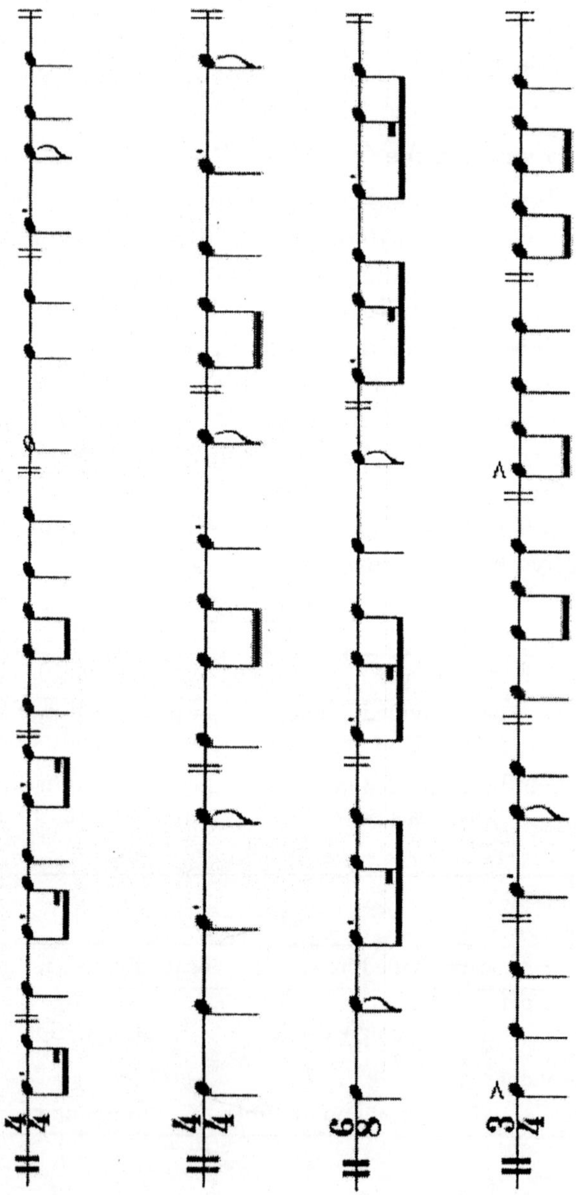

Fgure 1. Examples of Bo diddley pattern.

Most popular music is in 4/4 time, though often may be in 2/2 or cut time such as in bossa nova. Doo-wop and some other rock styles are frequently in 12/8, or may be interpreted as 4/4 with heavy swing. Similarly, most classical music before the 20th century tended to stick to relatively straightforward metres such as 4/4, 3/4 and 6/8, though variations on these such as 3/2 and 6/4 are also found. By the 20th century, composers were using less regular metres, such as 5/4 and 7/8. An example a use of this metre is Dave Brubeck's 'Take Five' written in 5/4 time.

Also in the 20th century, it became relatively more common to switch metre frequently—the end of Igor Stravinsky's The Rite of Spring is a particularly extreme example—and the use of asymmetrical rhythms where each beat is a different length became more common: such metres include already discussed quintuple rhythms as well as more complex constructs along the lines of 2+5+3/4 time, where each bar has a 2 beat unit, a five beat unit and a 3 beat unit, with a stress at the beginning of each unit—there are similar metres used in various folk musics.

Other music has no metre at all (free time) such as drone based music exemplified by La Monte Young, feature rhythms so complex that any metre is obscured such as in serialism, or is based on additive rhythms, such as some music by Philip Glass. Metre is often combined with a rhythmic pattern to produce a particular style. This is true of dance music, such as the waltz or tango, which have particular patterns of emphasizing beats which are instantly recognizable. This is often done to make the music coincide with slow or fast steps in the dance, and can be thought of as the musical equivalent of prosody.

Sometimes, a particular musician or composition becomes identifed with a particular metric pattern; such is the case with the so-called Bo Diddley pattern. Polymeter is the use of two meters simultaneously, or in regular alternation. Examples include Bela Bartok's "Second String Quartet." A stunning example from the rock canon is "Kashmir" by the seminal British hard-rock quartet Led Zeppelin, in which the percussion articulates 4/4 while the melodic instruments present a mesmerizing riff in 3/4.

Metric structure includes meter, tempo, and all rhythmic aspects which produce temporal regularity or structure, against which the foreground details or durational patterns are projected. Metric levels may be distinguished. The beat level is the metric level at which pulses are heard as the basic time unit of the piece. Faster levels are division levels, and slower levels are multiple levels. A metric modulation is a modulation from one metric unit or meter to another.

Process Music

Process music, often used synonymously with minimalism, is specifically music which arises from a process, and more specifically, music which makes that process audible. A number of Steve Reich's early works are examples of process music, particularly a specific process called phase or phasing. In his 1968 work Pendulum Music, a number of microphones are connected to a number of loudspeakers, and each is allowed to swing freely above the louspeaker it is connected to until it is still - the feedback that results from this process, as each microphone passes above its loudspeaker, makes up the music. György Ligeti's Poème symphonique, in which a hundred metronomes are set to different tempos and allowed to run down is another notable example.

Pulse (music)

In music, a pulse is an unbroken series of distinct yet identical periodically occurring short stimuli perceived as points in time. Ideally, this is opposed to a series of identical but aperiodically occurring stimuli, a series of periodically occurring yet otherwise differentiated stimuli, or an uninterrupted stream of sound (such as a drone). A pulse may be an unheard event underlining a piece or metric level, thus the tempo of the piece is how fast the pulse is running, implied by the performer or listener based on context or past experience, or audible such as in Terry Riley's In C. Non-ideal pulses varied according to strength or accents, which produce two or three pulse pulse groups (anything larger being a combination), strong-weak and strong-weak-weak (ibid).

In fact, given an ideal pulse, the most probable reaction for one to have is to perceptually group or differentiate the beats. A pulse which became to fast would become a drone, a pulse that is to slow becomes isolated sounds. A pulse that is regularly accented is a meter. An isochronal or equally spaced pulse on one level that uses varied pulse groups (rather than just one pulse group the whole piece) create a pulse on the (slower) multiple level that is non-isochronal (a stream of 2+3... at the eighth note level would create a pulse of a quarter note+dotted quarter note as its multiple level).

Pulse groups may further be distinguished as synchronous, if all pulses on slower levels coincide with those on faster levels, and nonsynchronous, if not. Process music can also be created using relatively traditional instrumental techniques - Reich's Piano Phase is an example. James Tenney is another composer who is concerned with process, such as in his tribute to Steve Reich,

Chromatic Canon, in which a tone row is eventually built up and, one note at a time, from what started as a repeated open fifth, before returning by the same path.

Texture (music)

In music, the word texture is often used in a rather vague way in reference to the overall sound of a piece of music. A piece may be described as having a "thick" texture, or a "light" texture, or other terms taken from outside of music (Aaron Copland's more popular pieces are described as having an "open" texture). The perceived texture of a piece can be affected by the number of parts playing at once, the timbre of the instruments playing these parts and the harmony and rhythms used, among other things. There are more precise terms which describe the number and relationships between voices:

— Monophony (base musical texture) is music with just one part (such as Gregorian chant). According to Adris Butterfield, monophony, "is the dominant mode of the European vernacular genres as well as of Latin song...in polyphonic works, it remains a central compositional principle."

— Heterophony is a kind of complex monophony - there is only one melody, but multiple voices each of which play the melody differently.

— Polyphony is music with several parts, each independent but related and each as important as the others - none of them are merely accompaniment.

— Homophony is music in which the top part has a dominant melody and other parts are subserviant to it, moving in the same rhythm.

— Monody is 17th century Italian song with a dominant melody and a separate accompaniment.

Note that none of these terms accurately describes the majority of western music made today, featuring a melody and rhythmically free accompaniment; in homophony the accompaniment is not rhythmically free, and monody is typically used in a historically specific way. A simultaneity is more than one complete musical texture occurring at the same time, rather than in succession.

Plunderphonics

Plunderphonics is a term originally coined by John Oswald for one of his recording projects, since applied to any music made by taking one or more existing audio recordings and altering them in some way to make a new composition. There is no attempt to disguise the fact that the sounds making up the composition have been "borrowed" in this way, and sometimes the sounds may be taken from very familiar sources. Plunderphonics can be considered a form of sound collage.

Although the concept of plunderphonics is seemingly broad, in practice there are many common themes used in what is normally called plunderphonic music. This includes heavy sampling of educational videos of the 1950's, news reports, radio shows, or anything with trained vocal announcers. The process of Sampling other sources is found in various genres (notably hip-hop), but in plunderphonic works the sampled material is often the only sound used. These samples are usually uncleared, and sometimes result in legal action being taken due to copyright infringement (some plunderphonic artists use their work to protest about what they consider to be overly-restrictive copyright laws).

Many plunderphonic artists claim their use of other artists' materials falls under the fair use doctrine. The name was first used as the title of an EP release by John Oswald. Oswald's original use of the word was to indicate a piece which was created from samples of a single artist and no other material. Influenced by William S. Burroughs' cut-up technique, he began making plunderphonic recordings in the 1970s. In 1988 he distributed copies of the Plunderphonics EP to the press and to radio stations.

In 1989, a greatly expanded version of Plunderphonics with twenty tracks was released — as on the EP, each track took material by just one artist, and included reworked material by both popular musicians like The Beatles, and classical works, such as Ludwig van Beethoven's Symphony No. 7. Like the EP, it was never put on sale. A central idea behind the record was that the fact that all the sounds were "stolen" should be quite blatant. The packaging contained sources for all samples used, but authorisation for them to be used on the record was neither sought nor given.

All undistributed copies of Plunderphonics were destroyed after a threat of legal action from the Canadian Recording Industry Association on behalf of several of their clients (notably Michael Jackson, whose "Bad" had been chopped into tiny pieces and rearranged as "Dab") who alleged copyright abuses. Later works by Oswald, such as Plexure, which lasts just twenty minutes but is claimed to contain around one thousand very short samples of pop music stitched together, are not strictly speaking "plunderphonic" according to Oswald's original conception (he himself used the term megaplundermorphonemiclonic for Plexure), but the term "plunderphonic" is used today in a looser sense to indicate any music completely — or almost completely — made up of samples.

69 Plunderphonics 96 is a compilation of Oswald's work, including tracks from the original Plunderphonics CD. Another important early purveyor of what can be described as plunderphonics were Negativland. While Oswald used easily recognisable and familiar sources, Negativland's sources were sometimes more obscure. Oswald and Negativland both made their collages by cutting up magnetic tape (or later using digital technology), but a number of DJs have also produced plunderphonic work using turntables (and in fact, "digging" for samples plays a large part in DJ culture).

Christian Marclay is a turntablist who has been using other people's records as the sole source of his music making since the late 1970s. He often treats the records in unusual ways — for example, he has physically cut up a number of records and stuck them together, making both a visual and aural collage. Sometimes a number of spoken-word or lounge music records bought from thrift stores are mashed together to make a track, but his More Encores album cuts up tracks by the likes of Maria Callas and Louis Armstrong in a way similar to Oswald's work on Plunderphonics.

Marclay's experimental approach has been taken up by the likes of Otomo Yoshihide, Philip Jeck and Martin Tétreault (although sometimes the records used are heavily disguised and unrecognisable, meaning the results cannot properly be called plunderphonics). Other DJs have worked in a more mainstream style: DJ Food (Kaleidoscope, for example) and DJ Shadow (Entroducing, for example) have both made albums consisting entirely of material plundered from other records. The Bran Flakes and People Like Us have both used thrift-store (or charity shop) records to create their music.

Vicki Bennett of People Like Us has extended the plunderphonic ideal to video, creating films to accompany her music by plundering the resources of the Prelinger Archives, the online part of the collection of film archivist Rick Prelinger. Another approach is to take two very different records and play them simultaneously. An early example of this is the Evolution Control Committee's Whipped Cream Mixes, which laid the vocals from Public Enemy's "Rebel Without a Pause" over Herb Alpert's "Bittersweet Samba." This gave rise to the so-called "bootlegging" phenomenon where an a cappella version of one song is mixed on top of a purely instrumental version of another. Soulwax and Richard X have both produced records along these lines.

There are also a number of web-based plunderphonics projects. The Droplift Project created a compilation CD of plunderphonic works which was then "droplifted" into record stores (this involved slipping copies of the record onto the shelves without knowledge of the store — a sort of reverse stealing). Dictionaraoke took audio clips from online dictionaries and stitched them together so they recited the words of various popular songs while instrumental versions of the music (often in MIDI renderings) played along.

Although the term plunderphonics tends to be applied only to music made since the 1980s and Oswald's coinage of it, there are several examples of earlier music made along similar lines. Notably, Dickie Goodman and Bill Buchanan's 1956 single "The Flying Saucer", features Goodman as a radio reporter covering an alien invasion interspersed with samples from a number of contemporary records. The Residents' "Beyond The Valley Of A Day In The Life" is made up of excerpts from Beatles records. A number of club DJs through the 1970s re-edited the records they played, and although this often consisted of nothing more than extending the record by adding a chorus or two, this too could be considered a form of plunderphonics.

Some classical composers have exercised a kind of plunderphonia on written, rather than recorded, music. Perhaps the best known example is the third movement of Luciano Berio's Sinfonia, which is entirely made up from quotes of other composers and writers. Mauricio Kagel has also made extensive use of earlier composers' works. Earlier composers who often plundered the music of others include Charles Ives (who often quoted folk songs and hymns in his works) and Ferruccio Busoni (a movement from his 1909 piano suite An die Jugend includes a prelude and a fugue by Johann Sebastian Bach played simultaneously)

Aleatoric Music

Aleatoric (or aleatory) music or composition, is music where some element of the composition is left to chance. The term was devised by the French composer Pierre Boulez to describe works where the performer was given certain liberties with regard to the order and repetition of parts of a musical work. The term was intended by Boulez to distinguish his work from works composed through the application of chance operations by John Cage.

An early genre of composition that could be considered a precedent for aleatoric compositions were the Musikalische Würfelspiele or Musical Dice Games, popular in the late 18th and early 19th century. (One such dice game is attributed to Wolfgang Amadeus Mozart.) These games consisted of a sequence of musical measures, for which each measure had several possible versions, and a procedure for selecting the precise sequence based on the throwing of a number of dice. Music related to the aleatoric idea may be found in works of John Cage, who was in part inspired by his friend Morton Feldman who was making experiments with chance in music in the 1950s.

Cage used the I Ching in the composition of his music in order to introduce an element of chance over which he would have no control. The first time he used it was in the Music of Changes for solo piano in 1951, to determine the sequence of notes or groups of notes that should be used and the precise timing of their occurrences. He used chance in other ways as well; Imaginary Landscape No. 4 is written for twelve radio receivers. Each radio has two players, one to control the frequency the radio is tuned to, the other to control the volume level.

Cage wrote very precise instructions in the score about how the performers should set their radios and change them over time, but he could not control the actual sound coming out of them, which was dependent on whatever radio shows were playing at that particular place and time of performance. One of Cage's other pieces, HPSCHD, itself composed using chance procedures, uses music from Mozart's Musikalisches Würfelspiel, referred to above, as well as original music. Other aleatoric composers include Henry Brant, Witold Lutoslawski and Lukas Foss.

The term "aleatory" is not always applied to music where there composer does not maintain full control over the piece. In pieces where certain decisions are left up to the performer, but are not a matter of chance, the terms indeterminate music or limited aleatory are sometimes used.

Cadence (music)

In Western musical theory a cadence (Latin cadentia, "a falling") is a particular series of intervals (a caesura) or chords that ends a phrase, section, or piece of music. Cadences give phrases a distinctive ending, that can, for example, indicate to the listener whether the piece is to be continued or concluded. An analogy can be made with punctuation, with some weaker cadences acting as commas, indicating a pause or momentary rest, while a stronger cadence will then act as the period, indicating the end of the phrase or musical sentence.

Cadences are called "weak" or "strong" the more or less final the sensation they create, with the perfect authentic cadence being the strongest type. In music of the common practice period, there are four main types of cadences: authentic, plagal, half, and deceptive. Each of these types can be further distinguished as perfect or imperfect. Each cadence can be described using the roman numeral system of naming triads:

— *Authentic cadence*: V to I. The phrase perfect cadence is sometimes used as a synonym for authentic cadence, but can also have a more precise meaning:

— *Perfect authentic cadences*: V to I, the chords must be in root position, that is the root of the chords must be in the bass, and the root of I must be in the highest voice also

— *Imperfect authentic cadences*: V to I, one or more of the chords are inverted or not in root position or the root of the I is not in the highest voice

— *Half (or imperfect) cadence*: any chord (frequently I or IV) to V

— *Plagal sequence*: IV to I, known as the "Amen cadence"

— *Deceptive (or interrupted) cadence*: V to any chord except I (typically vi)

It should be noted that these chord sequences do not necessarily constitute a cadence - there must be a sense of closure, as at the end of a phrase. Early music cadences, for instance, are different and more varied, being based upon dyads. Forbidden progressions may be reconsidered, for example, I-V-IV-I, such as in, which may be considered a doubled plagal cadence: I-IV/V-V-IV-I.

Clausulas

A clausula is a dyadic or intervallic, rather than chordal or harmonic, cadence. It requires at least two voices in contrary motion. According to Carl Dahlhaus, "as late at the 13th century the half step was experienced as a problematic interval not easily understood, as the irrational remainder between the perfect fourth and the ditone [4/3 / (9/8)2 = 256/243!]." In a melodic half step, no "tendency was preceived of the lower tone toward the upper, or of the upper toward the lower. The second tone was not taken to be the 'goal' of the first. Instead, the half step was avoided in clausulas because it lacked clarity as an interval." Beginning in the 13th century cadences begin to require motion in one voice by half step and the other a whole step in contrary motion.

Drone (music)

In music, a drone is a note or chord continuously sounded throughout much or all of a piece, sustained or repeated, and most often establishing an tonality upon which the rest of the piece is built. Similarly, a drone is the name of a part of a musical instrument intended to produce such a sustained tone, generally without the ongoing attention of the player). A sitar features three or four resonating drone strings and Indian sargam is practiced to a drone. Bagpipes (particularly the scottish Great Highland Bagpipe) feature a number of drone pipes, giving the instrument its characteristic "skirl".

The first string on a five-string bluegrass banjo is a drone string with a separate tuning peg that places the end of the string five frets down the neck of the instrument; this string is usually tuned to the same note as the fifth string produces when played at the fifth fret, and the drone string is seldom fretted when playing bluegrass. Composers of classical music occasionally used a drone (especially one on open fifths) to evoke a rustic or archaic atmosphere, perhaps Scottish or other early or folk music.

Drones are less often used in common practice classical music however because the longer and more central a drone the less functional it is and because equal temperament causes slight mistunings which become more apparent over a drone, especially when also sustained. On the other hand drones may be purposely dissonant, as often in the music of Phill Niblock. Contemporary classical musicians who make prominent use of drones, often with just or other non-equal tempered tunings, include La Monte Young and many of his students, David First, Pauline Oliveros and Stuart Dempster, Alvin Lucier (Music On A Long Thin Wire), Ellen Fullman, and Arnold Dreyblatt. Shorter drones or the general concept of a continous element are often used by many other composers.

A drone differs from a pedal tone or point in degree or quality. A pedal point may be a form of nonchord tone and thus required to resolve unlike a drone, or a pedal point may simply be a shorter drone, a drone being a longer pedal point.

Indian Classical Music

The origins of Indian classical music can be found from the oldest of scriptures, part of the Hindu tradition, the Vedas. Saamaveda, one of the four vedas describes music at length. The two main streams of Indian classical music are Hindustani music, from the North of India, and Carnatic music, from South India. Hindustani music is predominantly more liberal than it's south Indian counterpart. The prime themes of Hindustani music are Rasleela (Hindu devotionals) of Krishna and Nature in all its splendour. Bhimsen Joshi, Ravi Shankar, Hariprasad Chaurasia and Zakir Hussain are the arts' most popular living performers.

Carnatic music is similar to Hindustani music in that it is mostly improvised, but it is much more theoretical with stricter rules. It also emphasizes the expertise of the voice rather than of the instruments. Primary themes including Devi worship, Rama worship, descriptions of temples and patriotic songs. Among the most popular living performers are M S Subbulakshmi, Mangalampalli Balamuralikrishna, T V Sankaranarayanan, Madurai T N Seshagopalan and K J Yesudas.

Indian classical music (marga) is monophonic, and based around a single melody line. A composition, based on a particular raga, begins with the performers coming out in a ritualized order -- drone instruments, then the soloist, then accompanists and percussionists. The musicians begin by tuning their instruments; this process often blends imperceptibly into the beginning of the music. Players of the tabla, a type of drum, begin by tapping the edges with a hammer to make sure it is in tune with the soloist.

Another common instrument is the stringed tambura, which is played at a steady tone throughout the raga. This monotonous job traditionally falls to a student of the soloist. The raga begins with the melody being developed gradually, often over the course of a half-an-hour or more. The beginning of the raga is called an alap in Hindustani music and an alapana in Carnatic music. Many aficionados consider the alap their favourite part, but the alap is often inaccessible to others.

In Hindustani music, once the raga is established, the ornamentation around the mode begins to become rhytmical, gradually speeding up. This section is called the jor. After the jor climaxes, everything stops and the audiences applaud. Finally, the percussionist begins to play, interacting with the soloist, eventually reaching the spontaneous and competitive jhala section. Carnatic raga elaborations are generally much faster in tempo and shorter. The opening piece is called a varnam, and is a warm-up for the musicians. A devotion and a request for a blessing follows, then a series of interchanges between ragams (unmetered melody) and thaalams (the ornamentation, equivalent to the jor). This is intermixed with hymns called krithis. This is followed by the pallavi or theme from the raga.

Hindustani classical music

Hindustani classical music is a classical music tradition originating from regions in South Asia, extending east from Bangladesh through northern India into Pakistan and as far as Afghanistan in the west. In contrast to Carnatic music, another classical music tradition originating from South India, Hindustani music was influenced by, in addition to the Vedic philosophy and understanding of sound, by Afghan, Mughal and Persian performance practice.

Outside India, Hindustani classical music is often associated with Indian music in general, as it is arguably the most popular stream of Indian music outside India. A number of musical instruments are associated with Hindustani classical music. Some of the most famous instruments are sitar and tabla and the less well known instruments like sarod and sarangi. The most famous modern performer is undoubtedly sitarist Ravi Shankar, who helped popularize Hindustani ragas outside of India. Alongside the sitar in popularity are the bansuri (a sort of flute) and sarod, known among fans for recordings of virtuoso Ali Akbar Khan.

Music has long been important to Hinduism, especially for many Vaishnavite sects. The advent of Islamic rule under the Delhi Sultanate and later the Mughal Empire over northern India caused the traditional musicians to seek patronage in the courts of the new rulers. These Islamic rulers had strong cultural and religious sentiments focussed outside of India; yet they lived in, and administered kingdoms which retained their traditional Hindu culture. This helped spur the fusion of Hindu and Muslim ideas to make qawwali and khayal.

Perhaps the most legendary musician of this period is Amir Khusrau. Later, the Mughal Empire intermarried with Indians, especially under Jar ad-Din Akbar. Music and dance flourished during this period, and the Hindu musician Tansen is still well-remembered. Indeed, his ragas (which are based on times of the day) were reputed to have been so powerful that according to legend, upon his playing a night-time raga in the morning, the entire city fell under a hush and clouds gathered in the sky.

In the 20th century, the power of the maharajahs and nawabs declined, and thus so did their patronage. The

Indian Government-run All India Radio helped to stop this development and replaced the patronage system. The first star was Gauhar Jan, whose career was born out of Fred Gaisberg's first recordings of Indian music in 1902.

Types of compositions

The major vocal forms associated with Hindustani classical music are the khyal, gazal, and thumri. Other styles include the dhrupad, dhammar, and tarana.

Dhrupad

Dhrupad is a sacred style of singing traditionally performed by men with a tampura and pakhawaj accompanying. The lyrics are in a midieval form of Hindi and typically heroic in theme, or else praising a particular deity. A more ornamented form is called dhamar.

Bhajan

Religious vocal music, bhajan is the most popular form in northern India. Famous performers include Kabir, Tulsidas and Mirabai. It arose out of the Alvar bhakti movement of the 9th and 10th century.

Ghazal

Ghazals are an originally Persian form of vocal music that is popular with multiple variations across Iran, Central Asia, Turkey and India. Ghazal exists in multiple variations, including folk and pop forms. Notable performers include Ghulam Ali, Jagjit Singh, Mehdi Hasan and Pankaj Udhas.

Khyal

An informal form of vocal music, khyal is partially

improvised and very emotional in nature. Though its origins are shrouded in mystery, the 15th century rule of Hussain Shah Sharqi and was popular by the 18th century rule of Mohammed Shah. The best-known composer of the period was Sadarang, a pen name for Niamat Khan. Later performers include Faiyaz Khan, Abdul Karim Khan, Bhimsen Joshi, Bade Ghulam Ali Khan, Amir Khan and Mallikarjun Mansur. Some of the present day vocalists are Kishori Amonkar, Ulhas Kashalkar, Rashid Khan, Aslam Khan, Shruti Sadolikar, Chandrashekar Swami and Mashkoor Ali Khan.

Tarana

Tarana are songs that are used to convey a mood of elation and are usually performed towards the end of a concert. They have very few lyrics and are mostly composed of rythmic sounds. It can be compared to the Tillana of Carnatic music.

Thumri

Thumri is an accessible and informal vocal form said to have begun with the court of Nawab Wajid Ali Shah, 1847-1856. There are two types of thumri: Punjabi and Lucknavi. The lyrics are typically in a language called braj bhasha, and are usually romantic. Performers include Shobha Gurtu, Bade Ghulam Ali Khan and Girija Devi.

Hindustani music utilises a system of notation called sargam, a contraction for Sa Re Ga Ma. Re, Ga, Ma, Dha and Ni may be flat (komal), or sharp (tivra). The designation komal or tivra is never sung with the note's syllable, however they are notated as a line under or an acute accent above, respectively, the note's letter, such as &Macute&; and N.

Pygmy Music

The Pygmies are a broad group of people who live in Central Africa, especially in Congo, Central African Republic and Cameroon. Music is an important part of Pygmy life, and casual performances take place during many of the day's events. Music comes in many forms, including the spiritual likanos stories, vocable singing and music played from a variety of instruments. The African Pygmies are particularly known for their usually vocal music, usually characterised by dense contrapuntal communal improvisation. Simha Arom (2003) says that the level of polyphonic complexity of Pygmy music was reached in Europe in the 14th century, yet Pygmy culture is unwritten and ancient, some Pygmy groups being the first known cultures in some areas of Africa. Music permeates daily life and there are songs for entertainment as well as specific events and activities.

Formally Pygmy music consists of at most only four parts, and can be described as an, "ostinato with variations," or similar to a passacaglia, in that it is cyclical. In fact it is based on repetition of periods of equal length, which each singer divides using different rhythmic figures specific to different repertoires and songs. This interesting case of Ethnomusicology and Ethnomathematics creates a detailed surface and endless variations of not only the same period repeated, but the same piece of music. As in some Balinese gamelan these patterns are based on a super-pattern which is never heard. The Pygmies themselves do not learn or think of their music in this theoretical framework, but learn the music growing up.

Colin M. Turnbull, an American anthropologist, wrote a book about the Pygmies, The Forest People, in 1965. This introduced Pygmy culture to Western countries, many of whom were intrigued by the seemingly-simple lifestyle they led. Turnbull claimed that the Pygmies viewed the forest as a parental spirit that could be communicated with via song. Some of Turnbull's recordings of Pygmy music were commercially released, which inspired more ethnomusicological study, such as by Simha Arom, a French-Israeli who recorded a kind of whistle called hindewhu.

In 1993, the popularization of Pygmy music spread with the release of Eric Mouquet and Michel Sanchez's Deep Forest. Though the fusion of New Age spirituality with sampled Pygmy music and soft techno was heavily criticized, the album was a multi-million selling success. Soon after its release, controversy continued amid accusations that none of the money made from recording was given to the Pygmy performers. Pygmy styles include liquindi, or water drumming, and instruments like the bow harp (ieta), ngombi (harp zither) and limbindi (a string bow).

Popular Music

Popular music, sometimes abbreviated to pop music, is music belonging to any of a number of musical styles that are (at least in their heyday) broadly popular. A narrower sense of the term, usually "pop music", covers mainstream music that does not fall into any more specialized style such as jazz or hip hop. In the broader sense, "popular music" means any sort of music intended for mass consumption and propagated over the radio and similar media.

A defining characteristic of popular music (in the broader sense) is that it is the product of the modern business enterprise, and is disseminated for the purpose of earning a profit. Executives and employees of popular music businesses try to select and cultivate the music that will have the greatest success with the public, and thus maximize the profits of their firm. In this respect, popular music differs from traditional folk music, which was created by ordinary people for their own enjoyment, and from classical music, which was originally created to serve the purposes of the Church or for the entertainment of the nobility. (Today classical music is often subsidized by governments and universities.)

Although the controlling forces of popular music are business enterprises, young people who aspire to become popular musicians are certainly not always driven by the profit motive. Rather, they often want to find an outlet for their sense of expression and creativity, or simply to have fun. Historically, the conflicting motives of business people and musicians has been a source of tension in the popular music industry.

Many people play popular music together with their friends, often in garages and basements, on a casual amateur basis. This activity is one of the most widespread forms of participatory music-making in modern societies. As participatory music, "garage bands" are in a sense a resurrection of the old tradition of folk music, which in premodern times was composed and performed by ordinary people and transmitted exclusively by word of mouth. The difference between the old folk music and modern amateur performance of popular music is that the participants in the latter genre are well acquainted with the expert performances that they hear on recordings, and often try to emulate them. The older folk music of a society often lives on in a popularized version, which is likewise performed by experts and commercially disseminated. Such updated versions of folk music often have heavy amateur participation.

Genres

Popular music dates at least as far back as the mid 19th century. Below is a list of genres. Different genres often appeal to different age groups. These often, but not always, are the people who were adolescents or young adults when the music was new. Thus, for instance, Big band music continues to have a following, but it is probably a rather older group, on average, than the audience for rap. Musical genres usually not considered popular music would include the following:

— Children's songs (including Nursery rhymes and Jumprope songs)

— most Classical music, including Opera

— Folk music, as created by traditional performers

— Gregorian chant, Hymns, and many other forms of religious music

— Military music

— National anthems and other patriotic music

As noted earlier, these have a distinct character from popular music: either they are transmitted by word of mouth rather than in organized fashion (children's songs, authentic folk music) or else they are produced to fill the needs of a particular social institution (church, aristocracy, the military, or the state)

Folk Music

Folk music, in the original sense of the term, is music by and of the people. Folk music arose, and best survives, in societies not yet affected by mass communication and the commercialization of culture. It normally was shared and performed by the entire community (not by a special class of expert performers), and was transmitted by word of mouth. During the 20th century, the term folk music took on a second meaning: it describes a particular kind of popular music which is culturally descended from or otherwise influenced by traditional folk music. Like other popular music, this kind of folk music is most often performed by experts and is transmitted in organized performances and commercially distributed recordings. However, popular music has filled some of the roles and purposes of folk music where it has replaced it.

Armenian Folk MusiciansBecause of the changing meaning of "folk music", people asked to define it give widely varying answers. When Gene Shay, co-founder and host of the Philadelphia Folk Festival, was asked to define folk music in an April 2003 interview, he gave an answer similar to the definition above: "In the strictest sense, it's music that is rarely written for profit. It's music that has endured and been passed down by oral tradition. [...] And folk music is participatory—you don't have to be a great musician to be a folk singer. [...] And finally, it brings a sense of community. It's the people's music."

The jazz performer Louis Armstrong, is famously credited with saying, "All music is folk music, leastwise I ain't never heard a horse sing". This emphasizes the universality of people's love for music (which folk music also attests), and aptly expresses Armstrong's warm personal connection to his audience, but it also misses a distinction. Armstrong was not a folk musician, but a gifted performer within a sophisticated popular music tradition, which by his time had evolved to be very different from its folk origins.

The English term folk, which gained usage in the 18th century to refer to peasants or non-literate peoples, is related to the German word Volk (meaning people or nation). The term is used to emphasize that folk music emerges spontaneously from communities of ordinary people.

The appeal of folk music

The appeal of folk music is of a special kind, distinct from the appeal of classical or popular music. Typically, folk music lacks the technical sophistication and complexity that is often found in classical music and (to a lesser extent) in popular music. Yet the musical inventiveness of ordinary people, especially when acting together in a tight-knit musical community, should not be underestimated. Works of folk music are often experienced by modern listeners as extraordinarily beautiful or stirring. A particular virtue that often stands out in folk music is its purity: it often obtains exceptional aesthetic results from the simplest of musical means.

Variation in folk music

Music transmitted by word of mouth though a community will, in time, develop many variants, because this kind of transmission cannot produce word-for-word and note-for-note accuracy. Indeed, many traditional folk singers are quite creative and deliberately modify the material they learn. Because variants proliferate naturally, it is naïve to believe that there is such a thing as the "authentic" version of a ballad such as "Barbara Allen." Field researchers in folk song have encountered countless versions of this ballad throughout the English-speaking world, and these versions often differ greatly from each other.

None can reliably claim to be the original, and it is quite possible that whatever the "original" was, it ceased to be sung centuries ago. Any version can lay an equal claim to authenticity, so long as it is truly from a traditional folksinging community and not the work of an outside editor. Cecil Sharp had an influential idea about the process of folk variation: he felt that the competing variants of a folk song would undergo a process akin to biological natural selection: only those new variants that were the most appealing to ordinary singers would be picked up by others and transmitted onward in time. Thus, over time we would expect each folksong to become esthetically ever more appealing — it would be collectively composed to perfection, as it were, by the community.

Many feel, examining the folksongs that Sharp collected from traditional singers, that there is something to this theory. The Sharp material often shows a very striking, simple beauty, and there is little tawdry, cheap material that it might have temporarily picked up from external sources. This suggests that such material did indeed get "filtered out" by the collective efforts of the community. On the other hand, there is also evidence to support the view that transmission of folk songs can be rather sloppy. Occasionally, collected folk song versions include material or verses incorporated from different songs that makes little sense in its context. A perfect process of natural selection would not have permitted these incoherent versions to survive.

Folk music seems to reflect a universal impulse of humanity. No fieldwork expedition by cultural anthropologists has yet to discover a preindustrial people that did not have its own folk music. It seems safe to infer that folk music was a property of all people starting from the dawn of the species. However, the development of modern society--first literacy, then the conversion of culture into a salable commodity--created a new form of transmission of music that first influenced, then in some societies essentially eliminated the original folk tradition. The decline of folk music in a culture can be followed through three stages.

1.*Urban influence*: One of the first folk traditions impacted by modern society was the folksong of rural England. Starting in Elizabethan times, urban poets wrote broadsheet ballads that (thanks to printing) could be sold widely. The ballads probably didn't need musical notation, since they would have been sung to tunes that everybody knew, the folk tradition being very much alive at the time. These ballads heavily influenced the folk tradition, but did not override it. In fact, the folk tradition showed great resilience.

Through the process of folk transmission, the urban ballads were modified, keeping the more vivid content and ironing out the less "citified" material. The resulting body of folk lyrics is widely considered to be a very appealing blend. Thus, the printing press and widespread literacy did not suffice to destroy the English folk tradition, but in some ways enriched it. The English folk song legacy was probably affected by urban melodies as well as words. The clue here is that folk music in remote rural areas of the English-speaking world, such as Highland Scotland or the Appalachian mountains, abounds in tunes that employ the pentatonic scale, a scale widely used for folk music around the world.

However, pentatonic music was rare among the rural English villagers who first volunteered their tunes to researchers in the late 19th century. A plausible explanation is that life in rural England was far more closely affected by the proximity to the urban centers. Music in the standard major and minor scales evidently penetrated to the nearby rural areas, where it was converted to folk idiom, but nevertheless succeeded in displacing the old pentatonic music.

2.*Replacement of folk music by popular music*: The pattern of urban influence on folk music was intensified to outright destruction as soon as the capitalist economic system had developed to the point that music could be packaged and distributed for the purpose of earning a profit--in other words, when popular music was born. It was around Victorian times that ordinary people of the Western world were first offered music as a mass commodity, for example, in the phenomenon of Music Hall.

The introduction of popular music was simultaneous with the latter part of the Industrial Revolution. This was a time of great change in lifestyle for the great body of the people, notably the migration of the old agrarian communities to the new industrial ones. It is likely that the resulting social disruption helped cut people's emotional bonds to their old folk music, and thereby helped the shift in taste toward popular music. As technology advanced, succeeding generations became enticed with popular music in ever more accessible and desirable forms.

Gramophone records became LPs and then CDs; the Music Hall gave way to radio, followed by television. With the ever-increasing success of popular music, the musical life of many individuals eventually ceased to include any folk music at all. Moreover, since popular music for most people is passive music (that is, listened to, but not created or performed), the overwhelming success of popular music also entailed a sharp decline of music as an active, participatory activity.

3. *Loss of musical ability in the community*: The terminal state of the loss of folk music can be seen in the United States and a few similar societies, where except in isolated

areas and among hobbyists, traditional folk music no longer survives. In the absence of folk music, many individuals do not sing. It is possible that non-singers feel intimidated by widespread exposure in recordings and broadcasting to the singing of skilled experts. Another possibility is that they simply cannot sing, because they did not sing when they were small children, when learning of skills takes place most naturally. Certainly it is very common for contemporary Americans to claim that they cannot sing.

There is anecdotal evidence that the loss of singing ability is continuing rapidly at the present time. As recently as the 1960's, audiences at American sporting events collectively sang the American national anthem before a game; the anthem is now generally assigned to a recording or to a soloist.Inability to sing is apparently unusual in a traditional society, where the habit of singing folk song since early childhood gives everyone the practice needed to able to sing at least reasonably well.

Regional variation

The loss of folk music is occurring at different rates in different regions of the world. Naturally, where industrialization and commercialization of culture are most advanced, so tends to be the loss of folk music. Yet in nations or regions where folk music is a badge of cultural or national identity, the loss of folk music can be slowed; this is held to be true, for instance in the case of Ireland, Brittany, and Galicia, all of which retain their traditional music to some degree.

Fieldwork and scholarship

Starting in the 19th century, interested people - academics and amateur scholars - started to take note of what was being lost, and there grew various efforts aimed at preserving the music of the people. One such effort was the collection by Francis James Child in the late 19th century of the texts of over three hundred ballads in the English and Scots traditions (called the Child Ballads). Contemporaneously came the Reverend Sabine Baring-Gould, and later and more significantly Cecil Sharp who worked in the early 20th century to preserve a great body of English rural folk song, music and dance, under the aegis of what became and remains the English Folk Dance and Song Society (EFDSS).

Sharp also worked in America, recording the folk songs of the Appalachian Mountains in 1916-1918 in collaboration with Maud Karpeles and Olive Dame Campbell. Around this time, composers of classical music developed a strong interest in folk song collecting, and a number of outstanding composers carried out their own field work on folk song. These included Ralph Vaughan Williams in England and Béla Bartók in Hungary and neighboring countries. These composers, like many of their predecessors, incorporated folk material into their classical compositions.

In America, during the 1930s and 1940s, the Library of Congress worked through the offices of musicologist Alan Lomax and others to capture as much American field material as possible. Often, fieldworkers in folk song hoped that their work would restore folk music to the people. For instance, Cecil Sharp campaigned, with some success, to have English folk songs (in his own heavily edited and expurgated versions) to be taught to schoolchildren.

One theme that runs through the great period of scholarly folk song collection is the tendency of certain members of the "folk", who were supposed to be the object of study, to become scholars and advocates themselves. For example, Jean Ritchie was the youngest child of a large family from Viper, Kentucky that had preserved many of the old Appalachian folk songs. Ritchie, living in a time when the Appalachians had opened up to outside influence, was university educated and ultimately moved to New York City, where she made a number of classic recordings of the family repertoire and published an important compilation of these songs.

Folk revivals

As folk traditions decline, there is often a conscious effort to resuscitate them. Such efforts are often exerted by bridge figures such as Jean Ritchie, described above. Folk revivals also involve collaboration between traditional folk musicians and other participants (often of urban background) who come to the tradition as adults. The folk revival of the 1950's in Britain and America had something of this character. In 1950 Alan Lomax came to Britain, where at a Working Men's Club in the remote Northumberland mining village of Tow Law he met two other seminal figures: A.L.'Bert' Lloyd and Ewan MacColl, who were performing folk music to the locals there. Lloyd was a colourful figure who had travelled the world and worked at such varied occupations as sheep-shearer in Australia and shanty-man on a whaling ship.

MacColl, born in Salford of Scottish parents, was a brilliant playwright and songwriter who had been strongly politicised by his earlier life. MacColl had also learned a large body of Scottish traditional songs from his mother. The meeting of MacColl and Lloyd with Lomax is credited with being the point at which the British roots revival began. The two colleagues went back to London where they formed the

Ballads and Blues Club which eventually became renamed the Singers' Club and was the first, as well as the most enduring, of what became known as folk clubs. As the 1950s progressed into the 1960s, the folk revival movement built up in both Britain and America.

During the twentieth century, a crucial change in the history of folk music began. Folk material came to be adopted by talented performers, performed by them in concerts, and disseminated by recordings and broadcasting. In other words, a new genre of popular music had arisen. This genre was linked by nostalgia and imitation to the original traditions of folk music as it was sung by ordinary people. However, as a popular genre it quickly evolved to be quite different from its original roots.

Confusingly, popular (i.e., commercially-disseminated) music based on a folk tradition is called "folk music", no matter how different it may be from a folk music rooted in the community. As a result, some individuals in a modern society are unaware that folk music of the original variety ever existed. The rise of folk music as a popular genre began with performers whose own lives were rooted in the authentic folk tradition. Thus, for example, Woody Guthrie began by singing songs he remembered his mother singing to him as a child.

Later, in the 1930s and 1940s, Guthrie both collected folk music and also composed his own songs, as did Pete Seeger. Through dissemination on commercial recordings, this vein of music became popular in the United States during the 1950s, through singers like the Weavers (Seeger's group) and the Kingston Trio, who tried to reproduce and honor the work that had been collected in preceding decades. The itinerate folksinger lifestyle was exemplified by Ramblin' Jack Elliott, a disciple of Woody Guthrie who in turn influenced Bob Dylan.

Sometimes these performers would locate scholarly work in libraries and revive the songs in their recordings, for example in Joan Baez's rendition of "Henry Martin," which adds a guitar accompaniment to a version collected and edited by Cecil Sharp. Many of this group of popular folk singers maintained an idealistic, leftist/progressive political orientation. This is perhaps not surprising. Folk music is easily identified with the ordinary working people who created it, and preserving treasured things against the claimed relentless encroachments of capitalism is likewise a goal of many politically progressive people.

Thus, in the 1960s such singers as Joan Baez, Phil Ochs and Bob Dylan followed in Guthrie's footsteps and to begin writing "protest music", particularly against the Vietnam War, and likewise expressed in song their support for the civil rights movement. Such songs were newly written, but took their instrumentation and stanza forms from folk tradition. In Ireland, The Clancy Brothers & Tommy Makem (although the members were all Irish born, the group became famous while based in New York's Greenwich Village, it must be noted), The Dubliners, Clannad, Planxty, The Chieftains, The Pogues and a variety of other folk bands have done much over recent years to revitalise and repopularise Irish traditional music. These bands were rooted, to a greater or lesser extent, in a living tradition of Irish music, and they benefitted from collection efforts on the part of the likes of Seamus Ennis and Peter Kennedy, among others.

The experience of the last century suggests that as soon as a folk tradition comes to be marketed as popular music, its musical content will quickly be modified to become more like popular music. Such modified folk music often incorporates electric guitars, drum kit, or forms of rhythmic syncopation that are characteristic of popular music but were absent in the original. One example of this sort is contemporary country music, which descends ultimately from a rural American folk tradition, but has evolved to become vastly different from its original model.

Rap music evolved from an African-American inner-city folk tradition, but is likewise very different nowadays from its folk original. A third example is contemporary bluegrass, which is a modified development of American old time music. As less traditional forms of folk music gain popularity, one often observes tension between so-called "purists" or "traditionalists" and the innovators. For example, traditionalists were indignant when Bob Dylan began to use an electric guitar. His electrified performance at the 1965 Newport Folk Festival was to prove to be an early focal point for this controversy.

Sometimes, however, the exponents of amplified music were bands such as Fairport Convention, Pentangle and Steeleye Span who saw the electrification of traditional musical forms as a means whereby to reach a far wider audience, and their efforts have been largely recognised for what they were by even some of the most die-hard of purists. Since the 1970s a genre of "contemporary folk", fuelled by new singer-songwriters, has continued to make the coffee-house circuit and keep the tradition of acoustic non-classical music alive in the United States. Such artists include Steve Goodman, John Prine, Cheryl Wheeler, Bill Morrisey, and Christine Lavin.

Lavin in particular has become prominent as a leading promoter of this musical genre in recent years. Some, such as Lavin and Wheeler, inject a great deal of humor in their songs and performances, although much of their music is also deeply personal and sometimes satirical. Traditional folk music forms also merged with rock and roll to form the hybrid generally known as folk rock which evolved through performers such as The Byrds, Simon and Garfunkel, The Mamas and the Papas, and many others. More recently the same spirit has been embraced and expanded on by performers such as Ani Difranco.

At the same time, a line of singers from Baez to Phil Ochs have continued to use traditional forms for original material. A similar stylistic shift, without using the "folk music" name, has occurred with the phenomenon of Celtic music, which in many cases is based on an amalgamation of Irish traditional music, Scottish traditional music, and other traditional musics associated with lands in which Celtic languages are or were spoken (regardless of any significant research showing that the musics have any genuine genetic relationship; so Breton music and Galician music are often included in the genre).

Folk music is still extremely popular among some audiences today, with folk music clubs meeting to share traditional-style songs, and there are major folk music festivals in many countries, eg the Port Fairy Folk Festival is a major annual event in Australia attracting top international folk performers as well as many local artists.

Pastiche and parody

Popular culture sometimes creates pastiches of folk music for its own ends. One famous example is the pseudo-ballad sung about brave Sir Robin in the film Monty Python and the Holy Grail. Enthusiasts for folk music might properly consider this song to be pastiche and not parody, because the tune is pleasant and far from inept, and the topic being lampooned is not balladry but the medieval heroic tradition. The arch-shaped melodic form of this song (first and last lines low in pitch, middle lines high) is characteristic of traditional English folk music.

Another instance of pastiche is the notoriously well-known theme song for the television show Gilligan's Island. This tune is also folk-like in character, and in fact is written in a traditional folk mode (modes are a type of musical scale); the mode of "Gilligan's Island" is ambiguous between Dorian and Aeolian. The lyrics begin with the traditional folk device in which the singer invites his hearers to listen to the tale that follows.

Moreover, two of the stanzas repeat the final short line, a common device in English folk stanzas. (However, it should be noted that the raising of the key by a semitone with each new verse is an unmistakable trait of commercial music and never occurred in the original folk tradition.) Folk music is easy to parody, and it is not hard to see why: at present, it is a popular music genre that relies on a traditional music genre. As such, it is likely to lack the sophistication and glamour that attach to other forms of popular music. Folk music satire ranges from the worst excesses of Rambling Syd Rumpo and Bill Oddie to the deft and s1ubtle artistry of Sid Kipper, Eric Idle and Tom Lehrer.

Even "serious" folk musicians are not averse to poking fun at the form from time to time, for example Martin Carthy's devastating rendition of the "All the Hard Cheese of Old England", to the tune of "All the Hard Times of Old England", Robb Johnson's "Lack of Jolly Ploughboy," and more recently "I'm Sending an E-mail to Santa" by the Yorkshire-based harmony group Artisan. Other musicians have been known to take the tune of a traditional folk song and add their own words, often humourous, or on a similar-sounding yet different subject. Examples: The Wurzels, The Incredible Dr. Busker. The 2003 film A Mighty Wind is a particularly deft and cutting send-up of commercial folk music circa 1960.

Rock and Roll

Rock and roll, also called rock, is a form of popular music, usually featuring vocals (often with vocal harmony backing), electric guitars and a strong back beat; other instruments, such as the saxophone, are common in some styles. As a cultural phenomenon, rock's social impact on the world is likely unparalleled by any other kind of music. It has been credited with ending wars and spreading peace and tolerance, as well as corrupting the innocent and spreading moral rot. Rock has become popular across the globe, far from its birthplace in the United States, and evolved into a multitude of highly-varying styles.

The term rock and roll is vague. It is sometimes used to describe a number of genres only distantly related, including soul, heavy metal and even hip hop. In other circumstances, it is used strictly to apply only to the earliest incarnation of "rock" -- the 1950s scene that started the genre. Some make distinctions between rock and roll and rock music on these grounds, while others unapologetically use it as a synonym for modern Western popular music.

Rock and roll emerged as a defined musical style in America in the 1950s, though elements of rock and roll can be seen in rhythm and blues records as far back as the 1920s. Early rock and roll combined elements of blues, boogie woogie, jazz and rhythm and blues, and is also influenced by traditional Appalachian folk music, gospel and country and western. Going back even further, rock and roll can trace a foundational lineage to the old Five Points district of mid-19th century New York City, the scene of the first fusion of heavily rhythmic African shuffles and sand dances with melody driven European genres, particularly the Irish jig. Rocking was a term first used by gospel singers in the

American South to mean something akin to spiritual rapture.

Early North American rock and roll

Whatever the beginning, it is clear that rock appeared at a time when racial tensions in the United States were coming to the surface. African Americans were protesting segregation of schools and public facilities. The "separate but equal" doctrine was overturned in 1954. It can hardly be a coincidence, then, that a musical form combining elements of white and black music should arise, and that this music should provoke strong reactions, of all types, in all Americans. The rock 'n' roll music of the 1950s would change popular music forever.On March 21, 1952 in Cleveland, Alan Freed produced the first rock and roll concert. The audience and the performers were mixed in race and the evening ended after one song in a near-riot as thousands of fans tried to get into the sold-out venue.

By the end of the decade, rock had spread throughout the world. In Australia, for example, Johnny O'Keefe became perhaps the first modern rock star of the country, and began the field of Australian rock.

Rockabilly

It was two years later that the first major white rock star began recording. In 1954, Elvis Presley began recording with Sam Philips, starting with the hit "That's All Right, Mama". Elvis played a rock and country & western fusion called rockabilly, and he became possibly the first celebrity musician and teen idol. It was the following year's "Rock Around the Clock" by Bill Haley & His Comets that really set the rock boom in motion, though. The song was one of the biggest hits in history, and frenzied teens flocked to see him., even causing riots in some places; "Rock Around the Clock" was a breakthrough for both the group and for all of rock and roll music.

If everything that came before laid the groundwork, "Clock" certainly set the mold for everything else that came after. With its combined rockabilly and R & B influences, "Clock" topped the U.S. charts for several weeks, and became wildly popular in places like Australia and Germany. The single, released by indie label Festival Records in Australia, was the biggest-selling recording in the country at the time.

Cover Version

Through the late 1940s and early 1950s, R&B music had been gaining a stronger beat and a wilder style, with artists such as Fats Domino and Johnny Otis speeding up the tempos and increasing the backbeat to great popularity on the juke-joint circuit. Despite the efforts of Freed and others, black music was still taboo on many white-owned radio outlets. However, savvy artists and producers quickly recognized the potential of rock and raced to cash in with white versions of this black music. Covering was customary in the music industry at the time. One of the first successful rock and roll covers was Wynonie Harris's transformation of Roy Brown's "Good Rocking Tonight" from a jump blues to a showy rocker. The most notable trend, however, was white pop covers of black R&B numbers.

Black performers saw their songs recorded by white performers, an important step in the dissemination of the music, but often at the cost of feeling and authenticity. Most famously, Pat Boone recorded sanitized versions of Little Richard songs, though Boone found "Long Tall Sally" so intense that he couldn't cover it. Later, as those songs became popular, the original artists' recordings received radio play as well. Little Richard once called Pat Boone from the audience and introduced him as "the man who made me a millionaire".

The cover versions were not necessarily straightforward imitations. For example, Bill Haley's incompletely bowdlerized cover of "Shake, Rattle and Roll" transformed Big Joe Turner's humorous and racy tale of adult love into an energetic teen dance number, while Georgia Gibbs replaced Etta James's tough, sarcastic vocal in "Roll With Me, Henry" (covered as "Dance With Me, Henry") with a perkier vocal more appropriate for an audience unfamiliar with the song to which James's song was an answer, (Hank Ballard's "Work With Me, Annie").

American rock

With the runaway popular success of rock, the style began to influence other genres. Vocalized R&B became doo wop, for example, while uptempo, secularized gospel music became soul, and audiences flocked to see Appalachian-style folk bands playing a rock-influenced pop version of their style. Young adults and teenagers across the country were playing in amateur rock bands, laying the roots for local scenes, garage rock and alternative rock. More immediately, places like Southern California produced their own varieties of rock, such as surf.

Surf Music

The rockabilly sound reached the West Coast and mutated into a wild, mostly instrumental sound called surf music. This style, exemplified by Dick Dale and The Surfaris, featured faster tempos, innovative percussion, and processed electric guitar sounds which would be highly influential upon future rock guitarists. Other West Coast bands, notably The Beach Boys and Jan and Dean, would capitalize on the surf craze, slowing the tempos back down and adding harmony vocals to create the "California Sound".

Australian rock

After Johnny O'Keefe's last major hit in 1961, Australian popular music was dominated by clean-cut family bands. Bubbling beneath the surface, however, was a group of pioneering bands like the surf band The Atlantics.

British rock

American rock and roll had an impact across the globe, perhaps most intensely in the United Kingdom, where record collecting and trend-watching were in full bloom among the youth culture prior to the rock era, and where color barriers were less of an issue. Countless British youths listened to R&B and rock pioneers and began forming their own bands to play with an intensity and drive seldom found in white American acts. Britain quickly became a new center of rock and roll, leading to the British Invasion from 1958 to 1969.

In 1958 three British teenagers formed a rock and roll group, Cliff Richard and the Drifters (later renamed Cliff Richard and the Shadows). The group recorded a hit, "Move It", marking not only what is held to be the very first true British rock 'n' roll single, but also the beginning of a different sound — British rock. Richard and his band introduced many important changes, such as using a "lead guitarist" (virtuoso Hank Marvin) and an electric bass. Richard inspired many British teens to begin buying records and follow the music scene, thus laying the groundwork for Beatlemania.

British invasion

By the early 1960s, bands from England were dominating the rock and roll scene world-wide. First re-recording standard American tunes, these bands then infused their original rock and roll compositions with an industrial-class sensibility. Foremost among these was The Beatles, who became the single most influential act in the history of rock and roll. The Beatles brought together an appealing mix of image, songwriting, and personality and, after initial success in the UK, were launched a large-scale US tour to ecstatic reaction, a phenomenon quickly dubbed Beatlemania.

Although they were not the first British band to come to America, The Beatles spearheaded the Invasion, triumphing in the US on their first visit in 1964 (including historic appearances on the Ed Sullivan Show). In the wake of Beatlemania other British bands headed to the U.S., notably the Rolling Stones, who disdained the Beatles' clean-cut image and presented a darker, more aggressive image, The Animals and The Yardbirds. Throughout the early and mid-60s Americans seemed to have an insatiable appetite for British rock. Other British bands, including The Who and The Kinks, had some success during this period but saved their peak of popularity for the second wave of British invasion in the late 1960s.

Garage rock

The British Invasion spawned a wave of imitators in the U.S. and across the globe. Many of these bands were cruder than the bands they tried to emulate. Playing mainly to local audiences and recording cheaply, very few of these bands broke through to a higher level of success. This movement, later known as Garage Rock, gained a new audience when record labels started re-issuing compilations of the original singles; the best known of these is a series called Nuggets.

Folk-rock

As the British Invasion led by The Beatles picked up steam, a homegrown American trend was making itself felt, led by Bob Dylan. By 1963 the 22 year old Dylan had assimilated a variety of regional American styles and was about to work some alchemy to create an entirely new genre, usually dubbed "folk-rock". From 1961 to mid-1963 Dylan had kept his distance from rock and roll even though his first musical forays owed more to early rockers like Buddy Holly and Little Richard than to any of the more obscure folk and blues artists he would later embrace. He and others on the new folk circuit tended to view The Beatles as bubblegum, but admitted to a grudging respect for their originality and energetic style.

In 1963 Dylan's release of the album The Times They Are A-Changin'was a watershed event, bringing "relevant" and highly poetic lyrics to the edge of rock and roll. The Beatles listened to this album incessantly and moved away from the romantic themes of their work to date. In 1964 and 1965 Dylan threw off all pretense to roots purity and embraced the rock beat and electric instruments, climaxed by the release of the song "Like a Rolling Stone" which, at over six minutes, changed the landscape of hit radio and ushered in a period of intense experimentation.

Dylan would continue to surprise fans and critics with tour-de-force albums, but, after 1964, rarely strayed far from the rock and roll framework. His influence on all rock sub-genres is incalculable, probably equaled only by The

Beatles'. Among Dylan's most important disciples was Neil Young, whose lyrical inventiveness, wedded to an often wailing electric guitar attack, would presage grunge.

Counterculture

As part of the societal ferment in North America and Europe, rock changed and diversified in a number of subtle and not-so-subtle ways. As early as the mid-1960s, the image of rock and roll became less like previous musical forms. The Rolling Stones are credited with being the first band to dispense with band uniforms; band members simply wore whatever clothes they wished, and these clothes were often outlandish or controversial. Hair styles also became longer and less tamed. As trivial as these changes may sound today, this break from tradition was shocking to audiences used to clean-cut musical groups in matching suits.

Psychedelic rock

The music took on a greater social awareness; it was not just about dancing and smooching anymore, but took on themes of social justice. The counterculture that was emerging (partly as a reaction to the Vietnam War) adopted rock and roll as its defining feature, and the music began to be heavily influenced by the various drugs that the youth culture was experimenting with. In America, psychedelic rock influenced and was influenced by the drug scene and the larger psychedelic lifestyle. It featured long, often improvised jams and wild electronic sounds. Jimi Hendrix, Jefferson Airplane, and the Grateful Dead were leading practitioners of psychedelia.

A more esoteric form of British psychedelia and the Canterbury Sound is exemplified by the Soft Machine, who accompanied Hendrix on his first U.S. tour. Pink Floyd found their roots in British psychedelia, moving on to becoming more of a progressive rock, and arena rock band later in their careers. The culmination of rock and roll as a socially-unifying force was seen in the rock festivals of the late '60s, the most famous of which was Woodstock which began as a three-day arts and music festival and turned into a "happening", as hundreds of thousands of youthful fans converged on the site.

Progressive rock

The music itself broadened past the guitar-bass-drum format; while some bands had used saxophones and keyboards before, now acts like The Beach Boys and The Beatles (and others following their lead) experimented with new instruments including wind sections, string sections, and full orchestration. Many bands moved well beyond three-minute tunes into new and diverse forms; increasingly sophisticated chord structures, previously limited to jazz and orchestrated pop music, were heard.

Dabbling heavily in classical, jazz, electronic, and experimental music resulted in what would be called progressive rock (or, in its German wing, krautrock). Progressive rock could be lush and beautiful or atonal and dissonant, highly complex or minimalistic, sometimes all within the same song. At times it was hardly recognizeable as rock at all. Some notable practitioners include King Crimson, Genesis, Gentle Giant, The Nice, Yes, Gong, Magma, Can, and Faust.

Krautrock

In the mid-1960s, American and British rock entered Germany, especially British progressive rock bands. At the time, the musical avant-garde in Germany were playing a kind of electronic classical music, and they adapted the then-revolutionary electronic instruments for a progressive-psychedelic rock sound. By the early 1970s, the scene, now known as krautrock, had begun to peak with the incorporation of jazz (Can) and Asian music (Popol Vuh. This sound, and later pioneers like Kraftwerk, were to prove enormously influential in the development of techno and other genres later in the century.

Heavy metal music

A second wave of British bands and artists gained great popularity during this period dominant; these bands typically were more directly steeped in American blues music than their more pop-oriented predecessors but their performances took a highly amplified, often spectacular form. These were the bands that were led by the guitar; Cream and Led Zeppelin were early examples of this blues-rock form and were followed by heavier rock bands including Black Sabbath and Deep Purple. This style of rock would come to be known as heavy metal music.

Arena rock

The Beatles and the Rolling Stones had set the table for massive live performances in stadiums and arenas. The growing popularity of metal and progressive rock led to more bands selling out large venues. The corporate world saw the chance for huge profits and began marketing a series of what came to be called arena rock bands. Bands whose roots were in other genres, like Pink Floyd and Genesis, paved the way by putting on extravagent live shows drawing a large number of fans. Following in this wake, Boston, Styx, Foreigner, Journey, and many other bands began playing similar music, often less progressive and metal-like. This movement became a precurser to the power pop of future decades, and set the mold for live performances by popular artists.

Punk rock

Punk rock started off as a reaction to the lush, producer-driven sounds of disco, and against the perceived commercialism of progressive rock that had become arena rock. Early punk borrowed heavily from the garage band ethic: played by bands for which expert musicianship was not a requirement, punk was stripped-down, three-chord music that could be played easily. Many of these bands also intended to shock mainstream society, rejecting the "peace and love" image of the prior musical rebellion of the 1960s which had degenerated, punks thought, into mellow disco culture.

Punk rose to public awareness nearly simultaneously in Britain with the Sex Pistols and in America with The Ramones. The Sex Pistols chose aggressive stage names (including "Johnny Rotten" and "Sid Vicious") and did their best to live up to them, deliberately rejecting anything that symbolized "hippies": long hair, soft music, loose clothing, and liberal politics, and displaying an anarchic, often confrontational, stage presence; well represented on their first two singles "Anarchy in the UK" and "God Save the Queen". Despite an airplay ban on the BBC, the record rose to the top chart position in the UK.

The Sex Pistols paved the way for The Clash, whose approach was less nihilistic but more overtly political and idealistic. The Ramones exemplified the American side of punk: equally aggressive but mostly apolitical, more alienated, and not above fun for its own sake. The Ramones reigned as the kings of the New York punk scene, which also included Richard Hell and Television, and centered around rough-and-tumble clubs, notably CBGB's. Punk was mostly an East-coast phenomenon in the US until the late 1970s when Los Angeles-based bands such as X and Black Flag broke through.

New wave

Punk rock attracted devotees from the art and collegiate world and soon bands sporting a more literate, arty approach, such as the Talking Heads and Devo began to infiltrate the punk scene; in some quarters the description New Wave began to be used to differentiate these less overtly punk bands. If punk rock was a social and musical phenomenon, it garnered little in the way of record sales (small specialty labels such as Stiff Records had released much of the punk music to date) or American radio airplay, as the radio scene continued to be dominated by mainstream formats such as disco and album-oriented rock.

Record executives, who had been mostly mystified by the punk movement, recognized the potential of the more accessible New Wave acts and began aggressively signing and marketing any band that could claim a remote connection to punk or New Wave. Many of these bands, such as The Cars and The Go-Gos were essentially pop bands dressed up in New Wave regalia; others, including The Police and The Pretenders managed to parlay the boost of the New Wave movement into long-lived and artistically lauded careers.

Punk and post-punk bands would continue to appear sporadically, but as a musical scene, punk had largely self-destructed and been subsumed into mainstream New Wave pop by the mid-1980s, but the influence of punk has been substantial. The grunge movement of the late 1980s owes much to punk, and many current mainstream bands claim punk rock as their stylistic heritage. Punk also bred other genres, including hardcore, industrial music, and goth.

1980s rock

In the 1980s, popular rock included a wide range of variety. The early part of the decade saw pop-New Wave bands remain extremely popular, while the first pop-punk performers, like Billy Idol and The Go-Go's, saw widespread fame. Led by the American folky singer-songwriter Paul Simon and the British former prog rock star Peter Gabriel, rock became fused with a variety of folk music styles from around the world. This came to be known as "world music", and included fusions like Aboriginal rock and punta-rockero.

Hair metal

Heavy metal languished in obscurity during most of the 70s. A few bands maintained large followings, like Kiss and Aerosmith, and there were occasional mainstream hits, like Blue Oyster Cult's "Don't Fear the Reaper". Music critics overwhelmingly hated the genre, though, and listeners generally avoided it because of its strangeness. It left its mark on hard progressive bands like Chicago and flamboyant glam rock performers like Gary Glitter. Even while innovative metal bands like Metallica were forming numerous subgenres of metal, and the New Wave of British Heavy Metal was finding its own fans, a group of musicians were formulating what became known as hair metal.

Bon Jovi are often regarded as the first of these bands to gain popularity. They were known for long hair and feminized use of make-up, clothing and jewelry; nevertheless, their songs were defiantly masculine, even macho, focusing on girls, drinking and violence. Within a few years, hair metal dominated radio; bands like Def Leppard, Ratt and Extreme rose to fame, often collapsing under pressure later. Many were one-hit wonders.

By the end of the 1980s, a formula was developing in which a hair metal band had two hits, one a soft ballad, and the other a hard-rocking anthem. 1987 saw the release of Appetite for Destruction by Guns n' Roses, which skyrocketed to the top of the charts. Led by controversial frontman Axl Rose, Guns n' Roses rode the hair metal wave, wearing long hair and playing pop-metal. In contrast to other bands, they were not feminized in the slightest and incorporated influences from genres like thrash metal.

Chinese rock

Beginning about 1986, the Northwest Wind style of rock began to enter the burgeoning youth culture in China. The first Chinese rock song may be "I Have Nothing" by Cui Jian, now the widely-admired godfather of the Chinese rock scene. Spurred by pro-democracy activism, such as at Tianammen Square, and by governmental repression, rock flourished in the Chinese counterculture. Of especial popularity later in the decade were melancholy tunes called prison songs. By 1990, Chinese rock had begun to enter the mainstream, but almost immediately incorporated sounds and styles from the Cantopop style.

Though alternative bands remained, Chinese rock became subverted, often by bands working in cohesion with the Chinese government and in favor of the status quo; many of rock's fans in China became disillusioned as a result, leading to a general decline in popularity later in the decade.

Alternative music

The term alternative music (also often known as alternative rock) was coined in the early 1980s to describe bands which didn't fit into the mainstream genres of the time. Bands dubbed "alternative" could be most any style not typically heard on the radio, however, most alternative bands were unified by their collective debt to punk. Although these groups never generated spectacular album sales, they exerted a considerable influence on the generation of musicians who came of age in the 80s.

Grunge music

By the late 1980s rock radio was dominated by aging classic rock artists, slick commercial pop-rock and hair metal; MTV had arrived and brought with it a perception that style was more important than substance. Any remaining traces of rock and roll rebelliousness or the punk ethic seemed to have been subsumed into corporate-sponsored and mass-marketed product. Disaffected by this trend, some young musicians began to reject the polished, glamour-oriented approach and created crude, sometimes angry music.

The American Pacific Northwest region, especially Seattle, became a hotbed of this movement, dubbed grunge. Early grunge bands, particularly Mudhoney and Soundgarden, took much of their sound from early heavy metal and much of their approach from punk, though they eschewed punk's ambitions towards political and social commentary to proceed in a more nihilistic direction. Grunge remained a mostly local phenomenon until the breakthrough of Nirvana in 1991 with their album Nevermind.

A slightly more melodic, more completely produced variation on their predecessors, Nirvana was an instant sensation worldwide and made much of the competing music seem stale and dated by comparison, hair metal faded almost completely from the mainstream. Nirvana whetted the public's appetite for more direct, less polished rock music, leading to the success of bands like Pearl Jam and Stone Temple Pilots. Pearl Jam took a somewhat more traditional rock approach than other grunge bands but shared their passion and rawness. Pearl Jam were a major commercial success from their debut but, beginning with their second album, refused to buy in to the corporate promotion and marketing mechanisms of MTV and Ticketmaster, with whom they famously engaged in legal skirmishes over ticket service fees.

While grunge itself can be seen as somewhat limited in range, its influence was felt across many geographic and musical boundaries; many artists who were similarly disaffected with commercial rock music suddenly found record companies and audiences willing to listen, and dozens of disparate acts positioned themselves as alternatives to mainstream music; thus alternative rock emerged from the underground.

Britpop

While America was full of grunge, post-grunge, and hip hop, Britain launched a 1960s revival in the mid-90s, often called Britpop, with bands like Oasis and Blur. These bands drew on a myriad of styles from the 80s British rock underground, including twee pop, shoegazing and space rock.For a time, the Oasis-Blur rivalry was similar to the Beatles-Rolling Stones rivalry. While bands like Blur tended to follow on from the Small Faces and The Kinks, Oasis mixed the attitude of the Rolling Stones with the melody of the Beatles. Both bands became very successful, and for a time Oasis was given the title "the biggest band in the world" but slowed down after band breakups and slightly less popular support.

Indie rock

Alternative music and the rebellious, DIY ethic it espoused became the inspiration for grunge, the popularity of which, paradoxically, took alternative rock into the mainstream. By the mid-90s, the term "alternative music" had lost much of its original meaning as rock radio and record buyers embraced increasingly slick, commercialized, and highly marketed forms of the genre. At the end of the decade, hip hop music had pushed much of alternative rock out of the mainstream, and most of what was left played pop-punk and highly polished versions of a grunge/rock mishmash.

Following the lead of Pearl Jam, many acts who, by choice or fate, remained outside the commercial mainstream, became part of the indie rock movement. Indie rock acts placed a premium on maintaining complete control of their music and careers, often releasing albums on their own independent record labels and relying on touring, word-of-mouth, and airplay on independent or college radio stations for promotion.

Linked by an ethos more than a musical approach, the indie rock movement encompasses a wide range of styles, from hard-edged, grunge influenced bands like Superchunk to punk-folk singers such as Ani DiFranco. Currently, many countries have an extensive local Indie scene, flourishing with bands with much less popularity than commercial bands, just enough of it to survive inside the respective country, but virtually unknown outside them.

With the death of grunge-rock pioneer Kurt Cobain, rock and roll music searched for a new face, sound, and trend. In 1995, Canadian pop star Alanis Morissette released

Jagged Little Pill, a major hit that featured blunt, personally-revealing lyrics. It succeeded in moving the introspection that had become so common in grunge to the mainstream. The success of Jagged Little Pill spawned a wave of popularity in the late 90s of confessional rock releases by female artists including Jewel, Tori Amos, Fiona Apple, and Liz Phair. Many of these artists drew on their own alternative rock heroes from the 1980s and early 90s, including the folky Tracy Chapman and the hardcore punk girl bands called Riot Grrl. The use of introspective lyrics bled into other styles of rock, including those dubbed alternative.

The late 1990s brought about a wave of mergers and consolidations among US media companies and radio stations such as the Clear Channel Communications conglomerate. This has resulted in a homogenization of music available and the creation of artificially-hyped acts. In the early 2000s the entire music industry was shaken by claims of massive theft of music rights using file-sharing tools such as Napster, resulting in lawsuits against private file-sharers by the recording industry group the RIAA.

After existing in the musical underground for decades, garage rock finally saw a resurgence of popularity in the early 2000s, with bands like The White Stripes, The Strokes, and The Hives all releasing successful singles and albums. This wave is often referred to as the garage rock revival. In Britain, there is a new trend in copying 1970s rock bands in the form of wild clothing and long guitar solos, e.g. The Darkness. Though The Darkness have proved to be very popular it remains to be seen if this trend will become mainstream, with other bands emulating them.

Musical Instrument

A musical instrument is a device that has been constructed or modified with the purpose of making music. In principle, anything that somehow produces sound can serve as a musical instrument, but the expression is reserved generally to items that have that specific purpose. The academic study of musical instruments is called organology. Instruments are often divided by the way in which they generate sound:

— Wind instruments generate a sound when a column of air is made to vibrate inside them. The frequency of the wave generated is related to the length of the column of air and the shape of the instrument, while the tone quality of the sound generated is affected by the construction of the instrument and method of tone production.

— Percussion instruments create sound, with or without pitch, when struck. The shape and material of the part of the instrument to be struck and the shape of the resonating cavity, if any, determine the sound of the instrument.

— String instruments generate a sound when the string is plucked, strummed, slapped, etc. The frequency of the wave generated (and therefore the note produced) usually depends on the length of the vibrating portion of the string, the tension of each string and the point at which the string is excited; the tone quality varies with the construction of the resonating cavity.

— Voice, that is, the human voice, is an instrument in its own right. A singer generated sounds when airflow from the lungs sets the vocal cords into oscillation. The fundamental frequency is controlled by the tension of the vocal cords and the tone quality by the formation of the vocal tract; a wide range of sounds can be created.

— Electronic instruments generate sound through electronic means. They often mimic other instruments in their design, particularly keyboards.

— Keyboard instruments are any instruments that are played with a musical keyboard. Every key generates one or more sounds; most keyboard instruments have extra means (pedals for a piano, stops for an organ) to manipulate these sounds. They may produce sound by wind (organ), vibrating strings either hammered (piano) or plucked (harpsichord), by electronic means (synthesizer) or in some other way. Sometimes, instruments that do not usually have a keyboard, such as the glockenspiel, are fitted with one.

Many alternate divisions and further subdivisions of instruments exist. To learn about a specific instrument, consult the list of musical instruments or List of archaic musical instruments. All classes of instruments save the electronic are mentioned in ancient sources, such as Egyptian inscriptions and the Bible, and probably predate recorded history. The human body, generating both vocal and percussive sounds, may have been the first instrument, or, perhaps, found percussion instruments such as stones and hollow logs. Nine-thousand-year-old bone flutes or recorders have been found in Chinese archeological sites.

6

Technology in Next Generation Music

Music and Audio

All known historical societies have engaged in some form of musical activity. A society that neglects music probably does so to its own detriment. After all, music evokes emotion. Music provides identity. Music is intellectually stimulating. Audio is fundamental to many of our most important rituals and events. Memories involving audible phenomena also serve as powerful reminders of personal, national, and racial histories. Music has often been used as a means to communicate across linguistic and cultural barriers. As such, audio and music are core elements of understanding people.

Music is also a powerful tool for learning and growth. In fact, recent research has shown that music training can measurably increase performance by children and college students with such tasks as spatial reasoning. It is commonly accepted that the World Wide Web has changed much of the world experience. The pace of this change exceeds that of any in the history of humanity. New technologies have been developed on this infrastructure as the demand for more compelling experiences continues to grow. Streaming media is the most notable of these technologies. While the concept of packet-based audio was considered at the onset in the Internet, streaming audio did not emerge as a significant Internet "feature" until 1995.

The initial implementation relied on standard voice compression technology and had very low fidelity. In fact, many of the transmissions were simply inaudible or were too annoying to be useful. This technology has come far in subsequent years and now provides good fidelity audio at bandwidths in the range of ISDN connections. A new Internet needs to take a conscious step forward in this domain.

Audio and music are a very demanding test case

Musicians are extremely sensitive to very subtle (few-millisecond) shifts of temporal materials. They are also extremely sensitive to localization information. For example, a good orchestral conductor can isolate minor tuning imperfections among twenty or more string instruments. A truly gifted conductor will know which specific instrument in the section is sharp or flat. This is an impressive skill, which is learned by developing the ability to localize the position of competing sound signals using the temporal differences of arrival times of the sound at each of our ears. Audio over Internet2 needs to provide this kind of accuracy. As such, audio and music transmission will provide a critical test case, where errors can be readily perceived by one of our primary senses.

As we move from open-air analog-based audio transmission to packetized digital delivery systems, it is evident that there are many difficulties yet to be overcome. The subtle details contained in audio require very high resolution storage formats. For example, a 3-minute song on standard audio CD requires 32 megabytes of audio data. A higher quality format for audio research could require 260 megabytes. This order of magnitude storage difference makes Internet audio file transfer impractical. To view this problem from a different perspective, Table 1 shows bit rates associated with various forms of storage and transmission.

Table 1. Important bit rates

CAnet3 CANARIE-Bell Canada	40 GBit/s	optical Internet Oct.1998
Internet2 US new national backbone	9.6 GBit/s	network for end of 1999
Internet2 US new national backbone	2.4 GBit/s	network for end of 1998
Internet2 US national backbone	622 Mbit/s	infractructure April 1998
ATM OC-12	622 Mbit/s	
ATM OC-3	155 Mbit/s	
100-BaseT / FDDI LAN	100 Mbit/s	
T3	45 Mbit/s	
10-BaseT Ethernet LAN	10 Mbit/s	
T1	1.5 Mbit/s	
Digital HDTV	40-60 Mbit/s	5 1 audio uncompressed
Next generation DVD (Blue Laser)	23 Mbit/s	
DVD-ROM	11.08 Mbit/s	
Digital DVD-Audio (uncompressed)	9.6 Mbit/s	6 channels max. 96 kHz, 24 bit
Digital TV, DVD-Video (NTSC)	6-10 Mbit/s	5.1 audio, NTSC video compr.
Multichannel audio compressed	224-640 kbit/s	5.1 channels, Dolby Digital
Compact disc	1.14 Mbit/s	44.1kHz, 16 bit, stereo
Stereo audio uncompressed	1.536 Mbit/s	48 kHz, 16 bit, stereo

Stereo audio compressed ("MP3")	20-128 kbit/s	MPEG-2 Layer 3
Normal telephone channel	64 kbit/s	mono, limited bandwidth
Telephone modem	14.4- 56 kbit/s	ITU V.90 modem 56 kbit/s
Cable modem (with Ethernet card)	50-200 kbit/s	up to 10 Mbit/s theoretical
ISDN	64-128 kbit/s	FM stereo quality
ISDB (Integrated Services Digital Broadcasting)	150 Mbit/s	NHK trans. 21 GHz/ ch
ADSL (a new telephone service)	512 kbit/s	uses standard wires
ADSL high-speed modem	1 Mbit/s	
Program data	10 kbit/s	
Facsimile (fax)	20 kbit/s	
Still picture	70 kbit/s	
Tell Text	100-200 kbit/s	
Audio graphics	800 kbit/s/ch	

NOTE: Audio stream bit rate is expressed in bits/second (bit/s) or thousands of bits/second (kbit/s), or millions of bits per second (Mbit/s). A higher bitrate provides better audio fidelity but requires more Internet bandwidth. The required bit rate transmission capacity depends on the type of service, coding method, error correction, quality (resolution) of signal, number of channels, and other factors.

Time delays are caused by several factors-encoding and decoding latencies, routing and switching latencies and, of course, transmission latencies. Beyond problems with time delays, the vast majority of Internet users cannot stream Internet audio material that matches the fidelity achievable with common home stereo systems. The required bandwidth far exceeds that of even relatively expensive ISDN connections. The reliability of Internet connections continues to degrade, even for high-bandwidth users, as the population of Internet users increases faster than the supporting network.

Many pundits have predicted massive outages and failures due to this increased load. This sort of cataclysmic event is not necessary to render the Internet useless for high-quality audio applications. A single skip or pop will ruin a high-quality audio experience. As such, the network requirements for high-quality audio are difficult to meet. As for music, at present musicians are exploring interactive performance with MIDI (Musical Instrument Digital Interface) and with streamed audio.

MIDI is a serial control protocol used by manufacturers of electroacoustic instruments, audio signal processors, and a host of computer music software products. The maximum bit rate is 32.5 kbit/s per 16 multiplexed channels of information. MIDI is sufficiently rich to permit complex control gestures (playing notes on a keyboard, tracking and encoding pitches from voice or orchestral instruments, moving a slider on a mixing console, turning a knob on a digital signal processor, manipulating banks of lights) to be captured and encoded as a serial data stream. It is also sufficiently fast to permit real-time compositional algorithms or sound signal processing routines running on personal computers to interact with live performance. Even though packet latencies are at least 1 ms and may exceed 20 ms, practical experience and countless live performances have proven that MIDI is a powerful mechanism for interactive music creation.

Technical issues in network transmission of music and audio

Internet2 requires the infrastructure to support not only passive but also interactive audio experiences. A passive experience would be analogous to listening to a concert via streaming audio, or watching a movie with sound effects via an MPEG movie. An interactive experience requires the ability for the listener to affect the course of audio program creation or playback not only locally but even for other remote listeners as well. An example would be a quartet of musicians, each in remote locations, playing synchronous music while monitoring each other over the Internet2 network.

Latency

Interactive audio applications are dependent on a low-latency connection between network locations. The time between playing a note and its arrival at a remote location cannot exceed a small fraction of a second. It is very difficult to interact on a musical level when latencies exceed this threshold.

Time stamping

Continuously flowing audio streams, video streams, and discrete events between locations must be synchronized with each other.

Quality of service

The quality of service requirements for audio streams are particularly demanding. Lost or late data packets can easily destroy the continuity of the audio signal stream, thus seriously degrading the quality of the sound. Video streams are less sensitive to millisecond-range breaks in content continuity. Based on current practice, Internet2 will need to exceed a minimum point-to-point service at the level of OC-3. Transmitting IP packets directly, as is anticipated in the recently announced Canadian CANARIE network, will alleviate the overhead associated with ATM and SONET (synchronous optical network) layers. This alternative should also be explored by Internet 2.

Audio formats

To maintain cost-effective efficient access to Internet2, the protocols selected for streaming audio must be compatible with conventional digital audio equipment. Today's digital audio equipment streams linearly encoded PCM audio streams in a multiplexed two-channel format conforming to the AES3 (AES/EBU) standard. Additional audio channels are typically transported over multiple instances of AES3 (not multiplexed into one big stream). Today an emerging technology named IEEE 1394 is promising to replace AES3 as the multichannel digital audio interconnect, carrying multichannel data in packets. conforming to the IEC 61883-6 standard. Internet2 audio protocols should be consistent with either AES3 or IEC 61883-6 protocols to enable low-cost reliable bridge devices.

The emergence of multichannel digital audio utilizing some form of perceptual coding (such as Dolby Digital, DTS, and MPEG audio) is another important consideration in specifying audio delivery protocols. Compressed audio formats are typically transported over a IEC 60958 (SPDIF) bus, in accordance with the IEC 61937 standard. Again, it is recommended that Internet2 utilize the packet formats specified by these standards to ensure compatibility with legacy digital audio equipment. Another consideration is the selection of audio data formats, sample rates, and encoding methods.

Standard sampling rates include 32 kHz, 44.1 kHz, 48 kHz, 88.2 kHz, and 96 kHz. Standard data formats include linear PCM with 16-, 18-, 20-, 24-, and 32-bit word lengths. Internet2 should support all permutations of these sampling rates and data word formats, and in fact should support future formats when they someday appear. Support of 32-bit single-precision and 64-bit double-precision IEEE floating-point PCM samples is also recommended for optimal compatibility with personal computers.

Synchronization between the sending and receiving devices on the network is also important. It is necessary to convey the sampling rate of the digital audio signals as they are transmitted from one remote site to another. This is typically achieved by transporting time stamps with the audio samples, or by referencing sample rates to a global clock such as GPS. Time alignment is also necessary in some applications (such as a simulcast between disparate audio, video, and other data streams). The Internet2 must provide a quality of service (QOS) that ensures that audio data are delivered at a rate suitable for recovering sample rate clocks without jitter or dropouts, and maintaining proper time alignment between the signals.

Failure to observe these industry standard digital audio transport standards when specifying digital audio protocols for Internet2 could result in prohibitively complex bridge device implementations, thereby limiting Internet2 to high cost, highly complex installations. By following industry standards the Internet2 world can easily bridge to today's digital audio systems and institutions and provide a highly valuable service to the digital audio community.

Number of channels

For distributed performance to be meaningful, the auditory experiences of the performers and/or conductor must be simulated accurately at the remote site. The simulated space requires techniques quite different from those used in sound recordings. While we know little about truly realistic simulation, it is certain that many channels of audio and video will be required and that these channels must be carried in precise temporal synchronization for the remote experience to be accurate. Each sound transmission should be identified according to the number of channels and the arrangement.

If a tradeoff will have to be made between the number of channels and the quality of the signal within the available bitrate, the user should be given a choice of which characteristic to maintain at the highest level of priority, and which at the lower levels. In some situations, depending on the program material, the multichannel attribute may be the most important characteristic of sound from the music and sound perception point of view. Thus there should be the option to preserve the multichannel characteristic of the original at all costs in the transmission.

Client-server issues

Many tools have been developed and are still being developed that promise to deliver audio over networks for playback. For the most part, these systems use a client-server approach in which the materials to be delivered are contained on one or several servers of various types and delivered over a network to a client. The client is usually some type of personal computer or, in some cases, a dedicated playback device or yet another server.

Decompression requirements

Typical characterizations of decompression processing requirements specify some percentage of some commodity CPU such as a Pentium running at some specific clock speed. This does not always equate to being able to actually use a given decompression technique on a given machine and in most cases represents not the peak usage but an average CPU utilization. There is also the assumption of an entire machine dedicated to the task of decoding audio when in fact there may be background or foreground processes competing for resources. These competing processes can be unrelated operations, operating system functions, or even overhead from the audio receiver process.

A method is needed to provide an accurate profile and guarantee resources for audio decode. Resources come in two classes, negotiable and nonnegotiable. Typically nonnegotiable items refer to hardware capabilities. For instance, if a computer's sound system can handle only audio sampled at 22.05 kHz, 32 kHz, or 44.1 kHz, this profile information is nonnegotiable. The negotiable component of this may be the inclusion of an in-line real-time resample filter. The profile should include at a minimum the following items:

— Memory requirements
— CPU type
— Operating system
— Peak CPU utilization
— Maximum duration of peak CPU utilization
— Average CPU utilization
— Playback capabilities (16 bit 8 kHz to 48 kHz, stereo, etc.)
— Availability of hardware-assisted decode or encode
— Compression technique capability sets.

Once the audio server knows these things, it can determine the type of audio stream to supply to the client. In some cases this information will indicate that the various streams available from the server cannot satisfy the audio delivery request. In other cases, the server will use this information in order to secure resources for audio playback on the client machine that match one of the audio profiles within the server's range of delivery options. By delivering an audio stream based on negotiated parameters that are then guaranteed by the client to exist, the audio consumer can be guaranteed an experience that is trouble free while meeting the minimum standards set by the content author.

Standardization of content on server side

While major headway has been made in the area of advanced standard file formats for audio delivery, adoption of these formats is by no means settled. As an industry, producers of media should demand that their network broadcast equipment adhere to a standard format. Until server vendors have achieved an appropriate standard, we will be faced with the following problems:

- Content life cycles of 6 to 12 months
- Constant need for consumers to download new players
- Incompatibility between existing content and new servers from the same or different vendors.
- Lowest common denominator content encoding
- Duplication of nearly identical applications from multiple vendors
- No standard way to utilize existing HTML or other code with embedded clients when changing from one server to another.

Formats such as Advanced Streaming Format contain advanced capabilities and can be readily extended to encompass new technologies as they are conceived. Using a single robust standard such as this will support competition while introducing some measure of compatibility.

Client architecture

Lack of a single standard client architecture is becoming a problem as more and more server vendors appear. While it can be argued that independent architectures provide a platform for rapid enhancement and expansion of capabilities by each server vendor, it is also clear that this moving target has stifled proliferation of content, rendering the advancements largely meaningless. It is possible to deliver clients that have the same interfaces without stifling competition. The modularization of network layers, compression techniques, and file read and write capabilities is advised. These modular components can then be plugged in to a standardized client as needed.

Many systems already use a modular design that allows decompression techniques from any vendor to be utilized by the existing client. Currently this modularity is on a per-client basis rather than a per-system basis. In other words, it is not enough to know what your CPU and operating system are. You also need to know which of many clients you will be using in order to obtain the proper decompression technique. This raises the complexity considerably for all parties involved. Once you have simplified component selection, automatic component download can be accomplished in a much more straightforward manner.

Copyright protection

By developing a standard client it will also become possible to implement some level of compatibility for audio copyright management and protection. A particularly compelling application that would benefit from this advancement includes pay-per-play streaming of high-quality audio. Consumers could access a much larger library of music than is currently feasible with physical media. Such an improvement in content access would surely provide new growth potential for the music industry. This lowered barrier to musical exploration would also result in a more diverse and creative musical landscape.

Current standardization efforts for secure systems have focused on building frameworks that support a diverse application space. This approach should also be taken within Internet2. This type of framework promotes interoperability between systems while not restricting the development of diverse secure applications. Current security systems have no level of interoperability, which results in incompatible content for the consumer. By employing such a generic security framework, clients could download and embed secure modules for specific applications in the same manner that was described previously for audio compression algorithms. The result would be an integrated client that could render content protected by multiple security systems.

Envisioned Applications

We ride roughshod here over the question of whether Internet2 shall remain limited to the academic community. Since so many advances in audio and music are aimed at the consumer, surely the needs of the consumer and the commercial market will also push the envelope of the musical and audio capabilities of Internet2.

Digital libraries

One of the largest obstacles to the adoption of digital audio libraries is the lack of easy and rapid content location. There are many simple query-string-based approaches to this problem, but searching through a recorded audio library requires quick and high-quality rendering of content. One example of this application is the research into classical melodic structures. A student using this library needs to quickly compare and contrast melodic segments contained in a library. The reason for this quick comparison lies in the limitations of human music memory.

Humans can retain certain aspects of a music experience for only a few seconds. As a result, the digital library system must be able to deliver each musical segment consistently and rapidly. Otherwise the research and learning experience will be significantly degraded. Furthermore, the quality of these musical pieces must be very high to allow distinction of performances and recordings. Beyond text searches and content rendering, the capabilities for doing searches based on auditory and musical content have recently begun to be studied. For example, how do you search for a sound track containing a bell sound?

One company has developed technology for content-based retrieval of audio. Such a system can analyze all the audio in a digital library, representing each sound by a compact set of parameter values, which are then stored in a database. The user can construct various types of queries based on the audio content, including "query by example." With query by example, the user indicates the desired type of sound by selecting all or part of an existing sound file in the library, or even by recording a sample sound into a microphone. The system displays a list of all sounds in the library that are similar to the given sound, ordered by degree of similarity.

Such technology can also be useful for segmenting and classifying audio (whether in a file or in a live streaming input). For example, a sports broadcast can be segmented into useful chunks by identifying and distinguishing moments of cheering, narrative by different sportscasters, and other distinctive sorts of sounds. Thus, long, sonically heterogeneous recordings can be broken into segments of more or less homogeneous sound, either upon entry into the database or upon retrieval.

These technologies are clearly relevant not only in the context of a self-contained digital library, but also with distributed, Web-based resources. For example, an Internet2 search engine could allow a user to search the Web for sounds that are similar to a specified sound. To build the indexes for such a search engine requires periodic and automatic downloading of massive quantities of audio, a function that would benefit from the increased bandwidth of Internet2-as would the per-user auditioning of search results.

Three-dimensional audio

In addition to a rapid comparison of musical segments as mentioned, the system will need to render many audio segments simultaneously and in a complex manner. Users of interactive audio applications will require three-dimensional audio attributes like head-related transfer functions (HRTF) to provide a realistic and useful audio delivery platform. For example, in an educational VRML replication of an orchestra, children can move about the stage and visit the different instrument families.

As they get closer to the brass section, they will hear and understand the sound of that family of instruments; off to the left they will hear the timpani, and they can choose to move in that direction based on the three-dimensional audio source. Internet2 must support persistent environments where a dynamic change to the audio source is recognizable to all participants in real time. These changes must be persistent in that if a sound generator is affected by one user and later experienced by another user, the changes are audible to the second user.

Beyond virtual reality

Network-based real-time immersive audio-visual applications go a step beyond virtual reality that stretches the capabilities of current technologies. They provide an immersive (content-rich) framework,. permitting one or more individuals to observe and interact with things or individuals elsewhere in remote locations. While somewhat similar to today's applications in teleconferencing, these applications differ in three important ways: they require high-resolution audio and video content streamed in two directions across a network, they depend on precise synchronization of their events and audio-visual content streams, and finally, they require a significantly higher degree of network "quality of service." Such applications share certain basic requirements with teleconferencing systems. In teleconferencing, systems using ISDN-based technology have proven to be effective, while for immersive audio-visual applications, they have not; bandwidth requirements and quality of network service are almost always the determining factors.

Broadcasting (audio webcasting)

We are in a very early stage with regard to radiolike services on the current Internet-more or less the equivalent of the very early crystal radio phase in the development of radio. Audio quality is decidedly low fidelity. Transmissions are interrupted for no discernible reason. Competing transmission systems use incompatible players. Computers are not ideal radio receivers. And so on. But the Internet has proven the concept that people want to communicate with more variety than is available from the "old" mass media. With the bandwidth of Internet2, broadcastlike audio content can be distributed in a viable fashion. This is as powerful an enabling technology for the electronic media as the World Wide Web has been for the print media.

Audio webcasting follows an important technology trend from analog through digital to packetized digital. In line with this, the existing mass-broadcasting paradigm may be replaced by something modeled after what has happened in the book and magazine publishing business. The megabookstores now popular in the United States carry tens of thousands of books and a few hundred magazines, some of which are aimed at a mass audience, but most of which are targeted to very specific reader needs and interests.

The old mass magazines (Life, Look, Saturday Evening Post, and so on) are gone. Newsletters and "small-press" publications are growing rapidly, their cheap production enabled by the new technology of desktop publishing. That relatively few sources of audio programming are available currently is the result of a technology limitation, not for lack of a receptive market. Radio frequencies are a scarce commodity, and because they are valuable, they must be used in a way that optimizes numbers of listeners.

Because they are dependent upon advertiser support, radio stations must appeal in the broadest possible fashion. There is no place, with the present limitations in the radio-frequency spectrum, to provide programming with anything like the wide variety the public is demanding from a modern bookstore. That is why Internet delivery is so compelling: there is no limit to the number of channels. As a source of information, the Web is superior to radio and television today; as a source of entertainment, the Web has already overtaken competing media for many "early adopters."

Eventually it may even be possible to extend the Internet's reach to portable receivers. An analogy can be made to the existing print orientation of the Web: the Internet's variety compensates for lack of portability. Newspapers and magazines are often read nowhere near an Internet connection, so portability is an advantage there also, but this has not prevented the growth of the Web for text and graphics. Home, work, and university listening is likely to rise as the content becomes more varied and interesting. After all, the computer is not necessarily a bad audio receiver device. Audio can be listened to while a user is doing something else with the computer. It can be used as background, just as radio often is.

Audio production: standardization of Internet methods

Once the specifications for standard control protocols for studio mixing and production have been established, it will be possible to participate in the production process from a distance using the Internet. For example, mixing a sound file from a distance by sending mixing instructions over the Internet will be possible, while auditioning the results in real time.

An artist, engineer, producer, or teacher will be able to correct a mix from a distance by specifying a number of changes in the three-dimensional architecture of the mixdown file. This will be similar to the composer's ability to change a composition or performance (for example, by correcting a MIDI file). Soft access and control of any place in the mix will be available. Needless to say, a teacher located hundreds of miles away will be able to demonstrate changes to a mix to a group of students, or adjust a mix for each student separately.

Collaborative work

The standardization of audio compression techniques, for example, is a lengthy and expensive process. There is no purely objective measure for audio quality. As a result, audio compression algorithms must go through many stages of subjective listening tests. The listening tests take place at many worldwide locations and require the convergence of many professionals from around the world. In addition, the candidates for these tests come from a select group of "golden ear" listeners. These special listeners have the ability to detect problems in the audio that most humans would not hear. As such, it is critical to have them participate in these events.

If these listening tests could be conducted remotely throughout the world through a high-quality network, much time and expense could be saved. The audio material could be distributed to the remote locations via the network. The audio rating could also be logged in real time to a central scoring facility. This connection would remove many of the planning delays that are common in audio standards testing.

Music education

Following are the on-line documentation of Internet2:

> Interesting examples of learningware for the appreciation of music have been developed at several institutions. Migrating exemplars, such as those developed at... Purdue University..., to a Web-based environment is constrained by current limitations on

> the quality of streaming audio. Internet2 services could remove these constraints...

and:

> In an Internet2 environment, moreover, studio instruction in music also would have new opportunities. World-class musicians could be invited to offer their insight and expertise. For example, a two-way video/audio connection might link a high school jazz band with an artist-in-residence at a university. The high quality of the communication link would allow demonstration and critical review to occur. In addition, the students would literally be able to "jam" with the university-based instructor. This connection could be extended to musicians (whether students or professional artists) at additional locations. The instruction could be enriched by introducing recorded audio and video performances drawn from a network-based server. The student interaction with the instructor could be recorded for later review, either by the instructor or for practice by the students.

This kind of application provides a real-time interactive high-quality audio-visual framework within which the player in one remote location is coached by an expert ("coach," or even the composer) in another. Coach and player are separated by an arbitrary distance. The use of the application is effectively decoupled from notions of geographic distance, despite its degree of immersion. The implications of this on a cultural level are profound.

Even when coaching players of average ability, the coach's evaluation of the player's performance depends on the discernment of auditory detail operating on extremely fine time and pitch scales (on the order of milliseconds or cents). Though secondary, fine visual observations regarding fingering technique, posture, or breathing, for example, can also play an important role in the evaluation. The coach's keenness of discrimination relies on the stability and the time-frequency resolution of the audio and video signals received. The system must also provide the player with the same ability to evaluate the coach's musical performance (demonstrating technique).

In addition to the music curriculum, universities and colleges will be able to offer some of their sound recording curricula on the Internet, where participants will find entire lectures, experiments, demonstrations, exercises, or training programs fully accessible from a distance. For example, a student in. a distant location will be able to learn about an MS microphone, audition and control the stereo MS microphone from a distance, audition the microphone's on- and off-axis responses, as well as learn about the design and construction of the MS microphone without ever seeing one in real life. The student will also use an equalizer or a compressor, or reverberate a sound, without having to purchase the equipment.

Broadening musical participation

Interactive music can open up music enjoyment and appreciation to the greater population who never had the time or opportunity to learn to play music. One company has developed computer-assisted music performance technology that enables people of a wide range of musical abilities, from professionals to beginners, to perform and interact with music. By enabling an Internet2 browser with such technology, the following benefits can be realized:

— By providing an adaptable musical control layer, such technology empowers musicians to increase their physical performance abilities exponentially in terms of dexterity, harmonic depth, and rhythmic accuracy.

— Equipped with an extensive musical database, this technology enables musicians to exploit sophisticated chord voicings and scalar patterns well beyond their current musical vocabulary.

- The software assists musicians in original and authentic expression while performing new and unfamiliar stylistic material.
- The program allows musicians a migration path to other musical disciplines, that is, percussion players using their rhythmic skills to perform dynamic harmonic material in real time.

On a larger scale, the Internet2 network could facilitate collaborative television production and simultaneous performance of music by artists placed anywhere in the world. A very ambitious and successful project linking musicians from seven locations spread all over the globe was conducted during the opening ceremony of the Nagano Winter Olympics.

Using ISDN (384 kbit/s) and satellite television technology for audio and video signals, a chorus in Berlin, Cape Town, Beijing, New York (United Nations), and Sydney performed the final movement of Beethoven's Ninth Symphony together with the Winter Orchestra (a full symphony orchestra, chorus, and soloists) at the Nagano Kenmin Cultural Center Hall. Furthermore, a 2000-person chorus located at the Olympic Stadium joined the performance, which was mixed for a live broadcast to viewers around the world.

The setup coordinated by NHK involved the use of seven satellites, twelve uplinks with encoders and decoders, and multiple-delay compensation. Audio and video signals were sent from Nagano's International Broadcasting Center via an optical fiber network to Tokyo and further via the KDD High-Reliability Network to satellite uplink stations at Yamaguchi and Ibaragi. There the signals were beamed to seven satellites which retransmitted the signals to stations in Germany, South Africa, China, the United States, and Australia, as well as return signals back to Japan.

The Line-Operation Centre receiving the signals added delays to all signals until they matched the delay of the longest transmission to and from Berlin. Thus the video and sound of the orchestra playing in the Nagano Kenmin Cultural Center Hall and the five choruses were projected on a big screen in the Olympic Stadium and via a public-address system, and also sent to the broadcasting center where pickup of the chorus from the Stadium was added. From the technical standpoint, the event demonstrated the absolute need for precise compensation of transmission delay of audio and video signals to achieve perfect synchronicity.

As well, the issues of reliability of telecommunication systems and compatibility between audio, video, digital formats, compression systems, interfaces and standards became very apparent. The high cost of this operation and its complexity demonstrated the need for more effective and economical ways of networking high-quality audio and video on a worldwide basis.

Forensic applications

Internet-based forensic audio laboratories could offer services of decomposing and segregating audio signals, removing reverberation or noise from sound recordings, plus other processes involving pattern recognition, using complex signal processing engines and advanced software.

Automatic update of software tools

Manufacturers of audio equipment will offer new software

tools for sound processing, making their new product available to the consumers faster than it takes to build a hardware version. These "plug-in" software devices will be "auditioned" over the Internet, and used as "demo" units limited only by their expiration date, finally purchased directly from the manufacturer using the Internet. All modifications or upgrades to these soft tools will be automatically sent to every registered user. Learning of a new product that has just become available will be as quick as finding a new icon on the desktop, ready for testing at a click of a button.

Scientific and engineering data representation

One part of the Internet2 proposal foresees, in the context of scientific experiments, "tools for synchronizing temporal data (such as music) with related text and images (such as musical scores)." Actually, the field of sonification (or audification) is active if young. Our ears are adept at hearing many places in space at once, including receiving information around corners and through solid walls, and detecting events at distant locations. Moving this concept to the Internet, we should be able to model, render, and transmit an auditory portrait of our virtual surroundings. Sound can depict a composite of information surrounding us in cyberspace, whereas our visual browsing is accomplished only one page at a time.

Sound can provide vast amounts of information while we are still waiting for a few image frames to download. And when audio is synthesized locally, only the control instructions need to be transmitted from a remote location, further upping the interactive ante of audio over video. The Internet is not only a topology of personalized sources and sinks replacing the impersonal radio stations and record stores of yesterday. The topology is itself a metaphoric space for audio signals to propagate and resonate, capable of informing a listener of other listeners and players on-line, and indicating the relative locations of sites with desired information.

The subsystems that we specify and build should be capable to treat the Internet as a meta-instrument that resonates with sound propagation, and provides immediate feedback from interactive interface devices, as well as transmitters and receivers of prepackaged media. The parallel emphasis of local computation on the one hand and streaming of remote signals and control messages on the other captures both the broadcast metaphor and the music performance metaphor. The construction of a dual-metaphor cross-platform tiered approach to an "audio operating system" can sustain a new Internet well into the next century.

Twelve-tone Technique

Twelve-tone technique is a system of musical composition devised by Arnold Schoenberg. Music using the technique is called twelve-tone music. Josef Matthias Hauer also developed a similar system using unordered hexachords, or tropes, at the exact same time and country but with no connection to Schoenberg. Schoenberg himself described the system as a "method of composing with 12 notes which are related only to one another".

The basis of twelve-tone technique is the tone row or set, an ordered arrangement of the twelve notes of the chrcmatic scale (the twelve equal tempered pitch classes), or, rather, an ordered arrangement of intervalss which produce those notes. When the technique is applied most rigorously, an entire piece must be built up from statements of any transposition of this tone row in strict order or transformations of this row. Both melody and harmony may be created in this way. The set may be used in succession or simultaneously, the latter of which may be ordered up or down, or not.

The initial tone row, or set form, used is called the prime series (P), untransposed it is P_0. P can be used starting on any one of the twelve notes of the chromatic scale (P_X) - so long as the intervalss are the same, the rows are equivalent. $P_X = P_0 + X$.

Additionally, P can be transformed in two basic ways: it can be turned backwards to get the retrograde (R) or turned upsidedown to give the inversion (I) or the reverse contour direction. $I(X) = 12 - P_X$. These two transformative techniques can be combined to give the retrograde inversion (RI). As with the prime series, R, I and RI can be transposed to any note of the chromatic scale.

RI is:	RI of P,	R of I,	and I of R.
R is:	R of P,	RI of I,	and I of RI.
I is:	I of P,	RI of R,	and R of RI.
P is:	R cf R,	I of I,	and RI of RI.

thus:

P:	RI:	R:	I:
RI:	P	I	R
R:	I	P	RI |- |I: |R |RI |P

More recently composers such as Charles Wuorinen have also used multiplication of the row. However, there are only a few numbers which one may multiply a row by and still end up with twelve tones. Multiplication is indicated by MX, X being the multiplicator. As with the other compound operations multiplication is carried out and then transposition. $P_0 = M1_0$, $I_0 = M11_0$, $M7_0=I(M5_0)$. Thus, for the untransposed form of all:

M1:	M5:	M7:	M11:
M5:	M1	M11	M7
M7:	M11	M1	M5 |- |M11: |M7 |M5 |M1

Even numbers remain unchanged under M7 and all odd numbers become transposed by a tritone. The chromatic scale may be mapped onto the circle of fourths with M5, and the circle of fifths with M7.

Suppose the prime series is as follows:

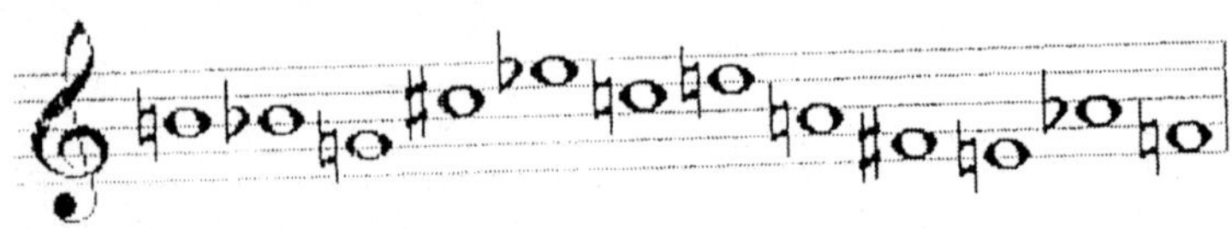

B, Bb, G, C#, Eb, C, D, A, F#, E, Ab, F

Then the retrograde is the prime series in reverse order:

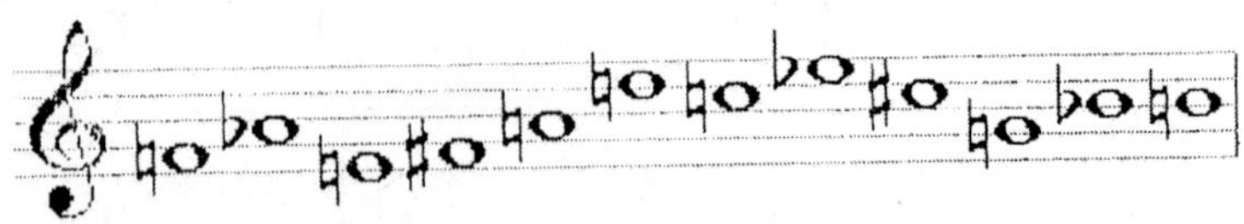

F, Ab, E, F#, A, D, C, Eb, C#, G, Bb, B

The inversion is the prime ser:es with the intervalss inverted (so that a rising minor third becomes a falling minor third):

B, C, Eb, A, G, Bb, Ab, C#, E, F#, D, F

And the retrograde inversion is the inverted series in retrograde:

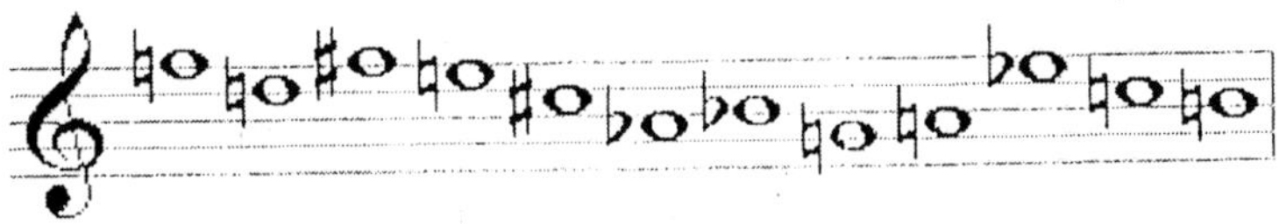

F, D, F#, E, C#, Ab, Bb, G, A, Eb, C, B

P, R, I and RI can each be started on any of the twelve notes of the chromatic scale, meaning that 47 permutationss of the initial tone row can be used, giving a maximum of 48 possible tone rows. However, not all prime series will yield so many variations because tranposed transformations may be identical to each other. This is known as invariance. A simple case is the ascending chromatic scale, the retrograde inversion of which is identical to the prime form, and the retrograde of which is identical to the inversion (thus, only 24 forms of this tone row are available).

When rigorously applied, the technique demands that one statement of the tone row must be heard in full (otherwise known as aggregate completion) before another can begin. Adjacent notes in the row can be sounded at the same time, and the notes can appear in any octave, but the order of the notes in the tone row must be maintained. Durations, dynamics and other aspects of music other than the pitch can be freely chosen by the composer, and there are also no rules about which tone rows should be used at which time (beyond them all being derived from the prime series, as already explained).

Schoenberg's idea in developing the technique was for it to act as a replacement for tonal harmony as a basic grounding force for music. As such, twelve-tone music is usually atonal, and treats each of the 12 semitones of the chromatic scale with equal importance, as opposed to earlier classical music which had treated some notes as more important than others.

History of the technique's use

Founded by Austrian composer Arnold Schoenberg around the late 1910s, the method was used during the next 20 years almost exclusively by the Second Viennese School (Alban Berg, Anton Webern, Hanns Eisler and Arnold Schoenberg himself). Rudolph Reti, an early proponent says: "To replace one structural force (tonality) by another (increased thematic oneness) is indeed the fundamental idea behind the twelve-tone technique," arguing it arose out of Schoenberg's frustrations with free atonality.

The technique became widely used by the fifties, taken up by composers such as Luciano Berio, Pierre Boulez, Luigi Dallapiccola and, after Schoenberg's death, Igor Stravinsky. Some of these composers extended the technique to control aspects other than the pitches of notes (such as duration, method of attack and so on), thus producing serial music. Some even subjected all elements of music to the serial process.

In practice, the "rules" of twelve-tone technique have been bent and broken many times, not least by Schoenberg himself. For instance, in some pieces two or more tone rows may be heard progressing at once, or there may be parts of a composition which are written freely, without recourse to the twelve-tone technique at all. Offshoots or variations may produce music in which: the full chromatic is used and constantly circulates, but permutational devices are ignored permutational devices are used but not on the full chromatic

Derivation

Derivation is transforming segments of the full chromatic, less than 12 pitch classes, to yield a complete set, most commonly using trichords, tetrachords, and hexachords. A derived set can be generated by choosing appropriate transformations of any trichord except 0,3,6, the diminished triad. A derived set can also be generated from any tetrachord that excludes the interval class 4, a major third, between any two elements. The opposite is partitioning, the use of methods to create segments from sets, most often through registral difference.

Combinatoriality

Combinatoriality is a side-effect of derived rows where combining different segments or sets such that the pitch class content of the result fulfills certain criteria, usually the combination of hexachords which complete the full chromatic.

Invariance

Invariant formations are also the side effect of derived rows where a segment of a set remains similar or the same under transformation. These may be used as "pivots" between set forms, sometimes used by Anton Webern, see George Perle.

Also, some composers have used cyclic permutation, or rotation, where the row is taken in order but using a different starting note. Although usually atonal, twelve tone music need not be - several pieces by Berg, for instance, have tonal elements. One of the best known twelve-note compositions is Variations for Orchestra by Arnold Schoenberg. "Quiet", in Leonard Bernstein's Candide, satirizes the method by using it for a song about boredom.

Unsupervised Learning of Meledic Segmentation

When listening to a piece of music, listeners often identify distinct sections or segments within the piece. Music segmentation is recognised as an important step in the abstraction of musical contents and researchers have attempted to explain how listeners perceive and identify the boundaries of these segments. Existing theories on music segmentation have employed Gestalt principles to identify discontinuities and create groupings between musical events.

The perception of parallelism and similarities are also known to influence the listener to relate different passages within a musical piece. In fact many Gestalt-based approaches rely on higher-level grouping rules or similarity functions to identify larger scale segment boundaries. It is suggested that Gestalt principles operate independently of the listeners musical knowledge. When familiarised with a certain musical repertoire, listeners memorise recurrent features in the music and use this knowledge to carry out musical analytical tasks. Empirical evidence shown, large sections of a musical piece can be recalled by listeners based on the recurrence of small musical cells, which act as markers within the piece. Leonard Meyer in his theory on music expectation also outlines the importance of learning in music understanding and relates expectation with information theoretical notions such as entropy.

The entropy (or unpredictability) associated with the occurrence of a musical event can change its prominence and hence make it salient to the listener, within a sequence of events. The notion of salience has also been referred as being associated with features that present intra-textual or inter-textual distinctiveness. Probabilistic methods have been widely used to acquire regularities in large sets of data, with many successful applications in natural language and speech processing. Some of these methods have migrated into the music domain however, probabilistic modelling has been used mostly for music prediction and generation and seldom to model musical analytical tasks or listening behaviour.

Some researchers seek the development of a system to learn and perform melodic segmentation in an unsupervised way. Applications for automatic music segmentation include the support to other analytical methods such as music search and pattern finding. The segments found can set the initial search points within a large piece, thus providing a reduction of the initial search space for complex algorithms.

They propose the implementation of a memory-based model to automatically predict the location of segmentation boundaries in a melody. The three main aspects of this model are described in this section. The first relates to the input of the model and deals with the representation of melodic information. The second and central part of the model is the feature learning module, which is implemented based on Markov models. The third relates to the output of the model and describes how it generates predictions about the location of segment boundaries, given a test melody.

Melody Representation

Music can be seen as a temporal process where sound events unfold in time. Melody information is converted directly from a Midi source into an event-based symbolic representation including the pitch, duration and the inter-onset interval between events. From these basic attributes they obtained two additional melodic features:

— Pitch step (PS): the interval distance between consecutive events (in semitones).

— Duration ratio (DR): the ratio between the duration of consecutive events.

Table 2 shows the melodic representation for an extract of Debussy's Syrinx, together with derived features PS and DR. For practical reasons the original DR values (in parenthesis) were converted into a logarithmic scale.

Table 2. Melody representation and two derived features.

No.	Pitch	Onset	Dur	PS	DR
1	82	3998	1000	-1	-5 (0.14)
2	81	4998	143	+2	-1 (0.80)
3	83	5141	115	-3	6 (8.70)
4	80	5256	1000	-1	-5 (0.17)
5	79	6256	167	+2	0 (0.99)
6	81	6423	166	-2	1 (1.64)
7	78	6589	273	-3	0 (1.18)
8	77	6862	322	—	—

These two features have the advantage of representing melodic information in a relative manner, thus avoiding the use of absolute pitch values or absolute durations. The latter is particularly important since in an expressive (non-mechanical) performance the durations of Midi events do not correspond exactly to the notated durations.

Feature Learning with Markov Models

Markov models are typically constructed from statistics obtained from a large corpus of data (usually referred to as the training corpus) using the co-occurrences of adjacent symbols to determine the probabilities of sequences of symbols.

An nth order n-gram model (a class of Markov models) assumes that the probability of occurrence of a symbol depends on the prior occurrence of *n-1* other symbols. Given a sequence $s=w_1 \dots w_l$ of length l, the probability $P(s)$ is given by,

$$P(s) = \prod_{i=1}^{l} P(w_i \backslash w_{i-1}, \dots, w_{i-n+1}) \tag{1}$$

If the training corpus is small and the order of the model is high, longer sequences will have relatively lower counts, resulting in less accurate probabilities. Independently of the size of the training corpus, it is unlikely that all possible symbol sequences will occur. This becomes a problem if, when computing probabilities using Equation 1, some of the terms in the product have zero probability.

Another disadvantage of n-gram models is that their size increases rapidly with an increase in their order since we may need to store the probabilities of all combinations of fairly long sequences.

Mixed-order Markov Models

Mixed-order Markov Models (MMM) provide a representation of higher-order models by combining several lower order models. Thus an n th order model over a random variable S (with *k* possible values) can be expressed as:

$$P(w_{i-1},\ldots,w_{i-n}) = \sum_{\mu=1}^{n} \phi(\mu)a^{\mu}(w_i|w_{i-\mu}) \tag{2}$$

where $a^{\mu}(wi \mid wi-\mu)$ is a *kxk* transition matrix containing the probabilities of the occurrence of a symbol at position i given the occurrence of a symbol at position $i-\mu$, The mixing coefficients $\Phi(\mu)$ are estimated using an iterative procedure, using the initial counts in the transition matrix. The MMM is trained with all pairwise dependencies found in the feature sequences generated from the training set and then the corresponding mixing coefficients are estimated.

Entropy and Boundary Prediction

Following the initial assumption, they propose that some segmentation boundaries are likely to occur close to accentuated changes in entropy, associated with some melodic features. Shannon showed that one of the ways of measuring the quantity of information of a particular message is to determine its unpredictability or entropy. We can determine the entropy associated with a given context *c* as,

$$H_c = \sum_{\forall w} P(w|c)\log_2 P(w|c) \tag{3}$$

where w denotes all symbols that can be successors of the context c. Context c is a sequence of size n-1, where n is the

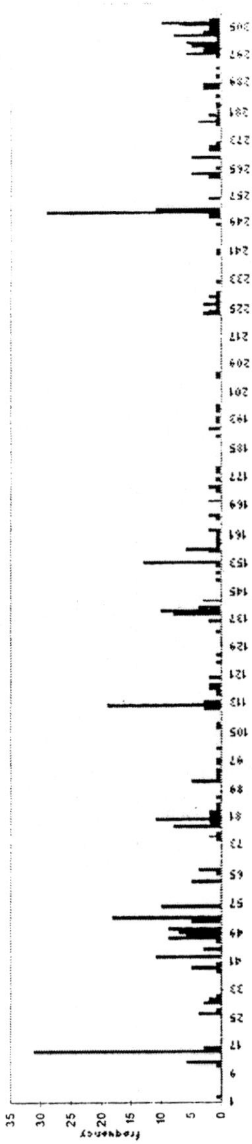

Figure 1. Histogram of segment boundaries (for all subjects) for Syrinx. Bins correspond to Midi events.

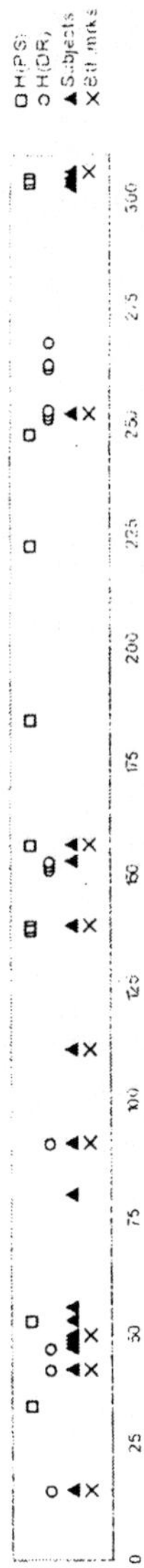

Figure 2. Segment boundary locations indicated by listeners, notated breath marks and boundaries predicted by the model.

order of the model. Conditional probabilities are obtained from Equation 2 and will reflect the statistics of the training set.

Entropy vectors are then calculated by taking all the successive context sequences from the feature vectors of the target melody. As mentioned earlier they are interested only in more prominent entropy changes across the melody. For every entropy vector they first determine the mean and standard deviation. Then all values outside the standard deviation are filtered from the vectors. Finally, from the remaining values in the vector, they considered only those that register a contiguous low-high or high-low variation with respect to the mean.

Data collection was performed by a computer program designed to guide the listeners through the whole listening session. Listeners were able to indicate a segment boundary by pressing the mouse button, while the melody was being played. To minimise the effects of priming, the program also guaranteed that no two listeners heard the melodies in the same order. The segment locations (time stamps) collected from the listeners were later synchronised with the MIDI data to associate them with the events in the melody.

A boundary is matched with an event if it occurs between the onset times of that event and the next. Figure 1 shows the histogram of segment boundary counts per event for Syrinx, for all subjects. The analysis of the separate boundary histograms for musician and non-musician subjects indicates that the differences between the two are not significant. This relatively low influence of the factor musical training in a segmentation task has previously been reported in.

Observing the graph of Figure 1 it is clear that listeners agreed on several segmentation locations, within the melody. The graph, also suggests that there is a delay or anticipation in some of the subjects' responses, particularly visible around the main segment boundaries at events 80, 112, 139 and 252. There are also areas in the graph that show a considerable number of responses that span over a fairly large number of consecutive events (e.g. 47-50 or 303-306).

Automatic Segmentation

Now look at the results obtained with their segmentation model on Syrinx, the larger melody of the study set. This melody was used both as the training set and the test set. Figure 2 plot the outstanding entropy transitions (white markings) for PS and DR, overlapped with the boundaries indicated by the listeners. In some cases the entropy variations stretch across more than two consecutive events and these, similarly to the L-boundaries, are depicted as several overlapped markings.

They considered that a prediction is correct if it indicates an existing *L-boundary location* within a distance of ±1 event. From a total of 14 L-boundaries considered, 11 were predicted correctly by the model (5 from H(PS) and 6 from H(DR)). The model generated also 5 excessive boundaries, 3 from H(PS) and 2 from H(DR). Excessive boundaries are those that have no correspondence with any of the L-boundaries.

7

Visualisation of Music in Virtual Environment

Listening and playing music is one of the oldest, the most entertaining and popular art form of the human race. Since the introduction of the phonogram and radio early this century, music has become an important part of our lives. One could argue that the hi-fidelity audio reproduction and broadcasting technologies are simple forms of virtual reality: their purpose is to fool the listener into believing that the music is as good and real as being performed in close proximity.

While enjoying music in the form of listening is a passive form of music appreciation, playing an instrument or conducting an orchestra might be classified as an active form of music appreciation, and such a skill may often require years of difficult training. Performing music at the quality, fidelity, and scale comparable to that of the music listening that current audio technologies offer is only practically possible for the professional musicians and rock stars (who, for instance, have the financial and technical means to gather the musicians and jam together).

As difficult as it is, this active form of music appreciation induces an even deeper sense of enjoyment out of the performers, because in addition to the sense of direct participation, the performers are given a total or at least partial control in expressing one's artistic taste. This fact is easily found in observing ourselves, humming and tapping to music, dancing to music, air-guitaring to the Rolling Stones, and air-conducting the Berlin Philharmonic.

Recent progress in digital music has enabled some form of active music appreciation. The digital synthesizer that can imitate various instruments with the "most common" keyboard interface and semi-automatic accompany/chord support is one such example. Another example is the Karaoke machine in which the tempo and pitch of a song accompaniment can be controlled. An even more ambitious approach is the application of virtual reality in hopes of allowing users to experience music in both passive and active fashion.

For example, at the Electronic Garden in SIGGRAPH 97, Takala featured a system called DIVA (Digital Virtual Acoustics) in which a user equipped with a glove and a special baton could control tempo and volume of an animated digital band. Another interesting development related to music appreciation is the trend from a purely auditory appreciation to a multimodal one. Music with animation and, especially, music videos have revolutionized the way in which music can be appreciated. The use of haptic feedback is being explored as well in the computer music community.

There are three dimensional space using multimodal interaction, should be designed for music appreciation and control. In particular, the use of three dimensional motion as the central medium for both music visualization and control. This is based on the music literatures that report the existence of human's internal representation of music in motion form, called the "inner motion" used for both music interpretation and performance. Therefore, in our approach, a given music is visualized using metaphorical motion models, and the interaction method is devised using principles from motor control/learning and multimodal interaction/interface design techniques in hopes of striking a chord with the internal motion-based music representation.

Music visualization and control have either been treated separately, or the emphasis has been put on only one or the other, resulting in "good visualization but difficult/ impossible to control" or "boring visualization but controllable" systems. The objective is the system to achieve an "interesting and inspiring" visualization, and at the same time, create a relatively easy-to-control music system in which the visualization serve as an effective feedback for better control of music.

The particular system is called the "Musical Galaxy". In the MG, tracks and melodic progressions are represented as orbiting planets (moving in direct relation to the music). Control-wise, we have adopted a two-handed interface, where the dominating hand controls the music progression and individual note volume through finger tapping (air piano playing) of the major melodic track, and the other hand controlling the global tempo through a simple squeeze/unsqueeze gesture.

The "air piano playing" interface is quite simple (well, if you had some basic piano training) and offers the sense of direct control and presence through the passive haptic feeling. The squeezing metaphor is based on the human's sense of proprioception (i.e. finger joints), and requires minimal cognitive load in the midst of simultaneous control of music progression and expression control by the dominating hand. The concept of musical motion, describe the visualization and interaction methods used in this work.

Music Visualization and Control

Perhaps, the most famous example of music visualization is the Disney's Fantasia, a musical animation that won special Academy awards in 1942 for "advancement of the use of sound in motion pictures and for widening the scope of the motion picture as entertainment and as an art form". Although at first it was criticized for having "cheapened" the music of Beethoven, Bach, and Tchaikovsky, and did not enjoy a commercial success, it is now considered a work of art and also enjoys a huge popularity. Since then, animated classical and rock music have been made and finally developed into the idea of music videos of today. Visualization of music (animated or not) is also considered an effective tool for teaching music to kids.

Although most of these animations or video productions are tailored made for the particular music pieces, some of them were based on abstract mathematical computer graphics. While the earlier computer graphic music visualization were mostly two dimensional and represented raw sound (rather than musical content), with the introduction of MIDI (the standards for representing digital music) and the fast development of algorithmic and hardware aspects of computer graphics.

With the advent of affordable VR technologies, many researchers are experimenting with the three dimensional and multimodal interfaces to control music to replace the current keyboard/mouse-based (piano or computer) interface to computer music. The on-line paper from IRCAM describes and offers many pointers to different approaches in using gestures for music performance [IRCAM 99]. They have classified the approaches into three main categories: instrumental gestures that imitate actual instruments (e.g. air-guitaring), dance oriented gestures that produce sound with whole-body movements, and conductor gestures modeled after conducting movements for global music control.

The motion or gestures may be captured using finger-tracking gloves, 6-DOF sensors, acceleration/velocity sensors (like the digital baton), EMG and ECG (e.g. to detect conductor's emotion), and even through digital images captured by a camera. It is also not clear what kinds of music can be produced or be controlled by such systems. For instance, it would be extremely difficult to reproduce even a simple two-track sonata through dance-oriented bodily gestures.

Music and Motion

The motivation is the desire to build a three dimensional virtual environment that reflects the musical content in a generic way (that is, not tied to a particular music piece), and the requirement that the virtual musical world must be conductive to the listener/conductor's representation of music so that one can control and appreciate the musical world in the most "cognitively-natural" way.

The rationale is based on music literatures that report the existence of human's internal representation of music in motion form, called the "inner motion" known to be used for both music interpretation and performance. According to Alexander Truslit, a German musicologist in the late 1930's,

"... To experience music fully, both the listener and the composer or performer must understand its most essential characteristics. This characteristics is the expression of inner motion, whose spontaneous manifestation in voice and movement formed the origin of song. This expression is the eternal driving force of music. In music, however, it is consciously shaped: inner experience and artistic form merge in to an integral process.

Many contemporary researchers agree on the strong relationship between music and motion in terms of their representation in the human mind. Interestingly, Truslit cites an episode by Carl Maria von Weber who described how, on his travel, the forms of the landscape moving past the coach window would evoke compelling melodic images in his mind. He also notes that there is also a more direct path from sound to the sensation of motion, through the human's vestibulum.

The simplest mapping between music and motion is the through the parameter of pitch (that is, melody) and rhythm. In two-dimensional space, the pitch/note represents the up and down motion and their velocity. The rhythm represents periodicity and impulsive force in the motion. These motion parameters are easy and natural for humans to exhibit and be captured through real-time gesture and motion capture.

While this abstract motion space is basically two dimensional in nature, the humans live and think in a multidimensional space. To visualize music using the "Galaxy" metaphor, in which various planets are orbiting ("moving") around the Sun. Each planet represents one or more music tracks, which are usually associated with certain instruments or hands (e.g. piano's right hand in one track, left hand in another, and clarinet in another). Planets move in orbit according to a profile characterized as a simple circular spline that dynamically change according to user input of tempo, and expression (in this case, just note volume). The performer/listener has a choice of two viewpoints, free (anywhere in the universe) and observational (fixed at close range from melody orbit).

One of the contrasting methods to using motion-central metaphor to music visualization is the less abstract instrument-oriented approach: for example, virtual orchestra, virtual band, virtual instrument (whether real or abstract metaphorical object). While these approaches may give the user the feeling of "I am conducting or leading the band myself!" by situating the user in such an environment, the actual visualization does not help the user very much in terms of controlling the music, that is the visualization is not very useful as an acoustic feedback. The conducting is done more through hearing the music.

Different approach has a different goal, to provide users with a more direct interaction with the music "objects" by materializing them (not the instruments) visually (or through other modes of display). With such a visualization scheme in hand, the next task is to design an interaction method most appropriate for it.

Interaction

The two main acoustic elements that an artist manipulates in shaping a performance are intensity and duration. Music played with tones of equal intensity and exact duration (as notated) sounds lifeless and mechanical. It is variations in duration and intensity that create the living shapes in music. Among the three major approaches to gestural control for music, disregarding the second approach (dance-oriented) due to its difficulty in performing a known score, combine the first and third type of gestural control, the instrumental and conductor-based. This is analogous to conducting a concerto in which the conductor also plays the major instrument, or to singing as playing the piano and leading a band.

The conducting based control alone offers easier control of the global aspects of the music, however, it is not appropriate for controlling the delicate note-level expression. The reverse is true for instrumental music control: it only controls the given instrument, and is not appropriate for controlling an ensemble of instruments.

Intensity and Note Progression

The three parameters available for the Musical Galaxy are the note intensity, progression, and global tempo/ expression (tempo variation may be used for expression such as ritardando). The note intensity and progression are controlled using an instrumental interface and the global tempo is controlled using a conductor like gesture. The instrumental interface is basically a virtual piano keyboard: the user needs to continuously tap (for each note of the melody) on the interface.

A special sensor (see Figure 5) that detects the user's tap and its intensity has been designed for this purpose (keyboard keys can be used as well for note playing only). In a multi-track musical score, there is one track, which we call the "Driving" track that represents the main melody (the other tracks are called the "Supporting" tracks), and this is the track (unless the user wants to control some other track) the user controls. As the notes in the Driving track are played upon finger taps (sent as MIDI notes to the sound processing hardware in real-time), all other notes from the supporting tracks that must be played until before the next melody note are played at the current tempo.

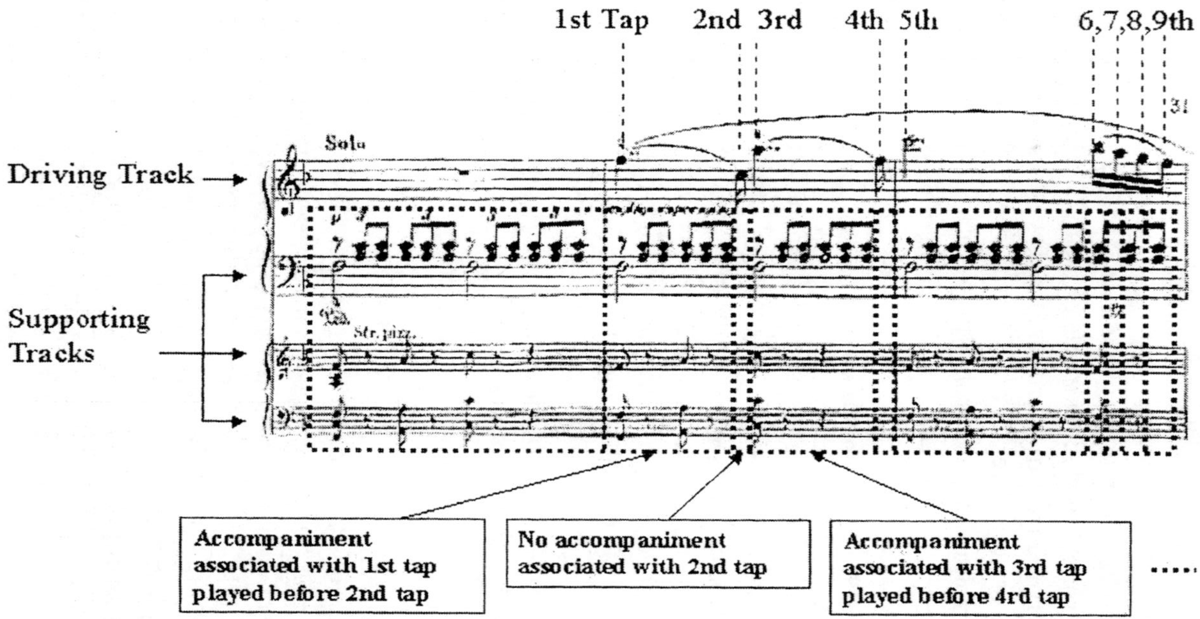

Figure 1. *As the notes in the Driving track are played responding to the finger taps, all other notes from supporting tracks are played automatically at the current tempo.*

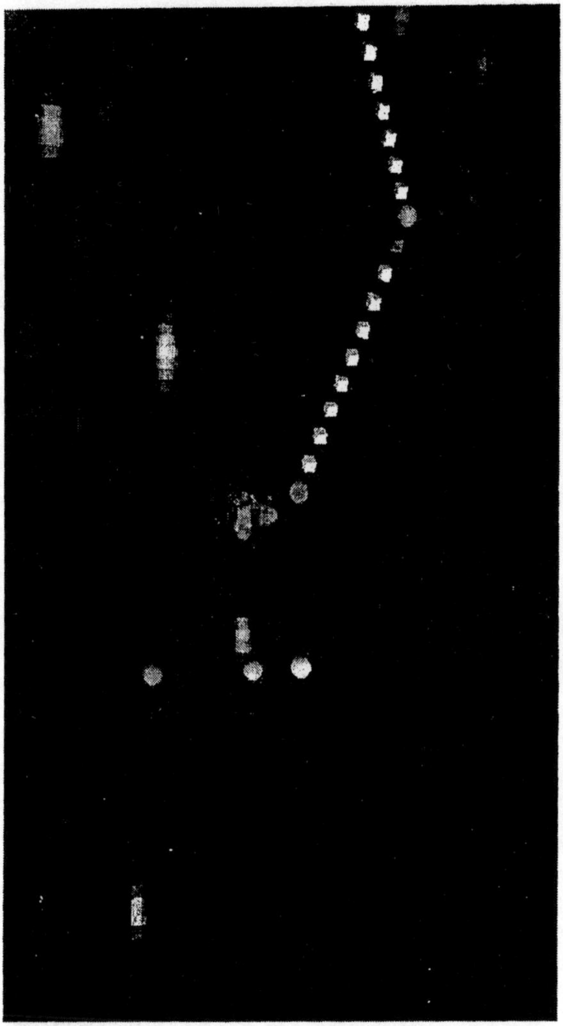

Figure 2. Musical Galaxy seen in the Observational Mode

Figure 3. Musical Galaxy seen in the Free viewing mode (Head Tracking Enabled).

Figure 1 illustrates how this is done. This is analogous to a soprano in a recital where the piano accompanist must follow (although the overall music profile is somewhat prearranged through prior practice) the singer's progression. Although not shown in the figure, the notes in the Driving track does not have to be "singular" (without harmony). If there are several notes to be played simultaneously in harmony, they are detected using the delta timing values among the melody notes.

The virtual tapping or piano keyboard interface thus requires minimal training in piano playing and prior familiarity with the music score, since the user needs to remember the melody and note durations to some degree. Usually, we are quite familiar (in terms of relative timing of the notes) with popular music pieces such as the famous 2nd movement of Mozart's Piano Concerto No. 21 (shown in Figure 1), and can hum to its tune. It is possible to even control the tempo, using the finger tapping, by constantly monitoring the relative timing between successive finger taps. There were two reasons for implementing: first it is not possible to introduce sudden changes in tempo, and if we were to employ both schemes (local tempo change with finger tap monitoring and global/sudden tempo change with the left hand), it could introduce confusion to the user's perception of the current tempo.

Another advantage of the finger tapping is that it uses the sense of touch: the player is given a distinct feeling of touch and transferring force through the interface. Although this is not the true form of haptic display with force feedback, a partial haptic display through touch still increases the feeling of direct interaction with the music and the feeling of participation in the virtual music world.

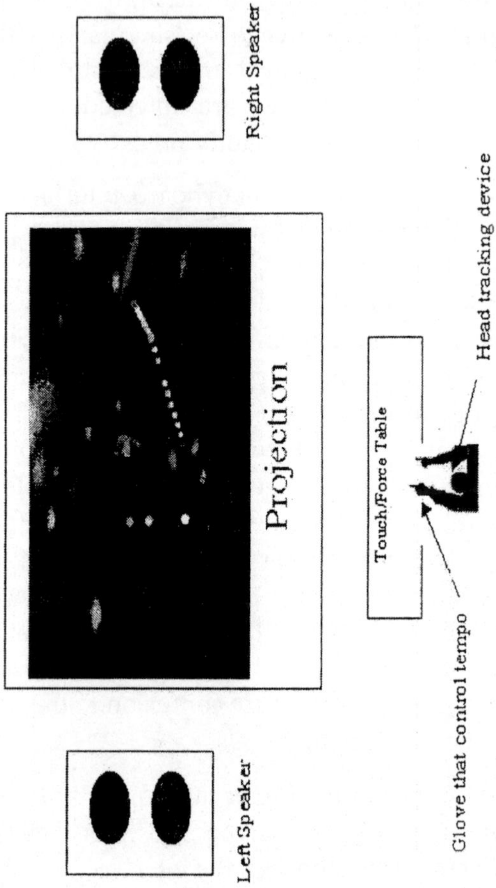

Figure 4. Musical Galaxy system set-up.

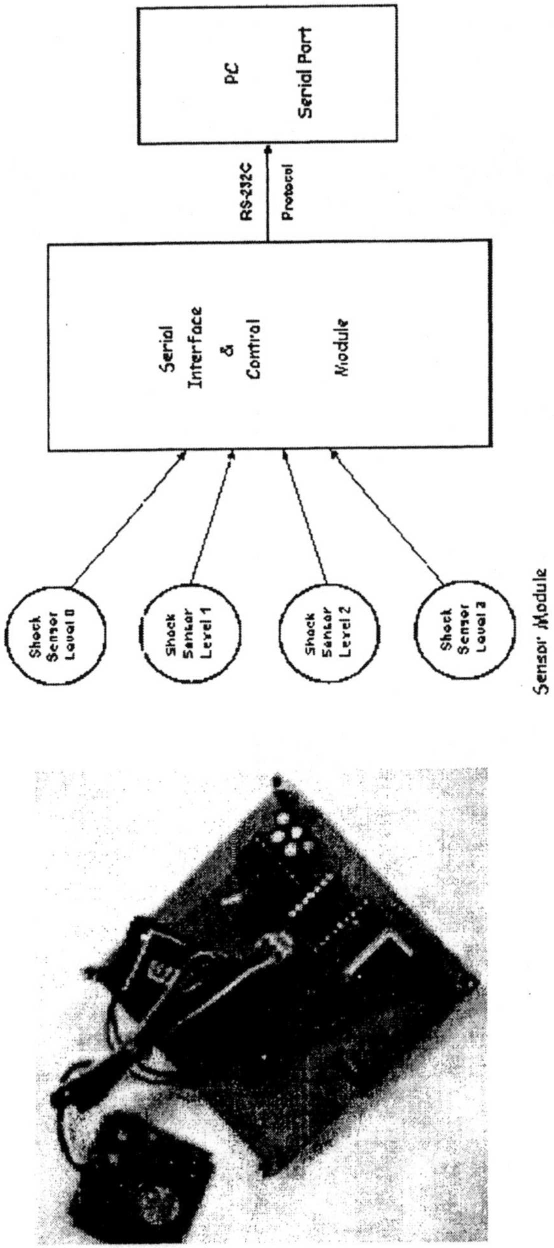

Figure 5. The Finger Tapping Sensor.

One of the hottest game introduced in Japan last year, called the "Beat Mania", is based on this simple idea. A note-like object progresses through time (moves from top to bottom) as the music plays, and the user is to strike one of the five virtual piano keys or scratch the turn table that matches the current note event, and as the player learns to match the note and the right key, it makes the user into believing that one is actually controlling the music instead of actually reacting to it. Similar types of such games are gaining wide popularity.

Global Tempo

The non dominating hand is used for global tempo control. The specific interface we have adopted is the gesture of squeeze/unsqueeze. The alternative methods we have considered were particular gestures that signal "tempo up" or "tempo down", and tracing the three dimensional position of the hand/arm (raising and lowering the hand). Using specific gestures burdens the user, even for just two gestures, with additional cognitive load and the user must make discrete kinesthetic changes with the finger configuration.

Both using specific gestures and raising/lowering arm method suffers from the calibration problem: it is difficult to designate a reference point in the empty 3D space. The squeeze/unsqueeze metaphor does not suffer from that problem because it is based on proprioception. The usefulness of proprioception has been well documented. The user is automatically aware of the current tempo through the direct mapping to the finger joint angles. Unlike specific up or down gestures, it can transmit continuous change in values as well.

There are several planets orbiting around the Sun, each representing a single music track. The orbit of the planet Earth represents the Driving melody track. Small spheres are rendered as "stepping stones" around the Earth to depict the current, past and future note positions. The positions and intervals of the stepping stones are according to the pitch and duration value of the corresponding notes. Figure 2 shows the snapshot of the Musical Galaxy seen in the Observational viewing mode.

The user is given two possible view points: Free and Observational. In the Free mode, the user is free to move anywhere in the universe and head tracking is enabled. In the Observational mode, the user position is fixed at close proximity from the position of the Earth (it moves relatively with the Earth). It is in the Observational mode where the user can interact and control the music at note by note level.

Figure 3 shows the Musical Galaxy seen in the Free mode. Although currently stereoscopy is not heavily used, in the future, to enrich the graphic content and experiment with direct manipulation of the stepping stones to control music, and feel that stereoscopy will become very important.

Figure 4 shows the current overall set-up of the Musical Galaxy. A Pentium based Intergraph Graphics workstation has been used for rendering and music processing (with just a general purpose sound board). The OpenInventor and Maximum MIDI Toolkit were used for graphics and MIDI programming. The 5th Glove was used to detect the hand gesture and the Polhemus Fastrak tracker was used to track the head motion (for view point control).

A Complex System for the Visualisation of Music

This self-authored system for translating musical

compositions into visual performance involves the interaction of multiple layers of information in a complex way. The art works which have emerged from this process have embodied principles of Intermedia as defined by Dick Higgins, the late avant-garde theorist and Fluxus artist. Intermedia is a completely different concept from multimedia, although it can be included in a multimedia environment. While with multimedia, content/information is presented in more than one medium simultaneously, Intermedia is a combinatory structure of syntactical elements which come from more than one medium but are combined into one. This "transformation" into another kind of entity is pointed to as an obligatory part of Intermedia by Yvonne Spielmann in her analysis of digital film and video.

There is an unpredictability of outcome based on a sensitive dependence upon the initial conditions (the music). The final form can only be seen after going through the entire process, the transformation into the new form of Intermedia.

The first part of the analysis task is to determine what are the structural parameters of the piece of music to be visualized, or in other words, what are the operating principles? Which data sets should be collected? Does the composition exist within a diatonic/chromatic harmonic frame work, or is it composed from layers of carefully chosen timbres? These two approaches mean very different things and are therefore visually depicted with completely different color systems.

For instance, if a piece of music can be reduced to a piano score then it is not dependent upon the timbre of different instruments in order to be that piece of music. Furthermore the vocabulary is based in language as all of the spoken/sung sounds are nonsense phonemes from German. A harmonic analysis would not have yielded meaningful information for translation of this composition. Nor would it have worked with music which depends upon carefully constructed timbre as its structure.

There are elements which have been contained in all of the compositions. They include patterns of rising and falling melodic lines, changes in dynamics (loudness), and also the rhythmic units and patterns including their articulation. This information is either gleaned from written scores, as in my work with Bruckner; a writing down of every note heard by hand from an *original audio performance* of Kurt Schwitters reciting his Ursonate; or lastly, as in the case of The Virtual Reality 21st Century Color Organ, the information comes directly from MIDI files.

Visual Vocabularies

Images re-ordering

One of the most important decisions to make is what kind of images will be used as the vocabulary through which the syntax of the music will be seen. Landscapes and/or architectural elements which are somehow close to the music, images which will carry meaning in style, structure, and/or historic connection. These images are cut up and reordered based on the previously mentioned analyses of dynamic changes, melodic and rhythmic structures. There are changes of image scale to represent louder or softer music. The width of the units representing a single note or chord is determined by its corresponding time value and melodic changes create shifts in the vertical placement of image units in both the two dimensional and three dimensional versions.

When the visual units finally appear in their new abstract formations, the original representational themes become subliminal in their appearance to the viewer. These multi-varied changes have come about through complex interactions of multiple simple systems. Analysis of the overall form of the music determines how the images are used. In the Bruckner work, images to the specific musical lines occupying the same place in the structure. The representation of silences is another contextually based element. Should the silence be read as an empty instant of time, or is it in an equal balance of power with the "on" notes?

Transparent color systems

A major part of the visual vocabulary which have been developed is based in the application of a transparent layer of color over the displaced and reordered images. Which information these overlaid color systems expresses is determined early on. As the music modulates through keys, the same pattern occurs with the movement through the colors.

Harmonic quality refers to the relative dissonance or consonance of two or more notes playing at the same moment. It is a sliding scale between the two extreme ends of pure consonance and the most extreme example of dissonance within a given style of music. For the music of Bruckner a pure consonance is represented by a pure hue from the color/harmony wheel and extreme dissonance is represented by a 50-50 mixture of the original color and its complimentary color, i.e.. 50% orange with 50% blue. This makes a grey hue.

Since there is no vertical harmony in the single voiced *Ursonate* and transformed the previous harmonic quality

Figure 6. Still shot from the Color Organ showing musical structure generated by piano chords.

system into one which maps how and where *vowels* are produced in the mouth. This system was developed at the Institute of Phonetics at the University of Cologne. The list of colors for unrounded vowels come from the warm side of the color wheel and rounded vowels are from the cool side. As the tongues moves down in the mouth to form different vowels, the color choice moves down the appropriate color list.

Vowels which are formed in the front of the mouth, like "i" and "e", are a pure color. vowels directly behind the teeth, like "I", have a 10% complimentary color component, the next step back in the mouth is 20% complimentary, and so on until the back of the mouth, as in "o" or "u", which has 50% complimentary color in the mixture. The last color system created is based on *timbre,* which literally means the color of sound. A vital component of music which is structured on timbre is the combination of specific and differentiated sounds, much like a painter can choose to use color.

Whereas the color system based on the *circle of fifths* maps harmonic movement and quality in order to visualize music which takes its structure from these concepts , this later system is effective with music when the actual sounds form the structure.

The 21st Century Virtual Reality Color Organ Project

The 21st Century Virtual Reality Color Organ is a collaborative project of David Britton. He is responsible for the graphics programming and the meta-architecture of the programming structure. The Color Organ is a computional system for translating musical compositions into visual performance. An instrument, like a musical instrument, it uses supercomputing power to produce 3D visual images and sound from MIDI files, and can play a variety of compositions. Performances take place in interactive, immersive, virtual reality environments such as the CAVE, VisionDome, or Immersadesk. Because it is a 3D immersive world the Color Organ is also a place; a performance space.

The Organ consists of three basic parts: First there is the set of systems or syntax which consists of logarithmic transformations from an aural vocabulary to a visual one. Second, there is the 3D visual environment serving as a performance space, and also the visual vocabulary from which the 3D environment was modeled. This visual vocabulary consists of landscape and/or architectural images and provides the objects upon which the syntax acts. Finally comes the programming which makes possible the interaction of the first two parts.

When the performance begins you are in this world of hand drawn *landscapes* which have been modeled into 3D. All of the landscapes are in black and white with the sky completely black. As the music plays a three dimensional colored and image embedded geometric structure takes shape in the space over the landscape. This is constructed from flat pictures of the landscape images representing the instrument family which produced them. They are colored a specific hue based on a timbre analysis of which instrument is being played and what the particular playing technique is at that moment.

The saturation of the color reflects changing dynamics (loud and soft). These flat strips of landscape are placed up and down in vertical space by their pitch. A higher pitch will be higher in space and a low pitch will be placed closer to the landscape below. The width of the strips is controlled by the volume (attack) of the signal. After the music has been played there remains a complete sculpture which can be further explored in an interactive way. The viewer can move at will through the space and touch elements of the sculpture and hear the sound which originally produced it.

Interactivity in a 3D environment gives the Organ another layer of complexity. The 2D wall works can be hundreds of feet long and therefore incorporate time into the viewing process, but it is a movement across a flat plane. When one is immersed in the Color Organ 's 3D environment you have the ability to move in all directions in and around the image embedded, colored geometry which is created before your eyes as you hear the music which is producing it. After the music has finished playing the structure remains to be explored from an infinite number of viewpoints. The viewer will also be able to point to a musical artifact and hear the sound which produced it.

The Color Organ will be able to function on two levels in the future. It will play pre-existent compositions as now, but Britton is re-doing the program architecture so that different musical parameters can be plugged in. The second goal is for the Organ to be able to translate the MIDI signals from live, improvising musicians, who could be located in different locations along the *AccessGrid* but the visualization and sound will appear including all parts in the immersive environments also located on the Grid. If the musicians are improvising it then becomes a complex adaptive system. There are many problems on internet 2, such as a lag of real time.

8

SOM: Application to the Organisation of Music Archive

With the increasing amount of data available digitally the potential of intelligent data analysis techniques has risen. The field of applications covers simple data surveys as well as sophisticated summaries for decision support. One important aspect of data analysis is to understand the inherent structure and organization of the data. Furthermore, algorithms which reveal the data structure are valuable tools in the automatized organization of digital libraries containing, for example, text-documents or pieces of music. One prominent algorithm with such capabilities is the Self-Organizing Map (SOM) which is frequently employed in the field of data exploration.

The SOM maps high-dimensional data to a 2-dimensional map display in such a way that similar data items are located close to each other on the map. Two of the main advantages of the SOM are the computational eficiency and the intuitive way the results are presented to the user. However, the basic SOM lacks the ability to extract the hierarchical structure of the data. This has been addressed for example in where the results of the SOM were used as input for hierarchical agglomerative clustering algorithms.

Other alternatives include, for example, the hierarchical SOMs. A top-layer SOM organizes the data into a few categories which are further refined on SOMs in sub-layers. However, the user is required to predefine the granularity of the individual SOMs as well as the overall depth of the structure. The Growing Hierarchical Self-Organizing Map (GHSOM) addresses this problem through a flexible structure which grows to fit the data.

A quality measure based on the variance of the data together with threshold parameters are used to decide which granularity is appropriate for a specific SOM, and which areas of the SOM are promising candidates for further hierarchical expansion. The Tension and Mapping Ratio (TMR) extension is based on two new measures which analyze the topological and cluster stability of the SOM. The result is an algorithm with improved decisions regarding the necessary granularity to represent the inherent hierarchical structure of the data and requires the user to adjust fewer parameters.

SELF-ORGANIZING MAPS

The Self-Organizing Map (SOM), as proposed in and described thoroughly in, is one of the most distinguished unsupervised artificial neural network models. The SOM maps high-dimensional input data to a usually 2-dimensional map display in such a way that similar data items are located close to each other on the map. The SOM consists of an ordered set of units i, which are often arranged on a rectangular grid. Each unit i is assigned a model vector m_i in the high-dimensional data space. A data item x_k is mapped to the best matching map unit c_k with the smallest distance between mi and x_k defined by

$$c_k = \arg\min_i \|\mathbf{x}_k - \mathbf{m}_i\|. \tag{1}$$

Two basic training methods exist to adapt the model vectors to fit the data. The SOM algorithm in its original form is an online algorithm which takes one data item per iteration as input and makes small adaptations sequentially. On the other hand, the batch-SOM algorithm takes all data items as input per iteration and thus makes bigger adaptations.

The model vectors are adapted iteratively in two steps. In the first step c_k is calculated for all x_k according to Equation 1. In the second step each model vector is adapted to better fit the data it represents. To ensure that each unit i represents similar data items as its neighbors, the model vector mi is adapted not only according to the assigned data items but also with respect to those assigned to the units in the neighborhood. The neighborhood relationship between two units i and j is usually defined by a Gaussian-like function $h_{ij} = exp(-d^2_{ij}/2r^2_t)$, where d_{ij} denotes the distance between the units i and j on the map, and r_t denotes the neighborhood radius which is set to decrease with each iteration t. The second step can be formulated as

$$\mathbf{m}_i^* = \frac{\sum_k h_{ic_k} \mathbf{x}_k}{\sum_k h_{ic_k}}. \tag{2}$$

where m^*_i is the updated model vector. An eficient implementation is to first calculate the mean $\bar{x}_i$ of the x_k which are mapped to mi and then calculate m^*_i as follows

$$\mathbf{m}_i^* = \frac{\sum_j n_j h_{ij} \bar{\mathbf{x}}_j}{\sum_j n_j h_{ij}}. \tag{3}$$

where n_j denotes the number of items mapped to unit j, which is basically a weighted sum of all data vectors in the neighborhood parameterized by the radius r_t.

The SOM algorithm and some of its properties are illustrated in Figure 1. The dataset was generated by a mixture of 6 Gaussian swith different covariances and priors. The model vecors of the SOM can be initialized randomly or based on more advanced techniques such as Principal Component Analysis (PCA). Figure 1 shows that after 5 iterations with a rather large neighborhood radius the SOM has roughly adapted to the structure of the data. Note that the model vectors are located around the center of the dataset because each model vector is representing many points due to the large neighborhood radius.

After 20 iterations with a smaller neighborhood radius the SOM has spread out over the whole set and has adapted to the fine structures in the data. The resulting map is a non-linear projection of the data space where the overall order is preserved. One characteristic of the SOM is that not all units represent the same number of items. For example, some units represent no items, and thus are not labeled with a number. These interpolating units are a result of the neighborhood constraints. The Smoothed Data Histogram (SDH) visualization utilizes this information to visualize the cluster structure.

The smoothed data histogram is a simple, robust, and computationally light cluster visualization method for self-organizing maps. SDHs using a simple 2-dimensional data set and discussed the similarities to other SOM based visualizations as well as to the posterior probability distribution of the GTM. Furthermore, the SDH was evaluated on a real world data set consisting of pieces of music.

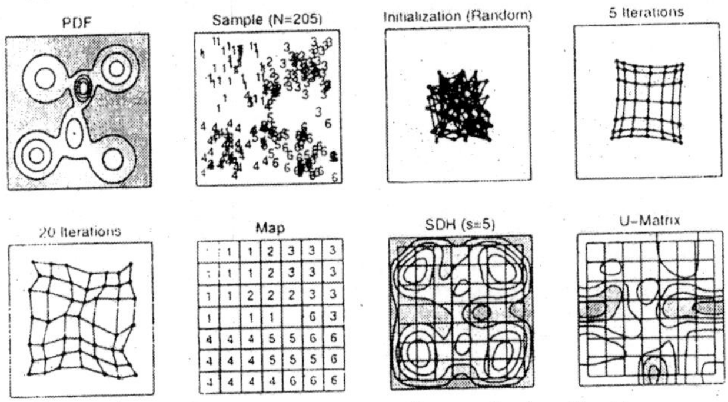

Figure 1. SOM training, mapping and visualization.

Note that all 6 clusters and their relation to each other can clearly be identified. Another important characteristic of the SOM is that areas in the data space with a high density are approximated by more model vectors than sparse areas. Thus, the distances between model vectors are large in sparse areas and small in areas with a high density, which is visualized by the U-matrix. The results of the U-matrix correspond roughly to those of the SDH. Clearly visible are the large distances between the clusters 1 and 4, 3 and 6, and between the clusters 4 and 6.

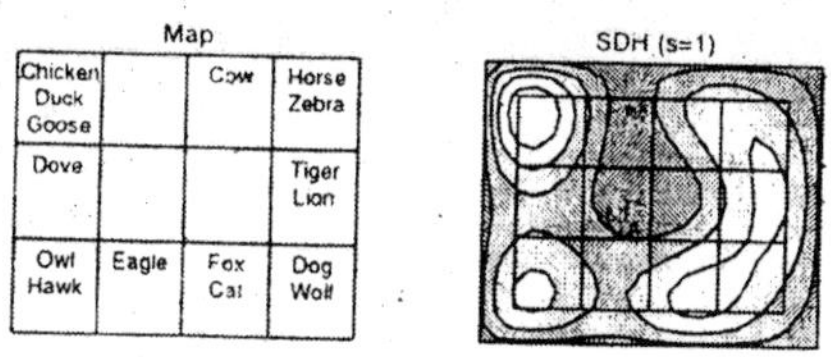

Figure 2. 4×3 SOM trained with animal dataset

The SOM mapping for a less abstract test set is depicted in Figure 2. The animal dataset consists of 16 animals which are described by several attributes, such as how many legs they have, if they can swim, hunt, and so forth. The map and the corresponding SDH visualization reveal that the dataset consists of three clusters, one larger one on the right representing mammals with a gradual separation of bigger ones in the upper regions and smaller ones below. On the left the birds are separated into two clusters.

The SOM has been employed in a wide range of applications, ranging from financial data analysis, via medical data analysis, to time series prediction, industrial control, and many more. It basically offers itself to the organization and in-teractive exploration of high-dimensional data spaces. One of its most prominent application areas is the organization of large text archives which scale up to millions of documents.

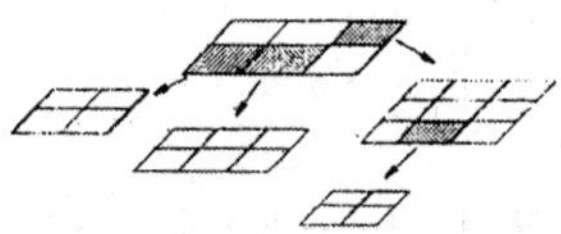

Figure 3. Example for a GHSOM architecture consisting of 3 layers. The shaded units are expanded on the next level.

Growing Hierarchical Self-Organizing Maps(GHSOM)

The Growing Hierarchical Self-Organizing Mapenhances the capabilities of the basic SOM in two ways. The frst is to use an incrementally growing version of the SOM, which does not require the user to directly specify the size of the map before hand, the second enhancement is the ability to adapt to hierarchical structures in the data. Both issues have been addressed separately by means of adaptive architectures, e.g. the Growing Grid, or the Growing SOM, or hierarchies of independent SOMs, e.g., the Hierarchical Feature Map or the Tree Structured SOM.

The key idea of the GHSOM is to use a hierarchical structure of multiple layers where each layer consists of a number of independent SOMs. One SOM is used at the first layer of the hierarchy. For every unit in this map a SOM might be added to the next layer of the hierarchy. This principle is repeated with the third and any further layers of the GHSOM. An example of a GHSOM architecture with 3 layers is depicted in Figure 3.

The training process starts with a small map of 2×2 units in the first layer which is organized according to the standard SOM training algorithm. After the model vectors have converged some decisions are made. Namely, (2A) if a new row or column should be inserted to improve the quality of the representation on this level, (2B) if the quality of the representation should be improved on the next hierarchical level by expanding one or more units, or (2C) if the SOM represents the data well in its current form. These decisions are the core of the GHSOM algorithm as they control the hierarchical structure and the shapes of the individual SOMs. In case of 2A a new row or column is inserted and the training process is repeated. In case of 2B for each map unit which needs to be expanded a new 2×2 SOM is created in such a way that the overall orientation is preserved. The training process is repeated for each of these new maps. Otherwise, (2C) if neither decisions 2A nor 2B are made no additional steps are necessary.

2A — Should a new row or column be inserted?

The intention is to increase the map size until all data items are represented well. This is measured based on the quantization errors, which describe how well a data item is represented by its best matching unit. The first step is to calculate the mean quantization error of each unit i (MQE_i),

$$MQE_i = \frac{1}{|U_i|} \sum_{k \in U_i} \|\mathbf{x}_k - \mathbf{m}_i\|, \quad U_i = \{k \mid c_k = i\}. \tag{4}$$

Then a summary which describes how well all units together represent the data is calculated as the mean of all MQE_i (MMQE). Alternatively, instead of using the mean the sum of all MQE_i (SMQE) can be used. The MMQE (or SMQE) is then compared to the mean quantization error of all data items with respect to a virtual unit with its model vector set to the mean of the dataset. Some researchers will refer to the mean quantization error of the virtual unit as MQE_0. If the following inequality is fulfilled a new row or column of map units is inserted in the SOM,

$$MMQE > \tau_1 MQE_0, \tag{5}$$

where τ_1 is a user defined parameter. Once the decision is made to insert new units the remaining question is where to do so. The GHSOM uses a slightly modified version of the Growing Grid heuristic. First the unit i with the largest MQE_i is defined to be the error unit. Then the most dissimilar adjacent neighbor, i.e., the unit with the largest distance in respect to the model vector, is selected and a new row or column is inserted between these.

2B — Should map units be expanded on the next hierarchical level?

If the Inequality 5 is not fulfilled, the next decision to be made is whether some units should be expanded on the next hierarchical level or not. This decision is not as critical as the previous since it is possible to expand additional units after the training process, or to remove a subbranch without in uencing other branches of the GHSOM architecture.

The original GHSOM algorithm checks if the following inequality is fulfilled to decide whether unit i should be expanded,

$$MQE_i > \tau_2 MQE^*_0; \tag{6}$$

where MQE^*_0 is the mean quantization error of the whole dataset with respect to the virtual unit located in center of the whole dataset. Again, τ_2 is a user defined parameter. To simplify matters, instead of using Inequality 6, it is possible to use $|U_i| > n$ as measure. For example, n=10 would mean that all units with more than 10 items are expanded.

Note that this will usually not lead to a balanced hierarchy. The depth of the hierarchy in different branches will rather re ect the diversity in the distribution of the dataset which should be expected in real-world data collections.

Parameters

The two main parameters of the original GHSOM algorithm are τ_1 from Inequality 5 and τ_2 from Inequality 6. Generally, the values for τ_1 and τ_2 are chosen such that $1 > \tau_1 >> \tau_2 > 0$. The choice of the parameter τ_2 is not critical as it is possible to set it to values smaller than necessary and to decide after the training process how many layers are sufficient. On the other hand, τ_1 leads to decisions which cannot be undone at later stages without retraining the GHSOM. Setting τ_1 to small values will lead to small maps and a deep hierarchy, while large values will result in large maps with a at hierarchical structure. Usually the user will train and manually evaluate several maps until an appropriate value for τ_1 is estimated.

Orientation

Without further precautions no relationship between

different sub-branches of the hierarchical structure would exist, other than the relationship defined by the parent map which they have in common. For example, in Figure 3 the maps of the second layer could have an arbitrary orientation (i.e., they could be rotated in any direction), and thus would not allow to draw conclusions on the similarity of the 3rd layer map to any of the other two 2nd layer maps, other than the relationships represented by the first layer map. A simple solution to this is to enforce a specific orientation on the sub-layer SOMs through initializing the model vectors of the 2×2 SOMs in such a way that they correspond to the orientation of the parent map.

For example, the 4 model vectors could be initialized with the means of the model vector of the parent unit and each of its 4 immediate neighbors. For units located at the border of the SOM they use the existing units to interpolate a virtual unit based on the assumption that the map can locally be approximated by a linear hyper-plane. For example, if the unit i is to be expanded which is located on the left border, then the unit to its right j is used to create a virtual unit v_{ij}' beyond the left border $m_{ij}' = m_i - (m_i - m_j)$.

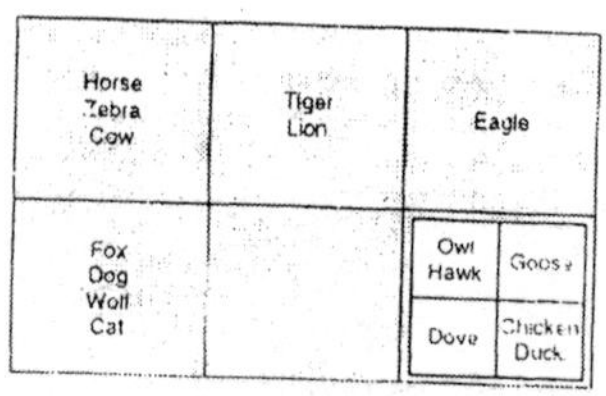

Figure 4. GHSOM trained with the animal dataset ($\tau_1 = 0.5$ using SMQE).

Tension and mapping ratio extension

The Tension and Mapping Ration (TMR) extension of the basic GHSOM algorithm introduced here addresses in particular Decision 2A: Whether new units should be inserted and in which row or column they should be inserted. This is the most critical part of the GHSOM algorithm. The TMR extension has two main effe cts on the GHSOM algorithm. First of all, the quality of the individual SOMs is improved by inserting new units where they are really needed. Furthermore, the appropriate map sizes are determined au-tomatically without requiring the user to guess a suitable value for the τ_1 parameter which controls Decision 2A.

Decision 2A is a model selection problem. In general selecting the model which best fits the data and avoids overfitting to noise in the data is a unsolved prob-lem. Several different techniques for model selection exist and have been applied to complexity selection of SOMs. However, the problem of Decision 2A is more subtle than it might appear on first sight since the aim is not necessarily to have a low quantization error on each layer, or to minimize, e.g., the Minimum Message Length necessary to decode the SOM and the data of a particular layer. Instead, the goal is to hierarchically cluster the data with clearly separated clusters on the top-layers and low quantization errors on the lower levels. Further-more, for computational efficiency it is of interest to take special characteristics of the SOM into account, such as the neighborhood relationships between units. The TMR extension addresses these issues.

The two principles of the TMR are straightforward. The first principle is to ensure stable mappings between two neighboring map units *i* and *j*. The stability is measured by inserting a virtual unit vij between the units *i* and *j* with its model vector $m_{ij} = (m_i + m_j)/2$. If a large number of items which are mapped to the units *i* and *j* would better be represented by vij then the arrangement is instable, on the other hand, if only a very small ratio of items would prefer v_{ij} then the relationship is stable. They refer this ratio as

Mapping Ratio (MR). The second principle is to ensure a stable structure of the neighborhood topology. The topology is stable if there is little Tension (T), i.e., if the distances between all neighbors are about the same. In particular, they calculate the Tension to avoid a disproportional ratio between the average pairwise distances between all adjacent rows and all adjacent columns.

Given a trained SOM the following 7 steps are executed before making the decision where to insert units is finalized.

Step 1, the 4 virtual units for each unit i are defined. For border units the same approach introduced for preserving the orientation of sub-layers is applied, i.e., the virtual units are linearly interpolated based on the assumption that the map can locally be approximated by hyper-planes.

Step 2, for all $x_k \in \mathcal{U}_i$ the best matching unit is selected from the 4 virtual units and the original unit. The number of items which are best represented by the original unit i is denoted as $n_{i(i)}$, the number of units mapped to the virtual unit vij as $n_i(v_{ij})$. Note that this information can later be reused in case unit i is expanded on the next layer, or in case a new row or column is inserted next to the unit.

Step 3, the Mapping Ratio MRij of each virtual unit vij is calculated as

$$MR_{ij} = \frac{n_{i(v_{ij})}}{n_{i(i)}} + \frac{n_{j(v_{ij})}}{n_{j(j)}}. \tag{7}$$

Virtual units located beyond the border are calculated as MR_{ij} where i denotes a border unit. Higher MR values correspond to less stable mappings since a relatively large amount of items is mapped between the map units. Step 4, the decision if the growth process should be continued or not is made. The sum of all MRij (SMR) is calculated. If the map is bigger than 2×2 and the SMR value has increased compared to the SMR of the previous, smaller map, then the current map is rejected and the growth process is terminated. Otherwise, the process is continued.

Step 5, for each row and column of virtual units z the average Mapping Ratio AMRz is calculated as the median of all MR_{ij} in the respective row or column.

Step 6, the Tension is calculated. First, the Average Distance AD_z is calculated as the median of the distances between the neighboring model vectors which define the row or column of the respective virtual units, i.e, for all v_{ij} belonging to z, $AD_z = \text{median}(||m_i - m_j||)$. Furthermore they calculate AD_r as the median of all AD_z where z represents a row, and AD_c as median of all AD_z where z represents a column. Then the Tension T_z for each z representing a row is calculated as $Tz = AD_z/AD_c$ and analogous for each z representing a column $T_z = AD_z/AD_r$.

For example, if a map with an equal number of rows and columns is trained on a 2-dimensional dataset with a high variance in the direction fitted by rows and a low variance in the direction fitted by the columns, then AD_r would be higher than AD_c and T_z for a row would be higher than for T_z for a columns. The Tension for rows and columns of virtual units beyond the borders of the map is set to the value of the respective row or column just before the border. Note that they use the median preferably because it is more robust towards outliers, however, using the mean will yield the same results for most applications.

Step 7, multiply the Tension T_z with the respective average Mapping Ratio AMR_z and select the row or column of virtual units z with the highest value as location for new units. The reason why we combine the Tension and Mapping Ratio by multiplication is that both become scale independent, higher values of one of the two will increase the outcome, and vice versa. Furthermore, both the Mapping Ratio and the Tension are considered of equal importance for the stability of a SOM.

Figure 5 illustrates an example where the SOM mapping is unstable. The 2×2 SOM is trained on the dataset consisting of 6 Gaussian clusters. Each of the 4 units represents 1.5 clusters, in particular the 2 units in the upper row share 3 clusters and the units below as well. Thus inserting a new column between these units would solve the problem. However, the GHSOM bases its decision on the error unit, which is the unit in the upper-left, and on the most dissimilar neighbor, which results in the insertion of a new row. In the fine tuning phase of the SOM algorithm each model vector is adapted to best fit the items it represents which leads to the suboptimal topology structure depicted in the upper-right subplot of Figure 5. On the other hand, the TMR extension correctly inserts a new column of units which results in the stable topology illustrated in the lower-right subplot.

Furthermore, using the TMR extension it is possible to analyze the global effe cts an insertion has while the original GHSOM draws its conclusions based merely on local observations. An illustrative example where the global effects need to be considered is depicted in Figure 6. The data is generated by 12 Gaussians with equal covariances which are arranged on a rectangular 6×2 grid with a local disruption in the center. The GHSOM identifies the error unit and its most dissimilar neighbor, in this case the most dissimilar neighbor has the second largest mean quantization error. Both units are very unstable as their model vectors lie in between clusters. From a local point of view inserting a new unit between them would increase the cluster quality.

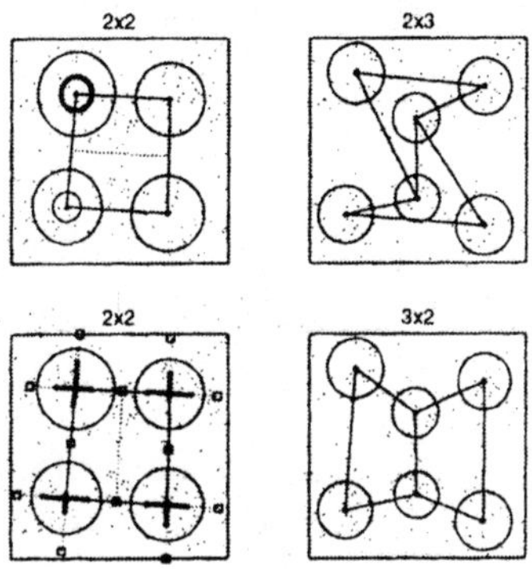

Figure 5. A wrong decision on the local level.

However, inserting a new row of units will effect the structure of 8 other units which represent their items very well. The result is depicted in the center-right subplot, where the overall topology does not correspond well with the data. On the other hand, when applying the TMR extension the effects on all units in the row or column are analyzed. Specific ally, the average benefit of the new units inserted in a particular row or column is calculated and the highest average benefit is selected. In this example, where obviously the mapping ratio is largest between the two center units the TMR extension decides to add a new column instead since all other units would not benefit from a new row.

Another advantage of the TMR extension is the improved decision regarding the required number of units for an individual SOM. To illustrate this the researchers use two 2-dimensional datasets, both generated by Gaussians with equal covariances located on a rectangular grid so that two immediate neighbors have unit distance. The first dataset was generated by 4 Gaussians, the second by 16 Gaussians. Thus, the best hierarchical SOM model would have 4 and 16 units at this level of detail while any number beyond could be interpreted as overfitting.

However, if each of the Gaussian clusters is generated by a mixture of other Gaussian distributions, the structure of these would need to be represented on the next hierarchical level. Figures 7 and 8 show the behavior of four different quality measures on these two datasets respectively. They compare the sum of all Mapping Ratios (SMR) to the MMQE, SMQE, and to the Davies-Bouldin (DB) cluster validation index. The curves depict the measured error for a 2×2 SOM initialized with PCA into which subsequently new columns or rows of units are inserted based on the TMR extension.

The DB index is used to determine the optimal number of clusters. Given the number of map units C and using the mean quantization errors the DB index can be calculated as

$$DB = \frac{1}{C}\sum_{i=1}^{C} \max_{i,j\neq i}\left(\frac{MQE_i + MQE_j}{\|\mathbf{m}_i - \mathbf{m}_j\|}\right). \tag{8}$$

For example, in the Figures 5 and 6, the Davies-Bouldin (DB) index would be large where the circles, which indicate the MQE, are close to each other or even overlap, and small if the circles are separated clearly.

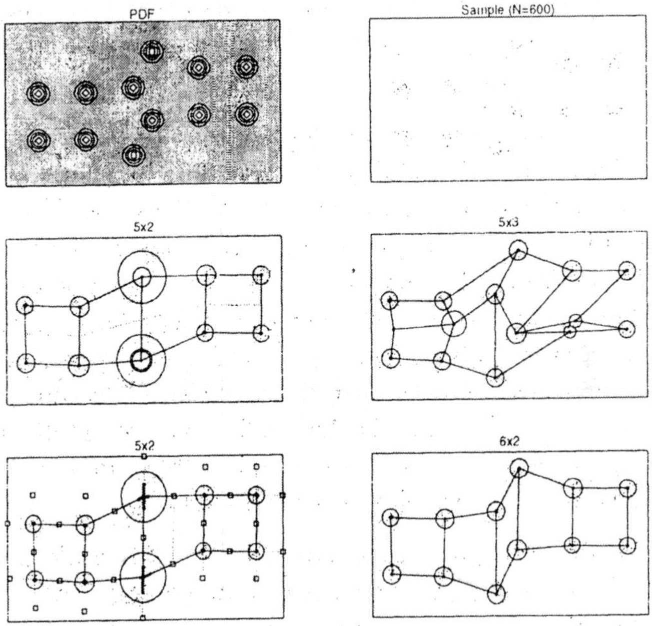

Figure 6. A wrong decision on the global level. The GHSOM is confronted with a situation in which the map generally fits the data quite well, except for a local disturbance. The first row depicts the probability distribution and the sample drawn from it. The second row presents the original GHSOM results and the third row the results of the TMR extension analogous to Figure 5.

Fifure 5 shows a wrong decision on the local level. The GHSOM is trained with the dataset presented in Figure 1. As in Figure 1 the model vectors which are adjacent neighbors are connected by lines. The larger circles around each model vector represent the mean quantization error. The first row represents the original GHSOM, the second row the TMR extension. In the upper-left subplot the error unit is marked by a circle with double lines (upper-left unit), the most distant neighbor with a simple circle (lower-left). The dotted line indicates where a new row of units is inserted, the second subplot in the first row presents the results after the GHSOM has been trained with the new row.

The lower-left subplot depicts the factors in uencing the decision of the TMR extension. The locations of the virtual units are marked as squares, the thick lines illustrate the ratio of items mapped to the respective virtual unit (MR). For example, many of the data items mapped to the unit in the upper-left would better fit the virtual unit located above. On the other hand, for example, hardly any of the items mapped to the unit in the upper-right would better fit the virtual unit located below it. Based on the TMR a new column is inserted, which is marked by the dotted line, and results in the map in the lower-right subplot.

Note, that neither the DB index nor the SMR can be calculated for a single cluster. This limitation does not apply to the MMQE or SMQE. However, the comparing the SOM which is under consideration with a bigger SOM leads to more reliable decisions whether the map size should be increased than comparing it with a one unit SOM (MQE_0).

In Figure 7, the MMQE error depicted is drastically reduced when 4 units are used instead of 1. Knowing that the correct number of clusters is 4 this could lead to the false assumption that it is sufficient to find the number of units after which the MMQE does not decrease significantly. The reason why this assumption is wrong is illustrated in Figure 8. Although there are 4 times as many clusters present the run of the curve is basically the same. Hence, trying to guess the optimal number of cluster from the MMQE is quite impossible.

On the other hand, the SMQE curve re ects the actual cluster structure better. However, to obtain the optimal number of clusters would require $1\leq \tau_1 \leq 0.38$ (see Equation 5) in the case of 4 clusters, and $0.27\leq\tau_1\leq 0.19$ in the case of 16 clusters. Thus, although both datasets are only 2-dimensional and consist of Gaussian clusters with equal covariances, it is not possible to use the same parameter setting for ½1 to obtain appropriate results.

The DB index responds better to the cluster structure than the SMQE. For example, in the case of 4 clusters, the index indicates that 4 units are a better approximation than 6 or 9 units, which would be sufficient information to terminate the growth process. However, in the case of 16 clusters the DB index does not have a local minimum at 16 units, although the index indicates only slightly better results for 20 units.

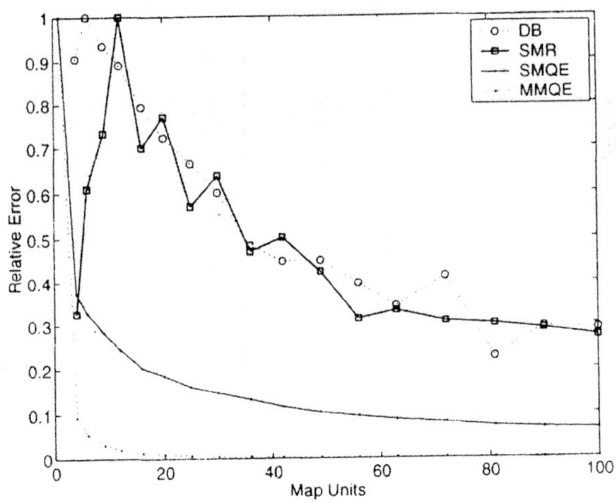

Figure 7. Relative errors for a dataset consisting of 4 clusters. The errors are normalized so that the maximum value equals 1.

In the case of 4 clusters the SMR in the range of 4 to 50 is smallest for 4. Note however, that if the number of units approaches the number of data items in the dataset, then all 4 error measures will converge towards zero, since all items can be represented without any error. In the case of 16 clusters the SMR rapidly decreases until the map size reaches 16 units, and then increases again to an error level more than two times higher than the minimum at 16 units. Thus, the SMR outperforms the SMQE and the DB index, while we have shown that the MMQE is an insufficient measure to determine the correct number of clusters.

The GHSOM with TMR extension trained with the animals dataset is presented in Figure 9. On the first level the animals are clustered into 3 groups, namely large mammals, medium mammals, and birds. On the second level the large mammals are further distinguished into carnivore and herbi-vore mammals. The hierarchical clustering result appears to have a slightly better quality than the one obtained from the original GHSOM.

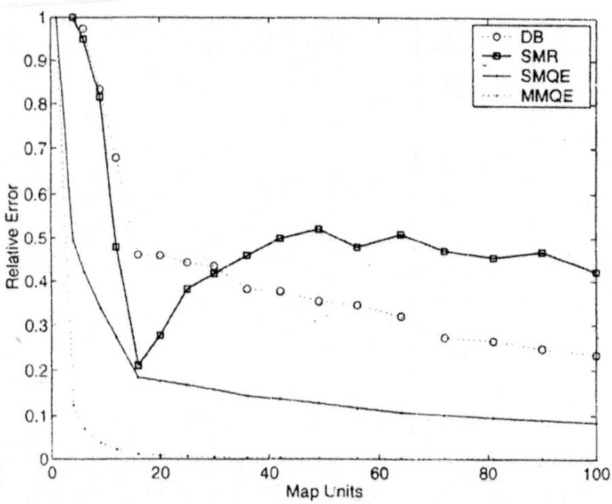

Figure 8 . Relative errors for a dataset consisting of 16 clusters. The errors are normalized so that the maximum value equals 1.

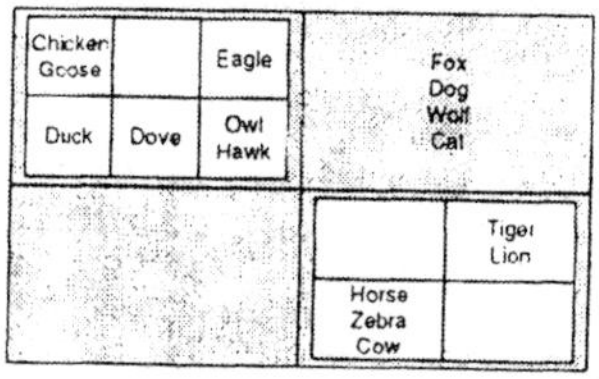

Figure 9. GHSOM-TMR trained with animal dataset.

There are two applications of the GHSOM with TMR extension. The first application is the content-based organization of a music archive. The second application is the identification of distinctive sequences in multi-variate time-series data representing musical performance strategies.

Content-based organization of music archives

The first dataset stems from the project Islands of Music whose goal is to create intuitive interfaces to music archives by automatically analyzing, organizing, and visualizing pieces of music based on their perceived acoustic similarities. The pieces are given in compressed-MP3 format and are decoded to the raw audio signal. From the time domain the signals are transformed into the frequency domain where the specific loudness sensation per frequency band is calculated based on psychoa-coustic models.

The loudness uctuation of the loudness amplitudes in each band are analyzed using a Fourier transformation. Furthermore, filters are applied to emphasize specific patterns. Finally, each piece is represented by 1200 low-level features describing the dynamic patterns of the loudness in frequency bands. Other than this data no additional information on musical styles, instruments, or musical content is given to the system.

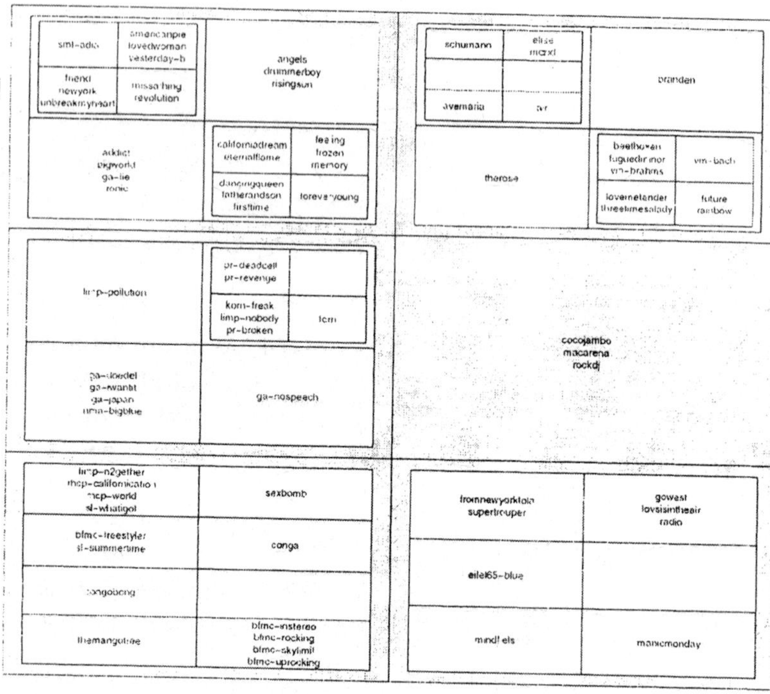

Figure 10. GHSOM of a music archive.

Figure 10 shows the hierarchical organization of a music collection consisting of 77 pieces with a total playing time of about 5 hours. On the first level the training process has resulted in the creation of a 2×3 map, organizing the collection into 6 major styles of music. The upper-right represents mainly classical music, while the lower-left mainly represents a mixture of Hip Hop, Electro, and House and specific ally music by Bomfunk MCs (bfmc). The lower-right and center-right represent mainly Disco music such as Rock DJ by Robbie Williams (rockdj), Blue by Eiffel 65 (eiffil65-blue), or Super Trouper by A-Teens (supertrouper). The upper-left represents Pop music while the center-left represents more aggressive Rock music. Please note that the organization does not follow clean 'conceptual' genre styles, splitting by definition, e.g. Hip Hop and House, but rather re ects the overall sound similarity.

Most of these 6 first-level categories are further refined on the second level. For example, the upper-right unit representing classical music is divided into 4 further sub-categories. Of these 4 categories the upper-left represents slow and peaceful music, mainly piano pieces such as Fur Elise (elise) and Mondscheinsonate 1st movement(mond) by Beethoven, or Fremde L.ander und Menschen by Schumann (schumann). The lower-right represents, for example, pieces by Vanessa Mae (vm), which, in this case, are more dynamic interpretations of classical pieces played on the violin.

Other pieces located in the cluster are the end credits of the film Back to the Future III (future) and the slow love song The Rose by Bette Middler (therose), and the Brandenburg Concertos by Bach (branden). Note that the third level refinement of the upper-left cluster separates the piano pieces from the slow violin piece Air from orchestra suite #3 by Bach (air) and the Ave Maria by Schubert (ave maria). The 3rd level refinement in the lower-right distinguishes for example the two love songs Three Times a Lady by Lionel Richie (threetimesalady) and Love Me Tender by Elvis (lovemetender) from the other orchestra pieces.

Some interesting insights into the music collection which the GHSOM reveals are, for example, that the song Freestyler by Bomfunk MCs (*lower-left*) is quite different from the other songs by the same group. Freestyler was the groups biggest hit so far and unlike their other songs has

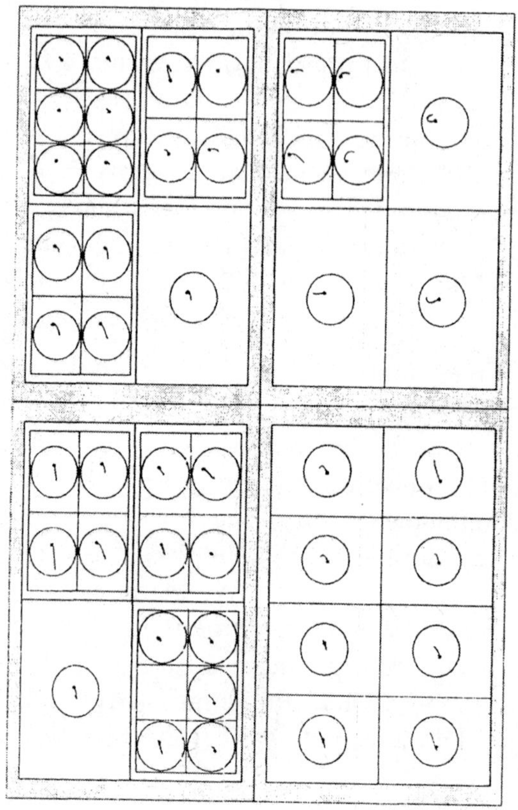

Figure 13. *All levels of the GHSOM trained on the music performances.*

been appreciate by a broader audience. Generally, the pieces of one group have similar sound characteristics and thus are located within the same categories. This applies, for example, to the songs of Guano Apes (*ga*) and Papa Roach (*pr*), which are located in the center-left of the 6 first-level categories together with other aggressive rock songs. However, the song Living in a Lie by Guano Apes (*ga-lie*) is another exception (*upper-left*). Listening to this piece reveals that it is much slower than the other pieces of the group, and that this song which is about the end of a relationship matches very well with, for example, Addict by K's Choice which is about addiction to drugs.

Identification of musical performance strategies

The second dataset stems from a large data mining project 3 whose goal is to study fundamental principles of expressive music performance. Performances by concert pianists are measured with respect to timing and dynamics (loudness) fluc-tuations; the goal is to find characteristic patterns that give insight into typical interpretation strategies used by pianists.

The dataset used for this particular experiment consists of performances of a piano piece by Frederic Chopin, played by 22 skilled pianists. Each performance is characterized by two series of numeric values that represent the measured tempo and loudness, respectively, over the course of the performance. A visualization of one such time series in the form of a trajectory in the two-dimensional tempo-loudness space is shown in Figure 11, with tempo on the vertical axis and dynamics (loudness) on the horizontal axis. The various trajectories were then cut into a total of 184 segments (according to bars) each represented by 80 attributes and subjected the GHSOM-TMR algorithm.

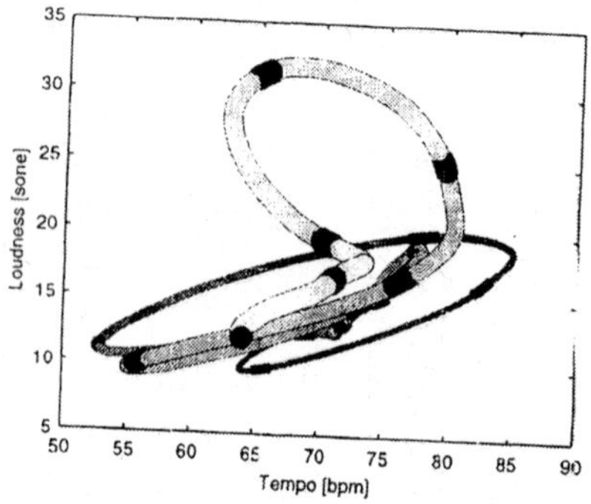

Figure 11. Time series in the form of a trajectory in the two-dimensional tempo-loudness space.

In the above figure the bar boundaries are indicated through the black sections. The time dimension is visualized through the thickness and the shading of the trajectory, the most recent bars are represented by lighter shadings and a thicker line, while bars played in the past are represented by darker shadings and a thinner line.

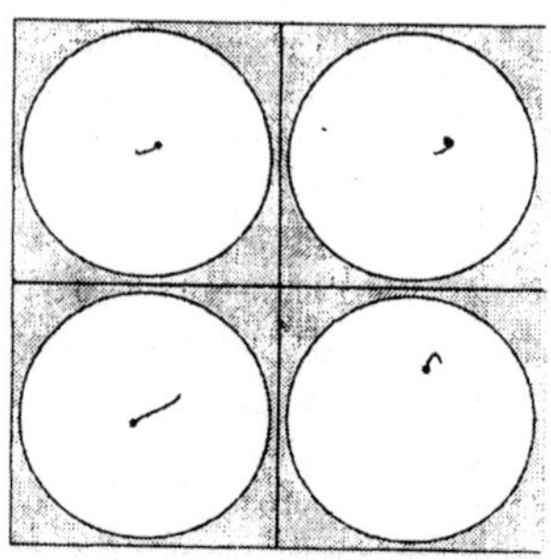

Figure 12. The top-level 2×2 SOM of the GHSOM trained on the music performances.

The purpose of the whole procedure is to find out whether there are indeed characteristic and interpretable classes of tempo/dynamics strategies that pianists apply consistently, and to quantify these. The results are shown in Figures 12 and 13, where the model vectors are visual-ized. The direction of the trajectory segments in time is indicated by a dot marking the end point. The shadows indicate the variance of the data items mapped to the specific model vectors.

At the top level (Fig. 12), four distinct classes emerge which have a clear musical interpretation: The upper two clusters are typical strategies used by pianists at the beginnings of musical phrases: a speeding up (accelerando — movement from left to right in this space) is accompanied by a slight increase in loudness (crescendo); the cluster in the lower left represents the opposite tendency of ending a phrase with a slowing down (ritardando) and a decrease in loudness; and the cluster in the lower right shows the typical way of shaping the middle part of a phrase, with a typical loudness maximum around the musical climax (the 'apex') of the phrase.

All this conforms well with current musicological theories of expressive performance. At more detailed levels (Fig. 13), these classes of elementary behavior are broken down into a number of interesting sub-categories. In the 'apex class' (lower right quadrant), a clear distinction between upward (towards the apex) and downward (after the apex) motions becomes visible — the crescendo and decrescendo parts of a typical phrase arch. Similarly, the 'phrase start' patterns in the upper two quadrants are now discriminated into accelerando-crescendo patterns and phases of 'stagnation' where the pianists keep tempo and loudness more or less constant (see the six classes in the upper right corner 4).

Untypical category members are collected in a separate set of subclasses (lower left in upper left quadrant, and lower right in upper right). In summary, these results are highly intuitive and conform with current mu-sicological theories. The hierarchical breakdown gives a nicely interpretable set of elementary performance strategies, at various levels of granularity — a sort of alphabet of elementary patterns that can be related to various types of musical structure, and out of which complex performances can be built.

Qualitative evaluation

The general problem of evaluating clustering algorithms is that for quantitative comparisons the true clusters in the data need to be known. This is usually the case in typical classification problems, or in artificial datasets. The former, as the name indicates, are not typical clustering problems, the latter can be tuned in such a way that any algorithm could outperform any other algorithm. The main field of application for the GHSOM is exploratory data analysis. Thus, to evaluate the TMR extension researchers applied both the original GHSOM and the GHSOM-TMR to explore the 2 datasets mentioned above.

In both cases the true cluster structure was unknown and the objective was to explore the data and gain new insights. Furthermore, in both cases any structure found in the data can easily be evaluated by either listening to music, or viewing 2-dimensional plots. In general, the first step to validate any results obtained from visual clustering techniques including the GHSOM-TMR is to compare the results to the results ob-tained from other techniques and even to the same technique with different random initializations. This is necessary to ensure that the structure perceived to be signif-icant is not only caused by some local minimum in an error function. In a second step the new insights gained from the clustering techniques need to be tested on new data.

For our evaluation both algorithms, i.e. the GHSOM with and without TMR extension, the first layer SOM was initialized equally using Principal Component Analysis to ensure equal starting conditions. Furthermore, the neighborhood radius rt for the batch-SOM training was set generously to ensure best possible convergence and to avoid randomly falling into local minima specific for the particular dataset.

In particular, they first trained the original GHSOM and searched for values of ½1 that lead to good hierarchical representations of the data. They found that the results were best when the GHSOM parameter controlling the size of the individual maps is set to $\tau_1 = 0.6$ in the case of the music archive and to $\tau_1 = 0.7$ for the musical performances when using the SMQE. They then trained the GHSOM-TMR (with the same τ_2; no τ_1 needs to be determined for the GHSOM-TMR) and obtained the same quality level.

Achieving significantly better results would have been a big surprise since, for example, the results obtained from the second dataset had previously been carefully analyzed and optimized manually. Thus, they would like to emphasize that the TMR extension is capable of creating the same hierarchical structures which were fine-tuned manually by GHSOM experts using the original algorithm.

Determining appropriate values for τ_1 requires the user to understand the GH-SOM algorithm, and even a GHSOM expert will need to calculate several maps and evaluate these manually before guessing the best value for τ_1. On the other hand, with the TMR extension the appropriate map sizes are determined automatically and the user does not need to worry about setting ½1 which simplifies the use of the GHSOM. The computational load of the TMR extension is about twice as high as the original GHSOM algorithm. The main reason for this lies in the 'look ahead strategy' of the TMR extension. However, the original GHSOM algorithm requires the user to make additional runs to test and understand the parameter setting. The evaluation of these additional runs usually requires more time than the training process.

Bibliography

Brill, Louis M., "Wavefronts Theatre of Performing Lights: On Light Shows with Music and Dance", Leonardo 13, p. 307 (1980)

Cook, Dick, "Kinetic Art: The Luminetic System With and Without Sound", Leonardo 8, No. 1 (1975).

DeWitt, Tom, "Visual Music: Searching for an Aesthetic", Leonardo 20, 115 (1987).

Evans, Brian, "Establishing a Tonic Space with Digital Color", Leonardo, Electronic Art Supplemental Issue, pp. 27-30 (1988).

Galeyev, Bulat, "Farewell Prometheus Readings: Light Music in the Former Soviet Union", Leonardo 27, No. 4, p. 351 (1994).

Grayson, John, "New Materials and Methods for the Musical Instrument Designer, the Audio-Kinetic Sculptor, Musician and Composer", Leonardo 3, p. 295 (1970).

Harrison, John and Simon Baron-Cohen, "Synaesthesia: An Account of Coloured Hearing", Leonardo 27, No. 4, p. 343 (1994).

Jablonsky, Stephen, "Graphic Artworks Based on Music: Musigraphs", Leonardo 12, p. 308 (1979).

Jack Ox with Peter Frank, "The Systematic Translation of Musical Compositions into Paintings", Leonardo 17, No. 3, p. 152 (1984).

Justesen, Aage, "Pictures Based on Voice Graphs: Pictonoms", Leonardo 11, p. 205 (1978)

Kostyniuk, Ron, "Electric Light Audio-Kinetic Artworks: 'Ecological Biomes'", Leonardo 12, p. 45 (1979).

Nicolas Schoffer, "Sonic and Visual Structures: Theory and Experiment", Leonardo 18, No. 2, p. 59 (1985).

Peacock, Kenneth, "Instruments to Perform Color-Music: Two Centuries of Technological Experimentation", Leonardo 21, No. 4, pp. 397-406 (1988).

Pierre Y. Karinthi, "A Contribution to Musicalism: An Attempt to Interpret Music in Painting", Leonardo 24, No. 4, p. 401 (1991).

Pocock-Williams, Lynn, "Toward the Automatic Generation of Visual Music", Leonardo 25, No.1, pp. 29-36 (1992)

Snyder, Robert R., "Video Color Control by Means of an Equal-Tempered Keyboard", Leonardo 18, p. 93 (1985).

Theo Goldberg and Gunther Schrack, "Computer-Aided Correlation of Musical and Visual Structures", Leonardo 19, No. 1, p.11 (1986).

Vadnerkar, S. V., "A Code for Representing the Occidental Musical Notation in Pictorial Art", Leonardo 9, p. 140 (1976).

W. Garner, "The Relationship Between Colour and Music", Leonardo 11, No. 3, p. 225 (1978).

Wagler, S. R., "'Sonovision': A Visual Display of Sound", Leonardo 3, p. 443 (1970).

Whitney, Sr., John., "Fifty Years of Composing Computer Music and Graphics: How Time's New Solid-State Tractability Has Changed Audio-Visual Perspectives", Leonardo 24, No. 5, p. 597 (1991).

Zajec, Edward, "Orphics: Computer Graphics and the Shaping of Time with Color", Leonardo, Electronic Art Supplemental Issue, pp. 111-116 (1988).

Index